STRANGERS
DROWNING

STRANGERS
DROWNING

—— GRAPPLING WITH ——

IMPOSSIBLE IDEALISM, DRASTIC CHOICES,

AND THE OVERPOWERING URGE TO HELP

LARISSA MACFARQUHAR

PENGUIN PRESS | NEW YORK | 2015

PENGUIN PRESS
An imprint of Penguin Random House LLC
375 Hudson Street
New York, New York 10014
penguin.com

ISBN 978-1-59420-433-3

Printed in the United States of America
3   5   7   9   10   8   6   4

Designed by Gretchen Achilles

FOR MY PARENTS

What are we? What is our life? Our goodness? Our righteousness?

—THE ASHAMNU, the Jewish shorter confession

CONTENTS

STRANGERS
DROWNING

A young man and an older man—a philosophy professor and his student—are having lunch together in a Thai restaurant in New Jersey.

YOUNG MAN: I'm not sure what the world would be like if everyone thought like me. In college we were given the thought experiment, Should you save your mother from drowning, or two strangers? I think I should save the strangers, but I would probably be too weak to, because I love my mom. And maybe it's good to have this disposition where you love your mom. I don't know what the world would be like if everyone saved the strangers rather than their mother. When I read books on Buddhism, and monks are talking about problems like this, they don't think of it as caring less for your mother—they think about it as caring about strangers more. And if you care about the strangers and your mother equally, it's just a numbers game at that point. But it's not a cold and calculating thing, it's extending empathy to others.

The young man's face is mostly blank. On first impression he seems to be deeply recessed inside himself—a person whose emotions are compressed under heavy strata of ideas about altruism and rationality and philosophical precision. But if he is questioned about his views on suffering, this word will recall to his mind facts he has encountered in books about terrible things endured by nameless human beings hundreds of years ago, or by prey animals in the wild, and the horror of this remote information will overcome him to the point where he starts to cry. What appears at first to be an absence of emotion then appears to be a need to control overwhelming emotion that is apt to surface without warning.

> OLDER MAN: But that's impossible. If you're going to care the same about everybody, you're going to care less about your mother. You're not going to be able to care the same about everybody as you care about your children.

The professor is thin and bearded; he has children.

> YOUNG MAN: Depends on what you mean by caring.
>
> OLDER MAN: It does depend on what you mean by caring, but to make your view plausible, caring is going to have to be divorced from feeling—it's going to have to be a disposition to act, or something like that. I mean, just imagine that you cared about everyone in the world the way you care about your own child. You would know that there were people dying horrible, painful deaths all the time, and if you felt about that the way you would feel about your own child's horrible, painful death, you'd be completely paralyzed with grief and anguish and wouldn't be able to go on living.
>
> YOUNG MAN: I don't think that's obvious. Suppose one of your children has died and the other child is about to die. You're not going to be paralyzed—you're going to do your best to save your other child.
>
> OLDER MAN: Yes. But I know that there are thousands of people in the world dying horrible deaths right now, and if I cared about each of those people the way I care about my own child, life would be intolerable. The Buddhist monks are wrong. I think it's very hard to understand the extremes of human caring until you've been a parent.

FOR DO-GOODERS,
IT IS ALWAYS WARTIME

> Love in action is a harsh and dreadful thing compared with
> love in dreams.
>
> —FYODOR DOSTOEVSKY, *The Brothers Karamazov*

This book is about a human character who arouses conflicting emotions: the do-gooder. I don't mean a part-time, normal do-gooder—someone who has a worthy job, or volunteers at a charity, and returns to an ordinary family life in the evenings. I mean a person who sets out to live as ethical a life as possible. I mean a person who's drawn to moral goodness for its own sake. I mean someone who pushes himself to moral extremity, who commits himself wholly, beyond what seems reasonable. I mean the kind of do-gooder who makes people uneasy.

This person has a sense of duty that is very strong—so strong that he's able to repress most of his baser impulses in order to do what he believes to be right. This is a struggle, but one that he usually wins. He rarely permits himself time off from his work, and spends little money on himself so he has more to give away. He has his joys and pleasures but they must fit—they must gain admittance. Because of this, there is a certain rigidity and a focused narrowness to the way he lives: his life makes ordinary existence seem flabby and haphazard. The standards to which he holds himself and the emotions he cultivates—care for strangers, a degree of detachment from family in order to care for those strangers, indifference to low pleasures—can seem inhumanly lofty, and separate him from other people.

The life of a zealous do-gooder is a kind of human sublime—by which I mean that, although there is a hard beauty in it, the word "beautiful" doesn't capture the ambivalence it stirs up. A beautiful object—a flower, a stream—is pleasing in a gentle way, inspiring a feeling that is like love. A sublime object, such as a mountain or a rough sea, inspires awe, but also dread. Confronting it, you see its formidable nobility, and at the same time you sense uncomfortably that you would not survive in it for long. It is this sense of sublime that I mean to apply to do-gooders: to confront such a life is to feel awe mixed with unease—a sense that you wouldn't survive in that life for long, and might not want to.

The do-gooder is both more and less free than other people. In the usual sense of the word he is less free, because he believes it's his duty to act in certain ways, and he has to do his duty. But in an older sense he is more free, because he can control himself, so his intentions aren't frustrated by weaknesses that he'd rather not have. He knows that if he makes a promise he will keep it; that if a thing is right he will do it; that he will not turn away because something seems too hard. Because of this, his life is what he intends it to be.

The usual way to do good is to help those who are near you: a person grows up in a particular place, perceives that something is wrong there, and sets out to fix it. Or a person's job suddenly requires heroism of him and he rises to the occasion—he might be a priest whose church becomes a refuge in wartime, or a nurse working in a hospital at the start of a plague. Either way, he is taking care of his own, trying to make their lives better—lives that he understands because they are like his. He may not know personally the people he's helping, but he has something in common with them—they are, in some sense, his people. There's an organic connection between him and his work.

Then there's another sort of person, who starts out with something more abstract—a sense of injustice in the world at large, and a longing for goodness as such. This person wants to live a just life, feels obliged to right wrongs or relieve suffering, but he doesn't know right away how to do that, so he sets himself to figuring it out. He doesn't feel that he must attend first to people close to him: he is moved not by a sense of belonging but by the urge to do as much good as he can. There is no organic, necessary connection between him and his work—it doesn't choose him, he chooses it. The do-gooders I'm talking about are this second sort of person. They're not better or worse than the first sort, but they are rarer and harder to understand. It can seem unnatural to look away from one's own people toward a moral idea, but for these do-gooders it's not: it's natural for them.

The first sort of person doesn't provoke the discomfort that do-gooders do. The first sort of person is often called a hero, and "hero" is a much less ambivalent word than "do-gooder." (I'm using the word here in a modern, colloquial sense—I'm not talking about Achilles.) A hero of this type comes upon a problem and decides to help. He is moved to do so by compassion for something he sees, something outside himself. When he's not helping, he returns to his ordinary life. Because of this, his noble act isn't felt as a reproach: You couldn't have done what he did because you weren't there—you aren't part of his world. You can always imagine that you would have done what he did if you had been there—after all, the hero is an ordinary person like you.

The do-gooder, on the other hand, knows that there are crises everywhere, all the time, and he seeks them out. He is not spontaneous—he plans his good deeds in cold blood. He may be compassionate, but compassion is not why he does what he does—he committed himself to helping before he saw the person who needs him. He has no ordinary life: his good deeds are his life. This makes him good; but it can also make him seem perverse—a foul-weather friend, a kind of virtuous ambulance chaser. And it's also why do-gooders *are* a reproach: you know, as the do-gooder knows, that there is always, somewhere, a need for help.

The term "do-gooder" is, of course, often demeaning. It can mean a silly or intrusive person who tries to do good but ends up only meddling. It can mean someone who seems annoyingly earnest, or priggish, or self-righteous, or judgmental. Benjamin Franklin gave up his quest for moral perfection when he realized "that such extream nicety as I exacted of myself might be a kind of foppery in morals, which, if it were known, would make me ridiculous; that a perfect character might be attended with the inconvenience of being envied and hated; and that a benevolent man should allow a few faults in himself to keep his friends in countenance."

But even when "do-gooder" simply means a person who does good deeds, there's still some skepticism, even antagonism, in it. One reason may be guilt: nobody likes to be reminded, even implicitly, of his own selfishness. Another is irritation: nobody likes to be told, even implicitly, how he should live his life, or be reproached for how he is living it. And nobody likes to be the recipient of charity. But that's not the whole story. There's a certain suspicion of do-gooders who work in NGOs, because aid money is often wasted and sometimes harms the people it's supposed to help. But that's not the whole story, either.

Ambivalence toward do-gooders also arises out of a deep uncertainty about how a person ought to live. Is it good to try to live as moral a life as possible—a saintly life? Or does a life like that lack some crucial human quality? Is it right to care for strangers at the expense of your own people? Is it good to bind yourself to a severe morality that constricts spontaneity and freedom? Is it possible for a person to hold himself to unforgiving standards without becoming unforgiving? Is it presumptuous, even blasphemous, for a person to imagine that he can transfigure the world—or to believe that it really matters what he does in his life when he's only a tiny flickering speck in a vast universe? Should morality be the highest human court—the one whose ruling overrides all others?

The philosopher Susan Wolf has written that a morally perfect person would be an unappealing, alien creature, driven not by the loves and delights of ordinary people but by an unnatural devotion to duty. In a life devoted only to duty, there's no room for art and little for enjoyment. "Morality itself," she writes, "does not seem to be a suitable object of passion." (It is a measure of how peculiar do-gooders have come to seem that a moral philosopher finds it unnatural to feel a passion for morality as such—and Wolf is not the only one who feels this way. A passion for morality is a passion for goodness—something like a secular version of a passion for God—and that did not used to seem so strange.) Wolf argues that if the ideal of the saintly do-gooder is not one we truly aspire to—if we feel that, in their strangeness or self-suppression, such people are missing some crucial human quality; if we believe, in other words, that the moral ideal is not a human ideal—then we should revise our ideas about the place of morality in life. Morality should *not* be the highest human court—the one whose ruling overrides all others.

So, yes, in the ambivalence toward do-gooders there can be petty defensiveness—resentment of being reproached and having to justify one's choices. There can be petty annoyance—irritation with earnestness or self-righteousness or priggishness. But there are also powerful forces that push against do-gooders which have nothing to do with any of those things, and which are not petty at all. Some of these forces are among the most fundamental, vital, and honorable urges of human life.

For instance: there is family and there are strangers. The do-gooder has a family like anyone else. If he doesn't have children, he has parents. But he holds himself to moral commitments that are so stringent and inflexible that they will at some point conflict with his caring for his family. Then he has to decide what to do.

To most people, it's obvious that they owe far more to family than to strangers. That's part of the very idea of family—family means those to whom you owe more. It might seem that caring for your family is the very heart of morality: charity begins at home. In some situations, it's true, preferring your family is called nepotism and is bad; in other situations, preferring your family is called incest and is very bad. But to most people, most of the time, the choice between family and strangers is no choice at all: caring for strangers' children as much as your own, say, would seem not so much difficult as unnatural, even monstrous. But the do-gooder doesn't believe his family deserves better than anyone else's. He loves his more, but he knows that other people love their families just as much. To a do-gooder, taking care of family can seem like a kind of moral alibi—something that may look like selflessness, but is really just an extension of taking care of yourself.

Political movements and religious orders have always known that a certain distance from the claims of family—sometimes to the point of celibacy or abandonment—is necessary for a total commitment to something larger. Abraham was ready to sacrifice his son; Agamemnon was ready to sacrifice his daughter; Buddha left his family behind. Saint Francis was brutal to his parents; Gandhi was brutal to his wife. Jesus says, in Luke: "If anyone comes to Me, and does not hate his own father and mother and wife and children and brothers and sisters, yes, and even his own life, he cannot be My disciple." Sometimes the claims of actual family have been not explicitly rejected so much as incorporated into spiritual family, to the point of disappearance: all humans become brothers; God becomes a husband.

A do-gooder might not go so far as hatred or abandonment, but the fact that he even asks himself how much he should do for his family and how much for strangers—weighing the two together in the same balance—may seem already a step too far. And not all religions permit the neglect of family for the sake of strangers. Under Sharia law, a Muslim must bequeath two thirds of his estate to his family, unless the family agrees otherwise. Sa'd Ibn Abi Waqqas, a wealthy convert, asked Mohammad whether he should leave two thirds of his estate to charity, since he possessed so much and had only one daughter; the prophet told him he should give away no more than one third lest he leave his daughter destitute. A Jew, by tradition, is obliged to give ten percent of his income to the poor, but must give no more than twenty percent, lest his family become poor itself, a public burden. In the Mishnah it is written: "If a man assigned his estate to strangers and leaves out his children, his arrangements are legally valid but the spirit of the Sages finds no delight in him."

Gandhi believed that the seeker after goodness is obliged to forswear close friendships and exclusive loves, because loyalty may tempt him to wrongdoing, and detracts from an impartial love of all mankind. Reviewing Gandhi's memoir, George Orwell found this belief repellent. He wrote:

> The essence of being human is that one does not seek perfection, that one *is* sometimes willing to commit sins for the sake of loyalty, that one does not push asceticism to the point where it makes friendly intercourse impossible, and that one is prepared in the end to be defeated and broken up by life, which is the inevitable price of fastening one's love upon other human individuals. . . . It is too readily assumed . . . that the ordinary man only rejects [saintliness] because it is too difficult: in other words, that the average human being is a failed saint. It is doubtful whether this is true. Many people genuinely do not wish to be saints, and it is probable that some who achieve or aspire to sainthood have never felt much temptation to be human beings.

At the same time, Orwell deeply admired Gandhi. Without him, the world would have been worse; and Gandhi could not have accomplished what he did without being the sort of saintly do-gooder that Orwell found so difficult to like.

There is one circumstance in which the extremity of do-gooders looks normal, and that is war. In wartime—or in a crisis so devastating that it resembles war, such as an earthquake or a hurricane—duty expands far beyond its peacetime boundaries. In wartime, it's thought dutiful rather than unnatural to leave your family for the sake of a cause. In wartime, the line between family and strangers grows faint, as the duty to one's own enlarges to encompass all the people who are on the same side. It's usually assumed that the reason do-gooders are so rare is that it's human nature to care only for your own. There's some truth to this, of course. But it's also true that many people care only for their own because they believe it's human nature to do so. When expectations change, as they do in wartime, behavior changes, too.

In war, what in ordinary times would be thought weirdly zealous becomes expected. In ordinary times, to ask a person to sacrifice his life for a stranger seems outrageous, but in war it is commonplace. Acts that seem appallingly bad or appallingly good in normal circumstances become part of daily life. In wartime, extreme malevolence is excused, and extreme virtue is also excused. People respond to this new moral regime in different ways: some suffer under the tension of moral extremity and long for the forgiving looseness of ordinary life; others feel it was the time when they were most vividly alive, in comparison with which the rest of life seems dull and lacking purpose.

In peacetime, selflessness can seem soft—a matter of too much empathy and too little self-respect. In war, selflessness looks like valor. In peacetime, a person who ignores all obligations, who isn't civilized, who does exactly as he pleases—an artist who abandons duty for his art; even a criminal—can seem glamorous because he's amoral and free. But in wartime, duty takes on the glamour of freedom, because duty becomes more exciting than ordinary liberty, and because war permits freedoms unheard of in peacetime, like the freedom to kill.

This is the difference between do-gooders and ordinary people: for do-gooders, it is always wartime. They always feel themselves responsible for strangers—they always feel that strangers, like compatriots in war, are their own people. They know that there are always those as urgently in need as the victims of battle, and they consider themselves conscripted by duty.

So is it good to try to live as moral a life as possible? Or is there something in the drive to extraordinary goodness that distances a person too much from ordinary humanity? I don't think this question can be answered in the abstract. In the abstract, there are ideas about saints and perfection. Only actual lives convey fully and in a visceral way the beauty and cost of a certain kind of moral existence.

For this reason, most of this book consists of stories about the lives of do-gooders: how they arrived at the moral principles they live by, and the choices they chose to face. Some of these are tiny, everyday choices, the kind that only a do-gooder's intense scrutiny would see as moral at all—whether to move a worm from a path, whether to buy an apple. Other choices are large and dreadful. One do-gooder decides she's willing to die in political protest, but knows that if she does she will abandon her son. A husband and wife create a refuge for lepers in a wilderness, knowing that their children may catch leprosy, or be eaten by panthers. Are all the choices these do-gooders have made the right ones? I don't know. Neither do they. It's a measure of their seriousness that they doubt and question themselves.

These do-gooders are very different from each other. Some are religious, others are not. Some have no children, others have dozens. Some care deeply about animals, others don't at all. Some think that suffering is pointless and wish it could be eliminated; others believe it makes compassion possible and is at the core of the human condition. They come from different walks of life and different parts of the world. One thing they have in common is that they consider it their duty to help other people. That is the form their morality takes; they are not interested in purity or asceticism. None of them is a world-historical figure—they are not Gandhis or Mother Teresas. Most

famous do-gooders come to public attention because they have a ge-
nius unrelated to their goodness: they're entrepreneurs or political
leaders who found institutions or alter the fates of populations, and
are judged on their success. But I want to separate the moral urge
from those grand forces, to try, insofar as it's possible, to see it by
itself.

Do-gooders are eccentrics, but their influence extends beyond
themselves, because where there's a sense that do-gooders are *too*
eccentric, too distant from ordinary people, there is also a sense that
doing good may be responsible for that distance. Where there's a
sense that extreme morality conflicts with humanity, there is also a
fear that to push yourself morally is to distance yourself from human
fellowship. Ambivalence about do-gooders can make trying to live a
more moral life seem less appealing, less necessary. You may wonder:
do do-gooders understand that it is flawed humans, weak humans,
ordinary humans, whom we love? And: if do-gooders are always
thinking of how the world is unjust and needs to be changed—if they
want to replace our world with another, better one—then do they
love the world that we know, which is the world as it is?

THE BODIES OF STRANGERS

Ayear after the betrayal, Dorothy Granada moved to Matagalpa. She had retreated to the capital to be alone and think about what to do next. It was 2010, she was nearly eighty, but she didn't want to stop working. Then the Ministry of Health asked her to move up here to put together a training program for the midwives of the campo, so that became what she did next. The Ministry of Health knew what she could do. She had not expected to start again in a new place at this point in her life, but that was the way it had worked out.

Matagalpa was a small city in the mountains, toward the Atlantic coast of Nicaragua, eighty miles from the capital. She rented a house in the hills south of the city and moved in there with a family she knew from the cooperative—the husband, a former guerrilla; the wife, who used to work for the police. She could have taken care of herself if she had to, but she was old now, slower and weaker than she used to be; it was better to have help. The house was made of concrete, on a dirt road, with a leafy porch and enough bedrooms for her and the couple and their children. There was a cleared space in the back for a cooking fire and drying laundry, and beyond that were woods. Down in the city it was very loud—there was always music blaring, and car horns honking, and motorcycles revving, and people riding around in trucks shouting political slogans from megaphones. If you looked up from the streets you could see the mountains, but in the middle of the day they seemed not to lift the city skyward but to close it in, to trap it in a bowl of noise. Here, up in the hills, it was quiet. Behind the house the dirt road dwindled to a path, cratered with puddles and muddied by streams over which people threw down wood planks for crossing, bordered by a mess of scrubby trees and bushes. She walked her dog there.

In the living room of the house she kept her books and old magazines, and there were a couple of comfortable chairs where she sat and read and drank her evening glass of wine. She read murder mysteries, when she could get them; most of the peace activists she knew read murder mysteries. How else to get out their aggression? she thought. They weren't allowed to kill people, so they read about it. There was a little room where she had a desk and a file cabinet and a computer. There was a photograph of her with Christopher, her son from her first marriage, their heads together.

The midwives she would be training lived in remote mountain settlements far from any medical care; they had been taught by their mothers. If a woman had a difficult labor out in one of these settlements, she would die; but difficult labors rarely came as a surprise, so the key was to teach the midwives how to recognize the signs of danger and get those women to a health center. They must monitor blood pressure to watch for hypertension; they must palpate the woman's belly to feel where the baby's head was. The settlements were not even villages but perhaps ten or twenty huts, far apart; her trainers, obstetrical nurses, would have to walk an hour in one direction, two hours in another. Some of the houses could be reached only on foot, along dirt paths that became treacherous in the rainy season.

Sometimes at the height of that season, when the rivers were swollen, it became impossible to leave the settlements, so it was also necessary to train the midwives to cope with dangerous labor by themselves. It wasn't just a matter of the labor itself; there were other ways a pregnant woman could die. If a man beat his wife, he often grew more violent when she was pregnant, so it was not only high blood pressure and diabetes that the midwife must look for in her women but also bruises and depression. Originally, Dorothy had planned to restrict the midwife training to women who were literate enough to keep records, but there were so few who met this standard that she had to drop it and improvise: if a midwife could not write, she needed to find a child who could. Dorothy raised money for basic equipment—blood-pressure gauges, bulb syringes, backpacks, rain boots, a few raincoats. The minute she started working again, she felt better. This was what she loved to do. This was what she was good at.

Some people try to help one person at a time, and other people try to change the whole world. There is a seductive intimacy in the first kind of work, but it can also be messy and unpredictable. People may resent help that is so intimate, and if the help goes badly, the blunder is personal. Even when the help succeeds, the victories are small and don't really change anything. The second kind of work is more ambitious, and also cleaner, more abstract. But success is distant and unlikely, so it's helpful to have a taste for noble failure, and for the camaraderie of the angry few.

Dorothy started out in the first kind of work: she was a nurse. But in the middle of her life she felt that nursing wasn't enough, she ought to do more, so she took up the second kind—she became an activist protesting poverty and nuclear weapons. She did that for many years, and then she realized that she didn't like the sort of person who tries to change the whole world. "I was out there doing civil disobedience and all that good stuff," she says. "It was all sacrifice, all for the cause, personal happiness was not important. We were confronting the powers and principalities, we were going to jail. And then I thought, We're so *serious*, all us peace-and-justice people. These people, they can't have fun, they have to be out on the firing line all the time." For years she had been like them. She carried the burden of duty around as they did—the world was on the brink of nuclear annihilation, and only she and these few others seemed to understand and care enough to stand up to it. "Those people did wonderful work, but they were really not nice people," she realized. "They were people you did not want to be around. They were so sharp. Everything was a matter of life and death: we've got to do this action because the world depends on it."

She thought: What makes me happy? What makes me happy is

being a nurse. And why shouldn't I do what makes me happy, as long as I am working for the good of the world? God didn't want you to be miserable—He wanted you to do good. In fact, she thought, it was better to be happy, because you did better work.

She had lived so many lives already that it didn't seem like much to her to throw out this one and begin another. It would be an adventure. She was an optimist, and anyway, it had been her experience that any new life was likely to be better than the one before. She was half Mexican, half Filipina, and had grown up in the ghetto in L.A. The old life usually wasn't so great that she regretted leaving it.

In the middle of her life, she was sick of the peace movement, and she was sick of being a brown person in North America, so in the mid-1980s she moved to Nicaragua with her husband, Charles Gray, to work with Latinas like herself. She thought: "The woman who gets up at three a.m. to grind the corn, she's had thirteen babies, half of whom have died either because of disease or because of the war, and this woman has never had five minutes to realize what sort of a human being she could be, because she's always cooking and having babies and burying her children—that is the woman I want to work with."

She wanted to work in a clinic for women, but she didn't want to start one—she didn't want to be a gringa do-gooder coming in with a plan. She wanted to find a group of women who were already organized and looking for a nurse. It took her some time to find one. Meanwhile, she and her husband went to live in an *asentamiento*—an encampment where refugees from the countryside gathered together for protection against the fighting—where she set up a clinic to train health workers. At the time, the war between the U.S.-backed Contras and the Soviet-backed Sandinistas was at its height—the Sandinistas were in power, and the Contras were trying to unseat them. She didn't know much about the Sandinistas before she got there, but she was quickly converted. She heard that on the first day after the insurrection in 1979, the Ministry of Culture was founded and the death penalty abolished, and she thought, I'm going to like this place. Health clinics were opening, even in the countryside; there were infant-care centers and school lunch programs. Volunteers showed up with shovels to clear up garbage dumps together. But most of all she was converted by the art. There were murals everywhere. It seemed that everybody was writing poetry and reading it aloud. Cultural centers were springing up, teaching people how to paint, how to dance, how to read and write. It seemed to her a kind of paradise. "Can you beat a revolution like that?" she says. "Oh, the eighties, what a holiday! All of us poured in from all over the world. What a celebration! It was marvelous."

After a few years, she heard about a women's cooperative in a town called Mulukukú that was looking for a nurse to run a clinic. The cooperative was having trouble finding someone willing to move there, because it was still so dangerous. The war was officially over by then, but there were still ex-soldiers everywhere, cut loose without any money, carrying guns, kidnapping people for ransom. There were no police.

Mulukukú was a new town, a frontier settlement in the middle of nowhere, one hundred and fifty miles northeast of Managua, the capital. People had started turning up there during the war. There was no town then—only an army training school near the Rio Tuma and a couple of cantinas that doubled as brothels. As the fighting in the countryside grew worse, refugees started collecting in Mulukukú in the hope that the soldiers would protect them. A few stalls with thatched roofs opened on either side of a dirt street—horses tethered outside, pigs wandering around. Many of the people who arrived were widows from the war, so often women did the building. They cleared the land, dug latrines, put up plastic shelters and houses made out of old boards and metal sheeting; then they established a day-care center and started a factory to make cinder blocks for proper houses. During the war, many had died from bullets shot through wood walls, so people wanted brick.

Once the houses were built, the women had formed a cooperative, led by a woman named Grethel Montoya. Grethel's husband, Noel, had been an engineer in Managua, but he had inherited a large tract of forest land around Mulukukú. Because farmers were fleeing the fighting, there was a shortage of food, and the government called on everyone who owned land of any kind to farm it, so Noel quit his job, cleared the land, and planted crops. By this time there were about a thousand people living in Mulukukú; many women were dying in labor and from unsafe abortions, and many were having more babies than they wanted. The cooperative realized the town needed a women's health clinic.

Dorothy decided that this was the place. Her husband had worked as a carpenter, and he built a house for them up in the hills on the edge of town, out of split bamboo held together with vines. They bathed in the creek at the foot of the hill, because it was too hard to haul enough water for a bath. The mosquitoes were vicious, but they had nets at night. The women of the cooperative wanted a carpentry shop; Charles Gray taught them how to build wooden frames for houses, frames for windows, and furniture.

Bit by bit, they built the clinic. At first she saw patients in a spare room in the school, and then, finally, when they had amassed enough donated money to build it, in a new cinder-block clinic, which had four consulting rooms and a waiting space and a dormitory for women waiting to give birth or escaping violent husbands. The clinic provided birth control; it administered prenatal tests and Pap smears. Some days there were a hundred people waiting outside the door when it opened. Because some women lived in settlements too remote for them to come to the clinic, they sent health workers out into the countryside, who traveled for many hours each way; when the roads ended, they proceeded on foot, or on horseback, or by boat.

If a patient needed to be operated on, Dorothy would put her in some kind of vehicle and drive to the nearest hospital that could do what needed to be done. Matagalpa was ninety miles away, but the roads were terrible; it was a hundred and fifty miles to Managua, and in the early days it could take twenty-four hours to get there. During the rainy season, the roads flooded and became nearly impassable. Sometimes she would set out hoping that the road would hold, and become trapped in the mud, in several feet of water, and have to wait for a tractor to pull her out. Sometimes part of the road would be flooded, so they'd get out of their vehicle, carrying the patient in a stretcher, and walk until they could find another vehicle on the other side of the water.

Dorothy would say to women who had had lots of babies in a few years, After this pregnancy you need to rest your body. Many women didn't want more babies—they couldn't afford it, they were exhausted, they had terrible uterine prolapses from too many pregnancies—but they were scared to use birth control, because their husbands or their church opposed it. One woman's husband found her birth control pills and denounced her to their church; the members of the church shouted at her that she was a whore, and they shunned her. The woman told Dorothy that she could not go through that again. She had almost died in her last labor, and she knew she might die if she had another baby, but death was better than exile.

There was one woman in Mulukukú, very overweight, with diabetes and toxemia, who had given birth to six children. When she was pregnant with her seventh child, Dorothy went to her home and told her she was in danger; she should get prenatal care; she should give birth in a hospital. But the woman had given birth to babies before without any problems, she couldn't understand what the fuss was about, and she refused. Dorothy pleaded with her; she went back to her home a second time to make her case, but the woman said no. Sometime later, the woman went into labor and showed up at the clinic, but by that time it was too late. The baby was dead inside her. They didn't have the equipment to do a C-section, so they had to pull the baby out. It was an enormous baby, twelve pounds, it took several people to pull it out, and they had no anesthetic for the woman. It was terrible; that scene haunted Dorothy for years. What else could she have done? she wondered. Should she have kidnapped the woman? Should she have brought in the police?

She saw a lot of terrible things in those days: babies dying in front of her, women dying in childbirth, women beaten by their husbands, women killed by their husbands. She tried not to cry in front of the patients; she cried at night. The cooperative organized women in their neighborhoods so that if one woman was being beaten the others banged their pots and pans to alert the neighborhood and scare the man off. If a husband went to jail, they tried to help the woman to support her kids—they might give her a loan to start a business. Mulukukú was a new village, everyone who lived there had run away from somewhere else, so nobody had any roots there, and neighbors didn't know each other. A lot of the men who beat their wives were soldiers who had been demobilized when the war ended. They had come in search of land, but many had not received any pay during the fighting, only equipment and food, so even when they found land they had no money to develop it, no money for seeds or fertilizer or fences or plows. They had no way to make a living and no purpose anymore, Dorothy thought, so they got drunk and beat their wives and felt like men again.

In the early days, many women in the cooperative thought the clinic should treat only Sandinista families, but Dorothy told them that if they wanted to do that she would leave. Though she didn't convince them at first, they needed her and backed down. To her, this wasn't so much a matter of fairness as a political tactic: she thought that health care could be used as a means of reconciliation. If you treated the Contras well and cured them when they were sick, they might stop hating you, and perhaps by extension they would stop hating other Sandinistas as well. Kindness changed people. Yes, it was possible that she might sometimes cure Contras and enable them to go out again and kill more Sandinistas, but that was a risk she had to take.

One time, she thought she might have done just that. A bus she was riding was stopped by a group of six or seven men carrying

AK-47s. They told everybody to get off the bus and line up. Two or three of the passengers started to run away; the soldiers shot at them and hit one man in the ankle. She took off her head scarf and wrapped it around the man's leg to stop the bleeding. The soldiers were Sandinistas, and the wounded man was a Contra, and they were going to kill him. She said to the other passengers, We have to stop them. Let's lie on top of him and make a pile of bodies. The passengers looked at her as if she were crazy, and the Sandinistas started to drag the wounded man off behind some bushes. She followed them, yelling, Don't hurt him! I can see what you're doing! I'm a witness! Then one of the Sandinistas said, Okay, we'll give him to you. She dragged the man back onto the bus and brought him to a health center in Rio Blanco. Later, she found out that he was a robber; he recovered nicely and went back to robbing once his leg was healed. Did he kill people? She didn't know—probably he did. But she still felt she'd done the only thing she could.

One afternoon, she was doing consultations in the clinic, and all the doors were open because it was so hot. She could see women and children outside in the corridor waiting to come in—and then, all of a sudden, everybody disappeared. She didn't know why until her next patient came in, and then she knew. He was a man with a terrible face. She had seen terrible faces like that on the men from the death squads in Guatemala. If you tortured and murdered, it did something to your face, she thought—the whole face looked hard and empty, as though it had been drained. She was told later that the man was the leader of a band of Contra who had done terrible things around Mulukukú, killing children, smashing a baby against a tree. He had come to the clinic because he had chronic pain in his head—a Sandinista bullet was lodged there. She told him she could give him something for pain, but he would have to see a neurologist in Matagalpa; she would make an appointment for him. He told her he could not go to Matagalpa, he would be killed. She told him she would take him there.

After that, the man brought his wife to the clinic, and the wife brought her brothers and sisters and all of their children. At last, the man brought his mother, and Dorothy knew they had won. Sometime later, the man heard of a group of Contras in the mountains who were planning to attack the clinic—the clinic got many death threats because they were associated with the Sandinistas. The man went to the group in the mountains and told them not to kill the clinic workers because they were taking care of Contra families, and the group did not come.

For a while, the clinic itself was safe, but only the clinic. Sometime around 1995, when Dorothy was living by herself in the bamboo house on the edge of town—after a dramatic argument in which she threatened him with a knife, she and Charles had split up and he had gone back to Oregon—the cooperative heard that a group of Contras was going to come and kill them. There was a list of names, and Dorothy's was on it. The cooperative held a meeting to discuss what to do. Dorothy said that if a group of Contras with machine guns showed up at one of their doors, they weren't going to be able to fight back—their only hope was to get the attackers to change their minds. So, instead of opposing them with violence, the cooperative members should offer them hospitality. The women decided that every night they would prepare some kind of food to offer the Contras, should they appear; Grethel said she would always have a plate of corn tamales ready. Dorothy said she didn't know how to make tamales, but she knew that Nicaraguans drank coffee day and night, so every evening, before she went to bed, just before she let her fire burn out, she prepared a fresh pot.

One night, the Contras came. They came to her house and called for her—Dona Dorotea!—to open her door. There were two of them, each armed with a rifle. They accused her of carrying guns for Sandinistas in the mountains, and said they were going to take her money. They figured that since she was a gringa she must have money, but when they ransacked her house they found nothing. They were furious. Why didn't she have any money? She told them that there was a medical delegation in town and she had given all her money to pay for transferring patients to the hospital. They kept poking her with their rifles, accusing her of running guns. She told them she was terrified of guns and never went near them.

Then they told her they were going to rape her. She had known she might be killed, but she hadn't thought about rape. In the end, they did not rape her—they left. And then, suddenly, as they were walking away, she remembered the coffee; she had been so frightened that she had forgotten all about it. She ran after them and called, Wait, I forgot something! Would you like a cup of coffee? The Contras told her they weren't going to drink her coffee, she would poison them. She assured them she would never poison them: she was a pacifist, she wasn't allowed to do that. They looked at her as if she were crazy and walked away. After that, she never spent another night in the bamboo house. She moved down into town, where someone would hear her scream if something like that happened again.

But the next bad thing that happened was so different that she was equally unprepared. In the 1996 elections, Arnoldo Alemán—head of the right-wing Liberal Alliance, known as El Gordo, the Fat Man—defeated the Sandinistan president Daniel Ortega. Alemán was convinced, she thought, that NGOs were allied with the Sandinistas, and seemed to be trying to shut them down. In 2000, he accused Dorothy of treating leftist rebels and performing illegal abortions and ordered that she be deported. She went into hiding, staying in one friend's house after another, moving around in a car, wearing a scarf and dark glasses, feeling as if she were in a movie. The clinic closed down—she had been the only nurse.

Human rights groups protested her persecution, and a group of U.S. congressmen sent a letter asking the government to change its mind. The case was written about so much in the press that Dorothy became famous throughout the country—referred to in the papers by her first name alone, Dorotea, as Daniel Ortega was always Daniel. After several months, a court suspended the deportation order, and she came out of hiding. She returned to Mulukukú and was received by happy crowds as, in the words of a newspaper article about the event, "a goddess, a martyr, a celestial messenger, a mother protector, a star, a sun that arrived to illuminate the lives of thousands." Six years later, Ortega, president again, presented her with the Order of Rubén Dario, the highest award given by the Nicaraguan government.

At some point in her time at the clinic, she had realized that she no longer believed in God. It was too difficult, surrounded as she was by pain and war. On the other hand, by the time she stopped believing in God, she had started to believe in human beings. She had seen people do a lot of terrible things, but she had seen a lot of people doing heroic things as well, and in the eighties, at least, she had seen what a revolution could be like.

She had lived a long time before she saw people doing heroic things. By then her expectations were so low, particularly of men, that it was not surprising that that brief surge of revolutionary fervor and public-spiritedness in Nicaragua should appear to her almost like a miracle. She had always been a nurse, had always wanted to take care of people, but not until the middle of her life did she manage to claw her way out from her dreadful childhood and her dreadful marriage, far enough to see that she could do more. It then seemed to her that it was not enough to be a nurse, doing work that someone else would do if she didn't. She would change her life, and she would do work that needed to be done but that other people would not do, because it was too hard or too dangerous.

She was raised Catholic in the ghetto in Central L.A. Her mother was Mexican, and they lived on the border of a Mexican neighborhood in what would later become Koreatown, but because her father was Filipino, as were all her mother's subsequent boyfriends, their family wasn't accepted there. Her mother was born in the States; her father had owned a farm east of Los Angeles, in Chino, but he lost it in the Depression, and soon after that both he and his wife died, so as a teenager, with three younger brothers to support, Dorothy's mother moved to the city to find work. She sold apples and newspapers on the street, and when she was sixteen, in 1930, she got pregnant and gave birth to Dorothy. Her mother was very pale, but Dorothy's father was dark, and she came out dark like him.

Her father was an immigrant from the southern part of the Philippines. She didn't know much about him. She knew that a lot of Filipinos had come over to California in the twenties to work in agriculture or build the railroads, so maybe he was one of them. He deserted her mother when Dorothy was an infant, and after that only reappeared from time to time. He was a violent man and used to beat her mother. Her only clear memory of him was of the time he tried to kill them. She was about three years old, and they were driving somewhere in the hills above Hollywood. He was shouting and her mother was crying, and he said he was going to drive them all off the cliff, and Dorothy, sitting in between her parents in the front seat, tried to pull the brake to stop the car. Later, she heard from someone she had grown up with that her father had been sentenced to life in prison and had been killed by another inmate in San Quentin.

Her mother kept moving in search of cheaper apartments and jobs—she worked in factories, she was too proud to clean houses—so Dorothy kept changing schools. At the end of grade school, she could barely read or write. Her mother had one boyfriend after another, and the house was chaotic and violent; the boyfriends would hit her and beat her mother. She started running away when she was ten; sometimes she would go to a relative's house; sometimes she would sleep in an abandoned building. One relative abused her sexually when she was a child; Dorothy was pretty sure he was also sleeping with her mother. A couple of times as a teenager she attempted suicide.

She skipped school a lot and went to the library or the museum. She was friends with a few Japanese kids until, when she was eleven, white people ransacked their homes and imprisoned them in horse stalls at the Santa Anita racetrack and then in internment camps farther away. She knew she wanted to be a nurse—she knew she wanted to take care of people—and she knew she couldn't be a nurse if she didn't graduate from high school, so she agreed to go with her stepfather to the Philippines to finish. He put her in a strict Dominican convent school, where she relieved her rage at the nuns by smoking in the bathroom, but she managed to graduate.

She came to hate Catholicism. All she heard about when she was little was pain and sacrifice and the bleeding Jesus. Life was a vale of tears; it was always Good Friday for the Catholics she knew. When she entered an Episcopal church as a teenager, she saw an empty cross for the first time in her life: no bloody corpse nailed onto it, just an empty cross. Of course, she thought: there had been a resurrection. The Episcopal church became her refuge. It felt safe, and it gave a form to her anger. But then the Episcopal pastor seduced her when she was still in school, and the abuse continued for years. At the time she didn't know it was abuse—she thought that she was being rescued and this was the price.

She moved away to live in Puerto Rico for three years—working as chief nurse in a hospital and directing a nursing school. She was working at the U.S. Army hospital in Heidelberg when she met her first husband. Robert Cutler was a few years younger than she was; he was serving as an army doctor in Mannheim, but he had a bleeding ulcer and so he ended up as her patient. He was a blue blood from New England. He grew up in Connecticut and played tennis and sailed at a summer home in Maine; his father was the head of a shipping company. She was dazzled, and she was as exotic to him as he was to her. They moved back to the States, married, settled in Chicago, and had a son, Christopher. Robert Cutler was a resident at the university hospital, and Dorothy was director of medical nursing. They lived in Hyde Park. She wore Peck & Peck shirtwaists and girdles and tried to be the perfect wife, but it didn't work. Robert

Cutler started coming home only to eat, returning to his lab to work into the night. Finally, after eleven years together, they divorced.

She pulled herself together and decided to change her life. She had realized long ago, when she was living in Puerto Rico, that it was only in Latino places that she really felt at home. She was done with middle-class life, she decided, done with privilege, done with being the exotic brown person among white people. She quit her job at the university hospital and went to work in the Mexican barrio, as a nurse at the free clinic of a community center. Most of the people who showed up at the community center were Mexican immigrants working on the railroad; some were Brown Berets, a militant Chicano group that came out of East L.A. At first she liked the Brown Berets, and they liked her for improving the clinic, but then they found out that she was still living in Hyde Park. Hyde Park was for white people, they said; why didn't she live in the ghetto? She came from the ghetto, she told them, and she wasn't going back. The Brown Berets turned against her, and she was driven out.

She thought: If I am not going to work in the barrio, I want to live someplace where Christopher can grow up canoeing and climbing mountains. She moved to Portland, Oregon, and got a job as a nursing supervisor for the county health services. Then, one Sunday morning in 1978, she was in church when she suddenly heard, as if for the first time, that the kernel of Jesus's message was to resist violence and stand with the poor. She thought to herself in wonderment: It's so easy—so simple. To her, standing with the poor meant being one of them. She was no longer married to a doctor, she had left Chicago, but she still had a full-time job, she was earning thirty-three thousand dollars a year. She had a car, and she and Christopher had an eight-room house just for the two of them. Now she wanted to get rid of those things. Normally if she made a decision she acted on it immediately, but she didn't want to do that to Christopher: he had been raised as a doctor's son, she didn't want to drag him down into poverty with her. She decided that she would stay in the middle class for a couple more years, until Christopher went to college, and then she would get rid of everything.

The resisting-violence part, though—that she could act on now. She started to think about violence, and she decided that the most violent thing she could think of was a nuclear bomb. There weren't any nuclear bombs in Oregon, but there was a nuclear power plant—the Trojan plant in Prescott, forty miles north of Portland on the Columbia River. Nuclear power plants and nuclear bombs were part of the same system, she thought. She joined the Fellowship of Reconciliation, a peace group that had been founded by Christians in Europe in 1914. It had supported conscientious objectors and the labor movement, freedom riders and civil rights activists. It was against war, the death penalty, and nuclear power. It was exactly what she was looking for.

The first time she got arrested, she spent four days in jail, locked in a cell with ten other women, all activists who'd been arrested with her. There were no beds, so they lay on the floor, and some of them were scared. But she wasn't scared—she was exhilarated. She said to the women, Do you know who is here in jail with us? Cesar Chavez! Dorothy Day! It is a *privilege* to be in here, she told them. She felt that she was in a place the saints had passed through. She felt that she was home.

Then, in the summer of 1980, she was involved in a break-in at the Trojan plant. She was too short to climb over the wall by herself, so a tall, skinny white man named Charles Gray lifted her up. It had been a long time since a man had touched her.

Thus began the middle period of Dorothy's life, which she spent with a complicated man who was consumed by a strange moral hunger. He had started out doing normal things like joining protests and giving sums of money away, but he craved more and more sacrifice and ended up nearly killing them both. A few years before he met Dorothy, he had committed himself to an extreme way of living that he believed justice required of him, whose radicalism was equaled only by its utter futility. He persuaded no one other than Dorothy to join him in it, and she had already decided to do something similar. And yet, over the years, many people read about his quixotic experiment and saw that they could change their lives more completely than they thought was possible.

Charles Gray was protesting at the Trojan plant because he was terrified of nuclear war. He had been terrified for years—so much so that after the Cuban Missile Crisis he had moved with his first wife and their young kids to New Zealand, which he had determined was highly unlikely to be attacked. At that time he was a college professor, but after they moved back to Oregon he got involved with some politically radical Quakers and quit academia to be an anti-nuclear and anti-poverty activist full time. He had a flair for the work: he was always coming up with attention-grabbing ways of publicizing information and statistics, and soon became locally famous. He put together a roving anti-nuclear production, Dr. Atomic's World Famous Medicine Show and Lending Library, and he and some other people drove it all over Oregon by bicycle and VW bus.

He had grown up poor, but his wife had inherited money, and now he and she set about giving it away to political causes. They gave away half their capital, and turned their house into a commune, but he wanted to do more: giving away so much money, he had experienced a thrill of liberation, and he wanted to feel it again. He had always felt guilty about having the money in the first place, and now he saw how easy it was to slough off that guilt. He kept thinking how wrong it was for them to have so much when so many others had nothing, and after some time he came up with the idea that he should live on his fair share of the world's wealth—what he called the World Equity Budget, or WEB. His first notion of this was simply to divide the world's total income by the number of people. But then he thought about future generations, and decided that, because the world population was growing, he would need to reduce his budget periodically to keep up. He ended up with a figure of about twelve hundred dollars a year. His wife refused to join him—she felt that giving away half her money was enough. She told him he had to choose between the World Equity Budget and her. Even though he still loved her, and they had been married for thirty years and had two children together, he chose the budget, and they got divorced.

He gave away all his possessions except for a few clothes and household items. His friends thought it was strange and awful that he had given up his marriage in order to identify with a bunch of poor people he'd never even met. People thought he was acting pure and self-righteous and judging them for being less so. They told him that what he was doing wasn't going to help any poor person, it had zero potential as a social movement, nobody gave a damn, he was starving himself for no reason—what was needed was institutional change, not personal witness. But to him those arguments just sounded like excuses for continuing to live like a rich person. He knew he wasn't starting a movement, though he did have a slogan for one ("Get poor now. Avoid the rush later"), and published a book-length manifesto, *Toward a Nonviolent Economics*. But he felt now that when he talked about equality and poverty he was no longer just spouting phrases. He knew, of course, that choosing poverty was very different from having it thrust upon you, and that his education set him apart from most poor people, but at least now he no longer felt complicit in their misfortune. He felt, after years of guilt and conflict, at peace.

At the end of 1980, Dorothy moved from Portland to Eugene. She had fallen in love with Charles Gray and taken on the whole package, World Equity Budget and all. He was funny and handsome and smart, and he was deeply committed to the same things she was committed to. It had taken him years of sorting out his financial affairs and psychological preparation before he was ready to change his life, but Dorothy dove in all at once. She had been waiting for this. She quit her job, sold her house, and gave everything else away, keeping only two boxes of books and her bicycle. She didn't need money anymore—Christopher's father was now a professor at Stanford, and Stanford would pay for Christopher's college tuition. She realized, with a grateful sense of the immense privilege of her situation, that she was free.

Dorothy loved living on the WEB; it was a challenge and an adventure. At that point, Charles was living on sixty-two dollars a month, earning a tiny wage working as a carpenter; Dorothy worked part time in a nursing home, and threw herself into her activism. Charles taught her how to Dumpster-dive for food, and where the best Dumpsters were, and she was an immediate convert; she never felt ashamed, as he had at first. She was astonished at the things you could find. There was a real bonanza once a year in the Dumpsters outside the University of Oregon dormitories, when departing students would throw away all sorts of things, even furniture. She tried not to patronize the Safeway Dumpsters, because she disapproved of Safeway: they sold products sprayed with insecticide, harvested by ill-treated farmworkers. She was aware this was a ridiculous position—as if Safeway would care that she declined to sort through their garbage—but she stuck to it nonetheless.

She realized that she could wear only one set of clothes at a time, and could be in only one room at a time, and could eat only so much food, and everything else was surplus. Most years, they spent even less than they were entitled to. They knew that if one of them got really sick, either they would have to break the budget or they would do what the world's poor generally did in such situations: die. But it didn't happen, so they didn't worry about it. Once, Charles ended up at the hospital and was classified as indigent, so he didn't have to pay, but in general they tried to avoid welfare programs, even though they recognized that by using parks, libraries, roads, and city water they were benefiting from America's wealth anyway.

At one point early on, when they were living in one room together in a shared house, Charles told Dorothy he thought they should live on the street. They were using money to pay rent that they could give away to people who needed it more; it had come to seem to him uncomfortably luxurious to live indoors. Dorothy told him she was not willing to live on the street—she didn't think it was purer, she didn't think anybody should live on the street. He was welcome to do it, but he would have to do it alone.

The WEB was not, for her, about simplicity or purity—she aspired to neither—but about justice. She loved nice things, good food, good wine, and pretty clothes; she loved the security of money. She just didn't love them enough to feel right about contributing to an unjust world. She believed that God wanted her to stand with the poor, and that was what she was going to do. To do it, she had to be poor herself. For Charles, the WEB was a moral absolute in itself that must not be violated: going over the budget was a crisis for him. To her, the WEB was an idea, a guideline, and if they went over, well, that was life. "I told Charles Gray, 'Okay, I'm in love with you. I love the project. I'll join the World Equity Budget. But I must have my glass of wine before dinner, and my coffee. I will not do without that.' We used to fight—he was always adding up every penny, he kept a notebook. Once, he told me that I was thirty-eight cents over budget. I said, 'Would you repeat what you just said?' And then I told him what he could do with his World Equity Budget."

Charles needed to push himself to the limit of what he could do—there was no lightness in him, he felt that he was chosen and his work was urgent—but she never felt that she or her life was particularly significant. She was just one small person among many others on the earth. "He was a purist and a puritan," she says. "I don't know how I got involved with a puritan—I'm Latina, I'm very loose. I don't know how I married him. It was an adventure. Plus, he was good in bed, because he'd had a lot of practice."

People said that if there was a woman in Eugene who stood still for more than five minutes, he would seduce her. Charles's first wife had put up with his ideas about sexual liberty, but Dorothy was very churchy and very jealous. She had no interest in free love, and no doubts at all about whether screwing whomever you wanted might be an essential part of the liberation of humanity, or the path to a new world, or keeping in touch with your feelings, or anything like that. Charles didn't give up easily. He took her to a house in Eugene where eight or ten men and women lived together and kept a calendar to determine who would sleep together each night. (They had to rotate regularly, or people might develop favorites.) One man showed her around the house and explained their system; after listening to him patiently, she said to Charles, These people are nuts. If you want to be with me, you have to be monogamous. I'm too old and not athletic enough for experiments like that.

They married in 1981, in a not-quite legally binding ceremony on the bank of the Willamette River. An Episcopal priest offered a Mass, and then performed the marriage ceremony from the Book of Common Prayer; since they didn't believe in involving the state, they didn't get marriage certificates. She wore a long white muslin dress, he wore a white shirt and white pants, and they both wore leis that a friend had made for the occasion. Someone played the guitar, and everybody sang.

All this time, Charles was still obsessed with the threat of nuclear war. He couldn't understand why it didn't terrify everyone. How could people just go about their lives as though everything was normal when the planet might be incinerated at any moment? It was crazy. The protests he had been involved in thus far, mostly climbing into nuclear plants, had clearly not had much impact. He had always been impressed by the effectiveness of Gandhi's fasts. Finally, in the late 1970s, he had decided that the situation was urgent enough that he had to oppose it with the strongest means available to him: an open-ended fast, possibly to the death.

He had already started planning what he called the "Fast for Life," in protest of the deployment of cruise and Pershing missiles in Europe, when he met Dorothy, and it was part of the package she signed on to—she agreed not only to accept it but to join him. She felt strongly about the issue as well, but they felt strongly about it for different reasons. He was against nuclear bombs because he was worried about the world blowing up. She wasn't so anxious about the world ending; she was against bombs because they were expensive and siphoned away government money that could have been used to feed people. When she thought about nuclear weapons, she pictured children starving.

They researched fasting, and discovered that a long fast required training, like anything else. You had to prepare your body and your mind. For three years they practiced: they did three-day fasts, week-long fasts, two-week fasts. For a year they traveled all over the country and to Europe and Asia, recruiting fasters and spreading the word. Their flights were paid for by donors to the fasting organization, and they stayed in people's houses wherever they went, but this program was so completely out of tune with the WEB that it made them uncomfortable. During these preparations, in 1981, Bobby Sands, a young member of the Provisional Irish Republican Army, died in prison while on hunger strike, and they saw that his death brought much sympathy and attention to his cause.

They began the fast on Hiroshima Day—August 6—1983. The core fasters set up headquarters in several cities: four people in Paris (including Solange Fernex of the Green Party), two in Bonn, and Dorothy, Charles, a Canadian, and a Japanese man in Oakland. In addition, thousands of other fasters fasted for less time—a day, three days, ten days. There was a communications office in Oakland with ten volunteers to take calls and read letters and deal with the press. Willy Brandt met with the fasters in Bonn and vowed to oppose deployment of missiles in Germany; two ministers from the Mitterrand government met with the fasters in Paris.

After four days, Dorothy stopped feeling hungry—she just felt empty. She knew from her research that it took three weeks or so for the body to burn through the easily metabolized fat and start in on the muscle. Later on, she felt very, very tired, but at the same time she felt a sense of spiritual well-being—a holy presence, as if God were with her. She came to feel that fasting was a kind of prayer.

She was open to the idea of fasting to death, but there was Christopher to consider. She had vowed to him that she wasn't going to die, but in fact she was waiting to see what would happen. At some point after the fast began, Christopher read an interview or saw something on TV and realized that the fast was open-ended. He became very upset; the fact that his mother could consider doing that to him, and that she had lied to him about it, destroyed something in him. Even thirty years after the fast was over, he was still determined never to believe a promise, or to make one himself.

On September 1, day twenty-seven of the fast, Korean Air Lines Flight 007, en route from New York to Seoul, was shot down by the Soviets over the Sea of Japan. Everyone on board, including a U.S. congressman, was killed. It was a terrible moment in the Cold War, and it soon became clear that if there was ever going to be a time when the United States might consider nuclear disarmament, this was not going to be it. Dorothy had lost forty pounds and was beginning to go blind. On the thirty-eighth day, Daniel Berrigan, a well-known Catholic anti-nuclear activist whom Dorothy had great respect for, called her up and told her, It's enough: stop. And she stopped. Two days later, on day forty, Charles stopped, too. Some activists were angry. They said, He said he was going to fast to the death—he went back on his word, the fast doesn't count. Others were angry that they were fasting in the first place; they thought it was a violent thing to do. Dorothy and Charles felt that they had done what they could.

After she and Charles recovered from the fast, Dorothy announced that it was her turn to set their agenda, and he agreed. The simple-living thing and the fasting-almost-to-death thing had been his ideas, and now she wanted to do something different. She told her fellow activists that she was moving to Nicaragua to be a nurse. They were shocked, and she was heavily criticized for leaving. Nobody could understand why she was doing it; nobody said, What a great thing to do, I hope it goes well. She had been one of the elect, one of the few who understood how important the nuclear issue was and was willing to risk her life to confront it, and now she wanted to be a *nurse*? Anyone could be a nurse! How could she abandon the higher calling of peace? How could she be so selfish?

One person said to her, If you're giving up the movement, who's going to deal with racism? For years she had been the brown person in the peace movement, helping the white people feel that they were working on race. She told that person that racism was his problem, not hers. This was another thing that had always bothered her: it was a privilege to take days off to stage a protest, to get thrown in jail on purpose, a privilege to give up a middle-class salary and become poor. Most brown people didn't have that privilege. "I remember talking to some black friends and they said, 'What are you doing with that white movement? Let them blow themselves up! To hell with it! Who cares?'"

She and Charles set off for Nicaragua. While stopping off in Mexico City, they received a message asking them to go immediately to Guatemala City. A friend of theirs, Alain Richard, a French Franciscan worker priest whom they'd lived with in Oakland during the fast, was alone and needed help. He was running a center that loaned meeting space to the Grupo de Apoyo Mutuo—the GAM—a group consisting mostly of wives of men who had been disappeared. Several of the wives were now also in danger and needed protection. The next day, Dorothy and Charles got on a bus and rode to Guatemala.

They arrived on Tuesday of Holy Week, 1985. While they were on the bus from Mexico, a member of the GAM was kidnapped and then found dead, his tongue cut out. The day after they arrived, there was a meeting at the house. At this meeting was Rosario Godoy de Cuevas, a young woman married to a student leader at the university who had disappeared; she had a little boy, Augustine, who was about two years old. The evening after the meeting, Holy Thursday, Rosario and Augustine disappeared. The president of GAM, Nineth

Garcia, called the center and said, Rosario is disappeared, we have to look for her; I will come for you. Nineth arrived in a taxi with four or five other women, all who were left of GAM's board of directors. Charles said he wasn't sure they should go, because they didn't have any authorization; Dorothy said, If you don't want to do it you stay here, but I'm going.

It was already dark. First they drove to the largest hospitals to see if Rosario was in one of their morgues, but they couldn't find her. By this time it was one in the morning. Nineth decided they should go to the DIT—the Departamento de Investigaciones Técnicas, the special police force under the control of the Ministry of the Interior, reputed to be staffed by members of the death squads. The DIT office they went to was a dirty room with not enough light. There was a small wooden bench in a waiting area, and a counter with some men behind it. The men were terrifying. Dorothy leaned against a wall: her knees were shaking so badly she thought she might fall down. Nineth pulled out a cigarette and asked her for a light. Right above them on a wall was a sign that said "No Fuma." Dorothy pointed to the sign, but Nineth said, They're smoking; ask them for a light. So Dorothy stumbled up to the desk and asked the men there if she could have a match, and Nineth lit her cigarette. Nineth amazed her. Something happened to people who had lost members of their families, she saw: they were fearless. It wasn't that they didn't care about staying alive; they cared more about finding out what had happened. It became clear that the DIT men didn't know what had happened to Rosario, so they set off again.

They decided to drive to Verbena Cemetery, to the oldest morgue in Guatemala City. By this time, it was three in the morning. It was now Good Friday, and the main streets of the city were blocked off, to be transformed into a Via Dolorosa, covered with flower petals; all night long, people had been strewing petals by lantern light to make the road of pain. They found their way through side streets and arrived at the morgue, and there was Rosario, on a slab. Her younger brother and Augustine were there, too, both dead. One side of Rosario's face was caved in and purple, and her hands were almost severed; they heard later that her brother and son had been tortured and murdered in front of her, and she had cut through her arms, which were tied up with wire, trying to stop it.

After that night, Dorothy decided that Nineth, as president of the GAM, was likely to be the next to go, so she, Dorothy, would protect her. She stuck to her twenty-four hours a day, everywhere she went. She hoped that since she was a U.S. citizen, registered with the embassy, the death squads might be reluctant to get involved in killing her. Alain Richard had heard from a diplomat that everyone on the GAM board was on a list of people to be killed.

She did this for three weeks. She was scared all the time. She knew that someone could dive out of a car any moment and seize Nineth, and she felt it was her job to stop them. There was a white van with darkened windows that followed them around and parked outside Nineth's house. Dorothy didn't have a weapon, and she didn't want one: carrying a gun scared her as much as the thought of being shot, and she knew that if the death-squad men wanted to kill her they'd do it, whether she had a gun or not. She figured if they tried to get Nineth she would scream bloody murder, and maybe that would put them off; she didn't know what else to do.

She was ready to die in Nineth's place—she thought Nineth's work was more important than her own—but she knew that wasn't likely to happen. More likely, she would just get hit on the head when the men came to take Nineth away. It drove Nineth crazy to have Dorothy next to her all the time, but Dorothy wouldn't let her alone for a moment—she considered it her job to keep Nineth alive. A few days after Rosario's death, the American State Department announced that the United States would be displeased if any more GAM members were killed. After three weeks, new people arrived to take her place—Peace Brigades International decided to make accompaniment by foreigners a regular part of its work—and she and Charles got on another bus and set out for Nicaragua.

Dorothy worked in the clinic in Mulukukú for nearly twenty years. Near the end of that time, a free government clinic opened in the town, offering curative care and vaccines. Dorothy suggested that the co-op clinic reduce its services to those the government didn't offer: Pap smears, preventive medicine. She would train the government doctors to go out to the campo and do prenatal care in the settlements. The other women in the cooperative agreed—or she thought they did. But when she returned from a fund-raising trip to the States, she discovered, to her astonishment, that the cooperative, led by Grethel, had decided to do something completely different: to turn the clinic into a private clinic that would charge fees for its services.

Dorothy was appalled. After twenty years, everything she had worked for had been rejected. She felt betrayed by the cooperative, but most of all she felt betrayed by Grethel. They had been close friends for two decades, almost family. She had thought they shared the same politics, the same ideals. And they had been through so many difficult times together. Sometimes, trying to help people, they had upset others. One woman said she had asked them to help her put her daughters up for adoption, to protect them from her husband, who was in jail for allegedly raping his stepdaughter. But then the husband was released and accused the cooperative of arranging the adoption without his permission.

Dorothy had thought that she would die in Mulukukú. Instead, she retreated to Managua and thought about what had happened. People had told her that U.S. donations were diminishing, so the clinic had no choice but to become more self-sufficient. Maybe that was true. She tried to remember that, even though it had gone against her and betrayed what she had thought was its purpose, the cooperative was still doing good things for Nicaraguan women.

In Matagalpa, Dorothy worked from one day to the next. When she was working, she was happy. There was still a lot she could do for a lot of women who had almost nothing. Working was the only form of happiness she aspired to now, but it was happiness, and it was enough.

She didn't believe in an omnipotent God anymore, so instead she hoped for decent governments, but her hopes even for those were much reduced. Nicaragua and the Sandinistas weren't what they had been. When the liberals came in, they had painted over the murals from the old days, and these weren't being replaced. When electricity finally came to Mulukukú, in the late nineties, right away every poor house had a television, houses where there wasn't enough food to eat, and there was everyone watching telenovellas from Brazil and Mexico about the woes of rich people. Things were better than they had been, undoubtedly—people weren't starving, and there were government health clinics everywhere. But what was the point of the revolution if it was only going to produce another nation of consumers? "Who cares if we have redistribution of wealth if the poor become just as greedy as the rich, but on a smaller scale?" she wondered. "What's that got to do with being a human being?"

She was eighty-four, but there was still much she wanted to do. She wanted to see places she had never been. She wanted to go to Peru and see Machu Picchu. Christopher had become a naturalist, working as a guide in the Amazon and Costa Rica, and every now and then she went on a trip with him.

She doesn't know how much time she has left. She survived so much malaria in Mulukukú that she knows she is pretty tough. Her mother lived to ninety-four, but she was demented when she died, and it was ugly, she doesn't want that. She has decided what she does want. When she is ready, when she can no longer take care of herself, she will stop eating, and then stop taking liquids. One day, she will drink a last glass of wine, and then, a few days after that, she will die. She heard that Charles Gray died that way, some years ago in Oregon, and that it was a good death. She has arranged everything with Christopher. He understands.

THE MOST OPPRESSED OF ALL

And why should the divine hospitality cease here? Consider, with
all reverence, the monkeys. May there not be a mansion for the
monkeys also? Old Mr. Graysford said No, but young Mr. Sorley,
who was advanced, said Yes; he saw no reason why monkeys
should not have their collateral share of bliss, and he had
sympathetic discussions about them with his Hindu friends. And
the jackals? Jackals were indeed less to Mr. Sorley's mind, but he
admitted that the mercy of God, being infinite, may well embrace
all mammals. And the wasps? He became uneasy during the descent
to wasps, and was apt to change the conversation. And oranges,
cactuses, crystals and mud? and the bacteria inside Mr. Sorley?
No, no, this is going too far. We must exclude someone from our
gathering, or we shall be left with nothing.

—E. M. FORSTER, *A Passage to India*

When Aaron Pitkin was a young man, he searched for a
cause to devote his life to—some way to lessen the suffering that he saw in the world—and the answer he came
up with was chickens. It was basically a numbers game. More than
eight billion chickens were killed each year in America, close to a
million an hour. The vast majority of animals killed for food were
chickens, because they were so small—the meat-to-life ratio was terrible. And what factory farms did to chickens before they died appalled him—the birds in chronic pain most of the six weeks or so
that they were alive, so fat that their legs couldn't hold their bodies
up, sitting in their own feces, covered in sores. Aaron realized that
if he could figure out a way to make chickens' lives better, then the
quantity of suffering he could eliminate would be many times greater
than in any other way he could think of.

It wasn't that he thought chickens were more important than people, or more innocent, or more moving. He cared about them because they were more helpless and more brutally trodden on than even the most oppressed people; their suffering was greater and their situation more unjust. He didn't spend time pondering how happy a chicken in better circumstances could really be. He wasn't interested in happiness; he was interested in pain.

Although he made animal suffering his life's work, it didn't affect him much emotionally. When he heard about some new terrible abuse, or even when he saw horrifying footage, half the time his immediate reaction was to think, Fantastic! This will be great for the cause! There was one video of a kosher beef-slaughtering plant in the Midwest in which the abuse of cows was so pornographically sadistic that it made him cry, but that was rare. This dispassion didn't affect how hard he worked or the lengths he was willing to go to, however. After Hurricane Katrina, he drove hundreds of miles to New Orleans in his car to save chickens, because he knew the factories would be flooded and nobody else would care enough to try.

Aaron is in his forties. (The names in this chapter are pseudonyms, adopted at Aaron Pitkin's request.) He works at a large animal-rights organization, and has been an extraordinarily effective chicken advocate, helping to bring about a dramatic change in both laws and attitudes. He is a vegan because he believes it's the right thing to do, but he is not a purist about it—he is a pragmatist who believes that relieving suffering is more important than adhering to principle. For this reason, he thinks he should probably eat meat when he is meeting with cattlemen (he also works on cows) in order to prove that he is not some marginal zealot out to destroy them but a regular Joe whom they can deal with. The trouble is, if anyone from the movement saw him eating meat, his authority would be irreversibly destroyed. He thinks about the example of a famous animal-rights activist who he'd heard was an awful person with a coke habit, given to sexual harassment and waving guns about, but the thing that really scandalized his followers was the rumor that he'd been spotted eating M&M's. True, the people who raised hell about the M&M's were a bit crazy, but they were Aaron's base; he needed them to do his work.

Aaron decided in high school that it was wrong to eat meat and he ought to be a vegetarian, but it took him six months to become one. Every day, he would get off the bus and go to Hardee's and eat a bacon cheeseburger and feel terrible about it. Then, that Christmas, he was supposed to go to his girlfriend's house for dinner, and he knew that they were going to serve meat in a way that resembled the animal far more than a bacon cheeseburger did—a whole turkey and a big ham—and he just couldn't face it. That was the end of his eating meat. Sometime later, he visited a place called Farm Sanctuary, an organization that rescued animals from agribusiness, and he discovered that animals were harmed in the production of eggs and dairy, too, so he decided that the only defensible position was to be a vegan. He thought, Boy, I am going to miss ice cream, but I have no choice.

Back in high school, he had been into death metal and wore his hair long and feathered. He had a pet python named Snaky, six feet long, that slept in bed with him at night. He didn't like being told what to do. He talked back at teachers and got whacked with a Ping-Pong paddle. One teacher put cayenne pepper on his tongue because he talked too much (he attributed to this his love of spicy food). He was always on the lookout for a good protest or a good scheme. At some point he realized that the jewelry he was buying for his girlfriends was a scam—from wholesale, it was marked up by crazy amounts. So for twenty-five dollars he bought a license that enabled him to go to gem shows and buy wholesale. He sold jewelry to friends and donated the profits to charity.

In college, he decided to dedicate his life to social justice. His initial plan was to work as a doctor in the Third World. And then he read an essay that changed his life: the philosopher Peter Singer's article "Famine, Affluence, and Morality." Singer argued that it was impossible to justify buying luxuries when a few hundred dollars donated to an international aid agency could save a person's life. After he read Singer's article, everything Aaron bought, even the smallest, cheapest thing, felt to him like food or medicine snatched from someone dying. Nobody would buy a soda if there was a starving child standing next to the vending machine, he thought; well, for him now there was always a starving child standing next to the vending machine. He became very, very frugal. He went Dumpster-diving for food. He never drank alcohol (though that was not just because of the expense—he couldn't stand the idea of losing control of his brain). Every time he spent money, no matter how little, he would write the amount down in a notebook. He read about a man named Charles Gray who had lived on less than twelve hundred dollars a year; though he couldn't fathom how to do that, he vowed to get closer.

Aaron now knew he had to donate as much money as he could to international aid, that much was clear to him, but what else should he do? He decided that animals were more oppressed than people, and among animals, the ones lower down the food chain—the non-mammals, the ones that weren't smart or cute—were the most oppressed of all. Nearly everyone cared about dogs and cats, many people cared about rabbits and cows, but very few people cared about chickens. At first, after making this decision to focus on animals, he made a point of spending some time each year in the library, reading anti–animal-rights literature in order to test his principles, to make sure there wasn't some compelling argument out there that would lead him to change his course. He wanted to be rational about it; after all, he was choosing animal-rights work for logical rather than emotional reasons. But after a while, he became convinced that he really was on the right track, and he stopped doing this research. It wasn't as if the rights of farm animals conflicted with the rights of humans: eating less meat was good for human health, it was good for the environment, and the undocumented immigrants who worked at slaughterhouses were some of the most ill-treated and miserable workers in the country.

After he decided that animal rights would be his thing, he began to see suffering animals everywhere. Once, in college, he was rushing to get to a final exam in a course he really needed to get into graduate school, and the final exam was a large part of the grade. But it was raining, and worms were coming up out of the grass and wriggling onto the paths. He knew that if he didn't pick them up someone would step on them and crush them to death. So he stopped and picked up the worms and put them back on the grass, and he was late. Then, at the end of the exam, he was racing to finish the final question, he had the answer on his calculator and was about to write it in his book when the examiner called out, Pencils down! Of course, other students were still scribbling away. And he had the answer already, right there on his calculator. But he put his pencil down.

That was a turning point for him. Before that day, he had believed in absolute principles and duties—never lie, never cheat, never this, never that. But when he thought of himself in that exam, putting his pencil down while everyone else was still writing, and getting a worse grade than he deserved, which might have prevented him from going to graduate school, all because of some idiotic, pompous sense of principle, he cringed. Being ethical was not about being pure, he realized; it was caring about suffering. From then on, he figured out the moral thing to do not by consulting inviolable principles but by thinking about consequences. Yes, it was generally better to be honest, but if Anne Frank is in your house and the Nazis are at the door, you lie.

During graduate school, in slivers of spare time, he sought emotional relief from its amoral isolation by working at charities. He arranged his classes so he could volunteer at Food Not Bombs on Fridays. That was awful work. He'd get up before dawn on a frigid Boston morning to show up in a tiny alley, with excrement everywhere, to lift box after box out of a van until his knuckles bled, and then he'd toil in a hot basement kitchen, making meals. The fun part was serving the meals, and seeing the faces of the people getting the food, but he usually left before that. He figured there would always be people wanting to do the fun stuff, but only he was willing to do the bad part, so he would do that and then go on to something else.

When he wasn't hauling food, he got involved in protests. He dressed up as a lobster and stood on the street, carrying a sign that read "Being Boiled Hurts." He had always loved that his mother had been arrested at a protest against racism, so he set about getting arrested himself. There was a law in Boston that he felt was unjust, prohibiting people from lingering in the Boston Common at night. Homeless people had been sleeping on the benches, and policemen had been dragging them away, so Aaron and some other people held a sleep-in and got arrested. When he joyfully called his mother to tell her all about it, she said, What took you so long?

Aaron's parents, Barbara and Mike, met as children—she lived in Flatbush, Brooklyn, and in the summertime she went to the beach near where he lived, on Long Island. They married in 1964. Barbara went to work for New York City as an investigator in the welfare department; Mike started out as a photographer, taking pictures of political protests. He and Barbara were members of Brooklyn CORE, the Congress of Racial Equality, and they went to a lot of demonstrations. Mike's most successful picture showed a black man in a demonstration against racism being arrested by the police. Hundreds of people were arrested that day, including Barbara. Mike took a photograph of a smiling Barbara sitting on the ground, shortly before her arrest, with a policeman standing to one side. Aaron, who kept a copy of this photograph on his desk, liked to describe it as his mother getting dragged away.

In 1965, Mike and Barbara left Brooklyn and moved to Colorado, where Mike had been offered a job as a news photographer on a local paper. Barbara loved living out west, but something seemed to have happened to Mike, and he was starting to act peculiar; he got fired from his job. Things went badly after that. He found a job in Wyoming, and then, when he was fired, he found another, working for the post office, but he was acting stranger and stranger. He showed people naked pictures of himself; he made threats; he was always chasing women; he barely slept. Barbara tried to hide his craziness from the boys; when she had to take him to a mental hospital, she told them he was away on a photography assignment. When he was at home, she was terrified: he was always taking Aaron and his brother to do crazy, dangerous things, and they loved it, he was so much more fun than she was.

When he was fired from his last job, in Arkansas, he began to deteriorate much more quickly. He became convinced that Nazis were pumping poison gas under his door, and insisted that everyone whisper in the house because he thought their neighbor was a Nazi and was spying on them. He started buying guns. He thought he was the Messiah. At a certain point, Barbara decided that she didn't feel safe with all the guns in the house. The people at the mental-health clinic where he was being treated didn't feel safe, either; finally, things got so bad that she sent him back to his parents, by himself.

Barbara always protected Aaron from knowing much about his father. She had never told him about his frequent infidelities. When she left Mike, she told Aaron, who was then about nine, that they were leaving because his father was sick. Aaron was horrified and started to cry. If his father was sick, surely they should be taking care of him, not abandoning him! What if he, Aaron, got sick—would his mother leave him, too?

After the divorce, Barbara decided to move the family back east, mostly because she was sick of their being the only Jewish family in town; Aaron was getting beaten up in school because Jews killed Jesus. But the damage was already done. When Aaron was getting beaten up for being Jewish, he had thought: If I had been born here, to these people, I would believe what they believe, and I would beat me up, too. So how can I be sure that my beliefs are right? When he was eight, he told his mother he didn't believe in God.

When he was in his mid-twenties, Aaron met Jen. She was working at the New England Anti-Vivisection Society when Aaron walked in and offered his services as an expert on mad-cow disease. She hated him immediately. He was aloof and arrogant and had terrible manners. He was already beginning to be something of a celebrity in the animal-rights movement, and there were always girls hanging around him. But a couple of months later, they were seated next to each other at a dinner, and he decided to be charming. She was duly charmed, and when he asked her out on a date, she accepted.

At the time, they felt they were quite similar. They both were wholly dedicated to overcoming injustice. She had come to animal rights by a more circuitous route than he had—she had started from feminism and moved through ecofeminism to an appreciation of what animals and women had in common in terms of being trampled upon—but they had ended up in the same place. They also laughed at the same things; they loved twisted little cartoons. To Jen's surprise, Aaron was funny. Even when he was giving talks about veganism, he could make people laugh. He had a chart with pictures of the seven different kinds of human poo, with descriptions of which poo was healthiest—and of course the best poo was the poo pooed by vegans.

Aaron and Jen moved in together, and then the trouble started. For one thing, Aaron was messy. Not just untidy—dirty. Laundry would pile up in his room, dishes in the sink. He would make huge batches of food to save money—pounds and pounds of lentil stew or hummus—and leave crusted pans and bowls all over the kitchen. When she complained, he told her that time spent washing dishes could be time spent working for animal rights, which were more important. She couldn't think of a good counterargument to that—

in fact, she thought he was right, from a moral point of view. So all she could say, when she felt herself going crazy, pressed to the brink by the filth in the kitchen, was, "But I *need* it, I *want* it, I'm *asking* you." Years later, she would wish she'd thought to yell at him, "You know what? It's all about balance, and we live in an imperfect world, and you're right, doing these dishes will take away from the animals, do the fucking dishes before I have a nervous breakdown." But back then she was young, and she wasn't sure what was right or normal or what she deserved. What killed her, too, was that she had always thought of herself as an extremely ethical person, and now she felt like the selfish one, the bourgeois one. Dishes? When animals were being tortured and people were starving? *Dishes?*

Jen came from a terrible family. Her mother had been raised in an orphanage and got pregnant when she was very young. Her father had owned a garage and made quite a bit of money, but then he became a violent alcoholic and lost it all. As a child, Jen was molested by her father and by her two brothers. When she told her mother about the abuse and that she was thinking about suicide, her mother told her she understood, and if Jen wanted to kill herself she should go ahead. Her father started buying guns, and at one point he tried to strangle Jen and her mother. (Years later, one of her brothers went to prison for murdering his wife.)

One night when she was fifteen, her mother woke her up and told her they had to run away, that minute, or her father was going to kill them both. Jen managed to escape, but for an hour her mother struggled to get out of the house as her father held her hostage at gunpoint. Jen waited outside in the snow, thinking, She's going to die, she's going to die. Finally, her mother managed to get out of the house, and the two of them fled to a battered-women's shelter. For a few months, they were homeless. Jen slept on friends' sofas, but she continued to go to school and get good grades, because she knew if she didn't she was doomed.

All through school, she worked for money to help her mother with the rent, and during college she sometimes recycled cans to earn money for food. She started racking up credit-card debt. But she believed in the women's movement, so when she graduated, instead of trying to get a high-paying job, she went to work for a battered-women's group for practically nothing. Still, with her history, Jen felt that if she wanted to make herself feel better by buying a pair of shoes occasionally, that was okay. She was careful with money, but Aaron was so much more so that he made her feel guilty. He kept the heat down low even in the middle of winter. He whittled his spending down to twenty-four thousand a year, then to twelve thousand a year, then nine. He never said anything when she came home with some purchase that he would have called unnecessary, but he didn't have to. She knew what he thought.

Jen worked hard, but Aaron was *always* working, and work always came first. He felt that there was so much suffering in the world—he felt the weight of it almost physically—how could he stop? How could he relax and watch TV when people were starving? Even when he was with her, she felt that he was itching to get back to it. If she objected, he was astonished that she could be so selfish. If she got upset, he would get upset, too, but he stuck to his principles. Sometimes she thought he was right to do that, but sometimes she thought that she, as his girlfriend, deserved special treatment—that people owed more to those they were close to than to strangers. Sometimes they would discuss this issue philosophically: Suppose there were two people drowning over there, Jen would ask, and I was drowning over here, and you could save either the two people or me, what should you do? These discussions always ended badly.

His activism, she realized, was the other woman in their relationship, and one with which she could never compete. When he wasn't going to classes, he would go on speaking tours and be on the road for weeks. She cooked for him and cleaned the house and packed his bags and shipped boxes to him at the post office. The only time he was fully there for her was when she was in a crisis so awful that he felt it justified diverting his attention. When her father died, she was scared to go to the funeral because her brothers, who had abused her, would be there. But Aaron took care of her. The day of the funeral, he helped her get dressed, because she was so numb she could barely move. He put aside his dislike of religion to say Kaddish with her, because she didn't want to pray alone.

It was not an accident that Aaron had ended up with someone from a background like Jen's. He had a history with traumatized women. When he was in high school, he began seeing a girl who had been abused since she was a child, raped by her stepfather and her brother. Her father was a gambler and an alcoholic. She had night terrors and couldn't sleep. Aaron resolved to save her. He felt that she was so deeply wounded and had had such a terrible life that she deserved to have someone who would treat her well. He had always felt an overwhelming desire to help people, but he was just a kid, he didn't know how; this was one thing he knew he could do. He knew that if she was left alone she would unravel, so he moved closer.

When she started to beat him up, he hid it from his mother. When she gave him bloody lips or bruises that he couldn't hide, he told his mother that he'd gotten into a fight at school. She stole his mother's money to buy cocaine, and he tried to hide that, too. One day, his mother walked into his room as he was cowering in the corner of his bed and the girlfriend was punching him, and after that his mother banned her from the house, but he still didn't break up with her. He could take the abuse, he figured—he was strong enough and came from a good enough family. He intended to marry her and take care of her and protect her for the rest of her life.

Just once, he hit back. He had driven her to her house, but she refused to get out of the car. She started hitting him, and he crouched down away from her, but the car was too cramped for him to shield himself. As she hit him, he got angrier and angrier; suddenly he lashed out and hit her back, in the head. She saw it coming and ducked, so the blow hit her on the back of the skull. His hand hurt like crazy, and they both began to cry, caught up in a hysteria of misery; in the middle of it, he realized what he'd done and felt sick. He had thought that his whole life was about protecting the weak, and now he had hit a girl who was horribly damaged—he had become one more brutal man in her life. At the same time, though, he understood that this was what she had wanted for a long time: she had wanted him to hit her back, because she could hold it over him. When he went off to college, she followed him and wouldn't let him work. Finally, one day, he was trying to get to a test and she was blocking his way and he realized, I cannot do this anymore, and he broke up with her.

At a certain point, Jen discovered to her astonishment that Aaron had money—not a huge amount, but a trust fund that was his to do what he liked with. She asked him to pay her credit-card debt. It didn't make any sense financially for the two of them for her to be paying all this money in interest, but, more than that, it was driving her out of her mind to be in debt after all these years. She was terrified of poverty, traumatized by her period of homelessness. But he wouldn't pay it. He told her that there were other people who needed that money more. He told her that she was well fed and had a place to live and there were people in the world who were starving. He had already allocated the money to a charity. It was blood money, in Aaron's eyes—his mother's father had started a company that manufactured gold bathroom accessories, and his father's father had amassed a fortune making fur coats—its taint could only be expunged by spending it to alleviate the worst sorts of suffering. There was Jen, and then there was Somalia. Or animals in cages. How could she compete with them? She couldn't. She knew he was right.

They got married in 1999. They had fought about this for a long time, because Aaron felt that since gays and lesbians couldn't yet get married in Massachusetts it was a discriminatory institution and they shouldn't participate in it. Jen told him she would spend the next ten years working for gay equality but she wanted to get married now. After all she had put up with from him, she wanted a ring on her finger. She knew he would never agree to having children, so she left that question alone, even though she wasn't sure what she felt about it. She spent the morning of the wedding throwing up.

The marriage lasted two years. One of the hardest parts of the breakup for Jen was that she now had to admit to herself that she wasn't the ethical person she'd thought she was. She was not just leaving Aaron; she was choosing selfishness. She was choosing her own happiness over the survival of other creatures. She could not justify it, she thought it was the wrong thing to do, but she couldn't help herself; she wasn't him.

For a while, it was awful. And then, bit by bit, all the resentment and misery she'd been repressing during the years she and Aaron had been together built up to the point where it exploded. She rebelled. She and Aaron had been rigorously vegan for years—and now *Jen ate cheese*. She went to Paris and gorged herself on cheese. She went shopping for clothes that were new. She drank alcohol for the first time in her life. She smoked pot and loved it. She revised her views on Israel. She worked as a dominatrix for foot fetishists. She stopped recycling.

Aaron, meanwhile, steered hard in the other direction. After he and Jen split up, he didn't have a place to live for nearly a year. He put the word out that he was willing to come and speak about veganism or nutrition or animal rights or social justice to anyone who would have him, for free, as long as they paid his fare and put him up for the night, even if it was on somebody's floor. At first, he was ecstatic. Now, after all the years of guilt living with Jen, he was free at last to devote himself completely to his activism. He earned nothing and he spent nothing. He was constantly on the move. He gave about forty talks a month, driving all over the country in a donated car, which he slept in if no one was putting him up. But then, after about eight months of this, he decided that enough was enough: he wanted a home again. He interviewed for a job at an animal-rights organization; that same day, he found a tiny, dingy apartment above a furniture store and rented it on the spot.

He loved his new work—so much so that after a while he began to feel that spending an entire day each week processing lentils was not an efficient use of his time. When he was younger, he had felt that his time was basically worthless, so the thing to do was to use it to save money. Now that he was a specialist with a degree and a platform, it occurred to him that his time wasn't worthless anymore. He still donated nearly half of his salary, but that wasn't his focus. Before long, he had become as obsessive about time as he had about money. He began to draw up flow charts and make lists, to figure out how he could use his days most efficiently. He set up his computer in his bedroom so that he could roll out of bed and push the on button with one movement; the fifteen feet he had to walk to the bathroom drove him crazy. He experimented with sleeping less—three hours a night, four hours a night—to see if he could get more work done that way, and to see how long he could keep it up before he collapsed. His doctor told him that he needed to exercise, and he found that he was nodding off at his desk anyway after so little sleep, so he decided to work while walking on a treadmill, which would serve the double function of keeping him alert and providing exercise without his having to take any time off. He wore a weights belt for stability, and he tied himself to nearby furniture with bungee cords to steady his body so he didn't get seasick. He looked insane, but what did that matter?

He rarely spent time with friends, and never allowed himself time to sit and reflect. He knew intellectually that spending time with friends or meditating on the course of his life could be good for his work—he might learn something important, or realize that he ought to change his direction—but he was risk-averse. If he spent time that way, he might learn something, or he might not. If he spent the evening working, he knew he would get something done.

After Aaron's grandparents were no longer able to take care of him, Aaron's father was placed in an assisted-living facility in California. But he grew depressed there and stopped eating, and the facility put him in a psychiatric hospital that allowed him to lie in the fetal position for so many hours a day that he lost the ability to straighten his legs. They called his family and told them they were referring him to hospice. Aaron, who knew that his father was still pretty young and that there had been nothing much physically wrong with him, was outraged, and had him transferred to a hospital in the city Aaron lived in. Mike was in a dreadful state. Because he couldn't walk, he would get lung infections and other kinds of infections and ulcers that went all the way to the bone; he was always in and out of the emergency room. For months he would slip into a catatonic depression, and then he would wake up into a manic state and become talkative and cheerful but at the same time deeply paranoid. He was convinced that the hospital staff were trying to poison him, and yet he would spend all day reminiscing happily about his life.

Now that his father was nearby, Aaron wrestled with the question of how much he ought to visit him. How should he weigh his responsibility to his father versus his responsibility to his work? And should that be affected by the fact that his father had been a terrible husband and made his mother miserable? He decided to do the minimum that was decent—he came in only for the crises (though there were many of these). He wondered how he would act if it were his mother in this position. He loved his mother a lot. He thought he would probably do the same thing, because it was the right thing to do, but it would be much more difficult.

When his father was lucid, Aaron would tell him what had happened to him when he was sicker, describe all the most gruesome scenarios that might come to pass in the future, and ask him if he wanted to be resuscitated in those cases; his father always said yes. Aaron couldn't understand it: his father stared at the ceiling all day, he couldn't even twist to look out the window, he hated TV and radio, his eyesight was too far gone for him to read, his greatest pleasure was eating Chinese food. Aaron thought he'd go crazy if he had to live like that. But his father wanted to live; he wanted to do whatever it took.

At last his father ended up on a ventilator, so he could no longer talk or eat. He became comatose. The doctors told Aaron that he would never come off the ventilator and would never wake up. They advised him to take his father off the machine, and Aaron gave them permission to do so. For a long time, he had been uncomfortable spending so much money on his father's treatment when that money could have relieved much more suffering spent on something else. He justified this because it was his father's money; since his father wanted to live, he felt he had no right to deny him. On the other hand, his father had been deemed incompetent years ago, so it was really Aaron's decision, and he couldn't pretend that it wasn't.

The day when his father was to be disconnected from the ventilator, Aaron arrived early at the hospital to say good-bye. He was sitting by his father's bedside, shortly before the nurse was to inject a final dose of morphine, when his father opened his eyes. It was like something out of a horror movie, Aaron thought—a corpse coming to life. His father's eyes followed Aaron around the room; he could move his head in response to questions. Aaron, appalled at what he had nearly done, told the doctor—only to discover that Mike had opened his eyes the day before as well, but the doctor, believing that his father's life was not worth living, and that Aaron was having difficulty letting go, had decided not to mention it. Aaron was furious. He called a halt to the disconnection plan and had his father's treatment restarted. This turned out to be the wrong decision.

It was too expensive to keep his father in the ICU, so the hospital sent him to a ventilator facility. There was enough money in trust to pay for a good one, but even so, the place was harrowing: bed after bed of humans barely alive, each attached to a machine. Many were in comas and had no brain activity at all. It was like a factory farm for people, Aaron thought. There were no families there, no visitors. What would be the point? But his father was not in a coma—he was in agony, even with the strongest painkillers the nurses would give him, and he was awake. He ended up back in the hospital with another infection, comatose, and the doctors again told Aaron to

pull the plug. This time he agreed, the ventilator was removed—
and, again, his father woke up. The doctors told Aaron that his father would die within minutes, because his lungs were far too
atrophied after all this time to work on their own, but he did not die.
He was breathing, he was conscious, and he was in pain. He could
not be given the morphine he had been given before, because it
would hasten his death and that would be illegal. Aaron sat there in
agony: now it seemed to him that he was actually murdering his father, and causing him to suffer, yet surely to send him back to that
ventilator farm would be worse than anything. Minutes went by, and
then hours, and still his father did not die. It took twenty hours
and then it was done.

Before he watched his father die, Aaron had thought mostly about
the pain of animals. He had seen so much footage of terrified animals bellowing in slaughterhouses, of crippled animals infected and
bleeding in cages, of animals whose legs hurt so much they couldn't
walk—he had spent so many years of his life with these images and
sounds in his head that suffering had come in his mind to mean
something that humans inflicted on animals, the anguish of the
weak and wordless inflicted by the strong. Now he had seen that
there were humans trapped in places as brutal as feed cages, and
when those humans suffered, their torment was as world-ending as
the torment of animals who lived in wretchedness only in order to
die. He had known that humans could suffer, of course. But that
humans could suffer as helplessly as animals could—that there were
humans who could not move, who could not feed themselves, who
did not have language to say what was happening to them or to beg
for relief—that, he had forgotten.

Shortly after he began work at the animal-rights organization,
Aaron met Leana, the love of his life. She worked there, too; he
did chickens, she did seals. She was a vegan from Waterford, Connecticut. She was nearly as frugal as he was, and she, like he, had

suspected that her principles, about money and other things, would mean that she would always be alone. She had decided when she was thirteen that it was unethical to have children, and she had never changed her mind. She, like him, considered family obligations tedious and generally tried to avoid them. In some ways she was even more ascetic than he was: she cared more about the environment than he did, so when they moved together to a building where the heat and air conditioning were included in the rent, he indulged himself in this free resource, but she shut off the vents in her room and froze or sweltered, depending on the season. Early in the relationship, he bought her a secondhand DVD player as a present, and she burst into tears: she had recently seen a film about the exploitation of children in China, and because the DVD player was made in China, it reminded her of that and was possibly tainted itself. Aaron was enchanted: she was a creature so pure, he felt, so morally sensitive, that she should not exist in a fallen world.

Aaron was determined not to mess things up with Leana as he had with Jen, so he told her that, during the first year they were together, he would devote serious time to their relationship. After that, he would revert to his normal habits. At first she was annoyed by this, but in the end she didn't mind too much; she liked to be alone a lot anyway. They decided that they would have dinner together most nights, and spend a long weekend together a couple of times a year, and that would be enough.

After several years at the animal-rights organization, things started to go really, really well. Aaron had a hand in bringing about a number of big, significant victories for chickens, both legislative and corporate. Several huge companies—Safeway, Bon Appetit, and Costco, among others—promised to purchase humanely raised poultry. Starbucks promised to use only cage-free eggs. California passed a law mandating that egg-laying chickens be given almost 70 percent more space to live in, and forbidding the sale of eggs from battery-caged hens elsewhere. American meat consumption had begun dropping nearly every year, which nobody had expected;

consumption had been going up and up and up since the fifties, but after all this time the message—his message—that meat was bad for you was finally getting through. Entire public-school systems had taken on Meatless Mondays.

He realized that it was silly to despair because people weren't becoming vegans; most people were never going to become vegans, or even vegetarians, but if they ate less and less meat, then little by little things for animals were going to get better. Sometimes he let himself hope that the whole country was turning his way: nobody wanted to see chickens tortured, and it was getting harder and harder to deny the awfulness of industrial agribusiness. Sometimes he felt that he was in on the cusp of a kind of civil rights movement for poultry that would build and build and build until a point, maybe even in his lifetime, when the dreadful practices of factory farms would seem as repellent and unimaginable as slavery.

When he felt this way, he felt that he was doing good work, that he had done good work, and he felt the sense of guilt and ineradicable debt that drove him when he was younger perceptibly ease. He still needed to accumulate a certain number of utility points each day to feel okay with himself—to feel that he'd done his duty—but since his work was going so well, those points were easier to come by. It had never occurred to him when he was younger that there might be a time in his life when he might feel he was doing *enough*. Mostly this was a good feeling, but he was also suspicious of it. What if the lesson of his effectiveness was not that he deserved to kick back a little, but that he was obliged to work harder than ever, now that he was getting more done? That would be more logical.

What if this sense of achievement was an illusion—what if he was just getting soft and complacent, as people so often did as they got older? It was not as though the world were fixed—there were still millions of people starving, and life was still horrific for most animals. He still felt the enormous weight of the suffering—a horror that existed just outside the door of his mind, and to open that door even a chink was to see how hideous and infinite the suffering was.

He saw that a lot of vegetarians felt so virtuous for not eating meat that they never pushed themselves to work for the larger cause. He didn't want to end up like that. He told himself he should never compare himself with other people, because most other people did so little for the world that he might start feeling he was ahead of the game. No, he had to compare what he was doing only with what he himself could possibly do.

He had always looked to the sixties, his parents' decade, as a time when many people were inspired into activism and rejected selfishness, but then he thought: What happened to all those people? Where did they slink off to, at right about the age that he was now? They weren't activists anymore. No doubt they told themselves some story about how making money and having a family were natural, and the sixties were a long time ago. He was pretty sure that wouldn't happen to him, but probably they had all thought that. Maybe there was some biological thing that happened to people at a certain age.

The odd thing was that he was happy. He loved his job, because he was doing work that only he could do. He was stacking up victories one after another. He was in love with a woman who didn't want more from him than he could give her. And he had joked with a couple of his closest activist friends that if they saw him getting too easy on himself and neglecting his duty, rather than let him grow old and complacent, they should take a pillow and smother him to death.

DUTY! THOU SUBLIME AND MIGHTY NAME THAT DOST EMBRACE NOTHING CHARMING OR INSINUATING, BUT REQUIREST SUBMISSION

How strange are the standards of do-gooders? Suppose you don't aspire to be a do-gooder; how much can morality demand of you? Is your life your own, to spend as you like, or do you owe some of it to other people? And if you do owe something, then how much? The moral question here is less one of quality—What should I do?—than of quantity: When can I stop?

Some do-gooders say they're only doing their duty: they're only doing what everyone ought to, and if most people think their sense of duty is bizarre and unreasonable, then most people are wrong. They reject the idea that what they do is saintly or heroic, because to them, that's another way of saying that most people needn't even try to do such things. Praise is a disguised excuse.

But of course it could be those do-gooders who are wrong. Nearly everyone believes that some acts go beyond the call of duty. Nearly every religion believes that there are some superior creatures, such as saints, who are capable of more than the rest of us. The philosopher J. O. Urmson has argued that it's a fundamental part of human morality to call some deeds saintly or heroic—meaning that they're very good to do but can't possibly be demanded of anyone, because the sacrifice or courage they require is too great. To reject the idea of saintliness and heroism—to say that there is no such thing as "beyond the call of duty"—is to say that everyone must be a saint or a hero, in the same way that everyone must pay his debts and avoid stealing; and that would be ridiculous, a morality for angels, not human beings.

Here's one way of thinking about this. It's not the only way, by any means, but right now it's one of the best-known arguments for the extreme morality of do-gooders. In 1971, there was genocide in East Pakistan, following closely upon a terrible cyclone, all in a place that was very poor to begin with. It seemed to some that if only enough money could be raised to pay for aid, then dreadful suffering could be avoided. People in rich countries heard about East Pakistan's troubles in the news, and some were sufficiently distressed that they donated money to aid organizations, whereas others were not so strongly affected; either reaction was acceptable, since to donate money for the relief of foreigners was to go beyond what most people considered a duty. Some money was raised, but not enough, and partly (though by no means exclusively) because of that, many thousands starved to death.

In response to this situation, the Australian philosopher Peter Singer wrote a now famous essay, "Famine, Affluence, and Morality," in which he argued that spending money on the trappings of middle-class life rather than on famine relief, or some other form of charitable aid, was not merely stingy but depraved. His argument went like this: If you walk past a shallow pond and see a child drowning, ought you to save the child, even if it would mean muddying your clothes? Most people would say that of course you should—muddy clothes are nothing compared with a dead child. Well, he argued, children are dying all the time, so if we can save them without sacrificing anything of equal importance, particularly something as unimportant as extra clothes, we ought to do it. Most of these children are nowhere near us, but what moral difference does it make if the child is in front of us or far away? If we spend two hundred dollars on clothes that could have bought lifesaving food or medicine, we're still responsible for a death. And, by extension, if we don't give much of what we own and earn for the relief of suffering, then we're responsible for many deaths.

This article had a profound effect on many people—particularly those who, like Aaron Pitkin, had been searching for a moral direction, prompted by an uncomfortable sense that the suffering of the world demanded of them a personal and painful response. The shallow-pond argument resolved this moral queasiness into sharp focus. It seemed, to Aaron at least, irrefutable. This experience was frightening—Aaron realized that he had been living even more immorally than he had imagined, and that he was going to have to change a great deal about his life—but it was also bracing. For a dyed-in-the-wool do-gooder like him, a convincing moral argument, one that dictated a clear path forward, was ultimately a comfort, even if that path involved a greater degree of asceticism than he had bargained for. To him, moral uncertainty, and the feeling of indeterminate guilt and taint that came with it, were more dreadful than any sacrifice. For this reason, he accepted the argument without worrying too much about the many complexities it left out—such as political questions about people in the First World presuming it to be their business to rescue impoverished foreigners, and practical questions about the limited ability of charities to solve problems, particularly in places where governments were incompetent or corrupt.

But the shallow-pond argument affected not only people like Aaron, who were primed to accept it; even many of those who felt instinctively and strongly that it must be wrong were hard-pressed to say exactly how. Surely, buying a pair of shoes could not be as bad as letting a child drown in front of you, such a person might think. Surely, a person who declined to reduce himself and his family to penury could not be as bad as a *serial murderer*. If either of these things were true, then our moral intuitions must be so badly flawed that we should shut our ears to them altogether—and if our intuitions were all wrong, then how could we trust them to judge anything at all? And yet, for all this sense of unraveled absurdity, the questions posed by the shallow pond remained uncomfortably unresolved. Why should it make a difference whether a dying child was right in front of you or not? And if it were your duty to rescue one child, then why not five children—or a thousand?

How did this happen? How did one drowning child become thousands of children drowning in an infinite succession of shallow ponds and the prospect of a lifetime spent frantically racing from one rescue to the next? How did the price of morality rise with such startling speed, and so staggeringly high? How did this simple argument manage to make a conclusion so foreign to common sense appear to arise from the most conventional and robust of moral instincts? It did so by blurring the difference between what to most people appear to be completely different moral situations: charity and rescue. Rescue—helping a person right in front of you, such as a child drowning in a shallow pond—seems to most people to be a duty, as long as it isn't dangerous. Charity—in the sense of helping an unseen person far away—does not. (Some people, of course, consider charity a duty, but a limited one, not the near-infinite duty that Singer was talking about.)

To most people, the distance between themselves and another person—physical as well as emotional—is a deep moral fact: it makes a profound difference to their sense of duty. A person who is far away, whom you cannot see or hear, and with whom you have no memories or loyalties in common, cannot compel your help in the same way as a person who is right in front of you, or who is in some sense one of your own. Ignoring the cries of a drowning child is a violation of the most basic kind of compassion; anyone who did that would seem less than human. Cultivating sympathy for unseen and unknown people, on the other hand, seems an abstract, second-order, extra-credit sort of moral emotion—admirable enough, but more than can be required of an ordinary person. Singer knew that to most people these differences were significant, but he set out to show that they shouldn't be. Physical distance in particular appeared to him to carry no moral weight whatsoever. How could a person who would consider it unforgivable to allow a child to drown in front of him be content to let an equally helpless child die, just because he was farther away? It made no sense.

Peter Singer is a utilitarian, which is to say that he believes that a person should figure out the moral thing to do not by consulting a list of rules—don't steal, don't murder, honor your father and mother, help old ladies across roads—but by trying to bring about the most well-being possible in the world. In principle, this means that a person ought to be concerned with well-being as such, and neutral about whose well-being it is, which means that we ought to be as much concerned about faraway strangers as about people right in front of us, or even our families. In fact, many utilitarians believe that it's usually best if people care more for their families than for strangers, because the world works better that way, but this is merely a pragmatic concession. Singer even includes animals as well as humans in his calculus of obligation, because when it comes to well-being, he believes, as Jeremy Bentham, the founder of utilitarianism, famously put it: "The question is not, Can they *reason?* nor, Can they *talk?* but, Can they *suffer?*"

To accept this idea—that, in principle at least, we owe as much to distant strangers as to people we are close to—is to reject a core part of what most people believe. Even to dismiss the importance of physical distance is extremely radical. As the philosopher Kwame Anthony Appiah has pointed out, a strict utilitarian would not rescue the child from the shallow pond at all: he would leave the child to drown, sell his unmuddied clothes, and donate the proceeds to a charity that could save more than one child with the money. That is how bizarre it is to dismiss physical distance. But of course displacing the preeminence of duty to family is a far greater leap. You might say that this question of family versus strangers is one of quality rather than quantity: *whom* must I help, rather than how much. In practice, though, there are almost always many more strangers, in direr need, than relatives.

But it's not only in its embrace of impartiality between family and strangers that utilitarianism is radical: it's even more radical in how *much* it demands. In some rules-based moral systems, after all, there is the possibility that as long as you follow the rules, once you have done your duty, you are free to use the rest of your time and resources as you like. You haven't stolen anything or murdered anyone, you have honored your parents, you have helped old ladies across the road, and now you can go about your business assured that you are a decent human being. But utilitarianism claims that you should act so as to bring about the most well-being possible in the world. Taken literally, this means that every single thing you do, at every moment of your life, should be motivated by that goal. Which is to say that there is no point at which you can say, I have done my duty, I have followed the rules, and I am now free to do what I want.

Singer is pretty extreme as utilitarians go, but he isn't the most extreme. Probably the most astonishingly demanding utilitarian was one of the first of the breed, William Godwin—a contemporary of Bentham's, husband of Mary Wollstonecraft, father of Mary Shelley. Writing soon after the French Revolution, Godwin declared that the desire to take special care of one's family and friends was a pernicious impulse that should be classed with the passions, alongside avarice, or the love of fame. To him, there was no life outside duty, because duty was infinite. A man "has no right to dispose of a shilling," he wrote, "at the suggestion of his caprice. So far from being entitled to . . . applause, for having employed some scanty pittance in the service of philanthropy, he is in the eye of justice a delinquent, if he withhold any portion from that service." This position was pure, consistent, and invigoratingly radical, but it proved so universally repellent that utilitarianism hastily retreated to the safety of moderation.

In utilitarianism's sensible middle years—the years of John Stuart Mill and Henry Sidgwick, the second half of the nineteenth century—it emerged as a gently pragmatic doctrine, definitely progressive, but with all traces of Jacobin outrageousness removed. For

Mill and Sidgwick, instincts such as love for one's children and loyalty to one's friends were so obviously useful that they should be encouraged, even if in some cases they worked against the general good. In fact, much of conventional morality should be left intact. After all, Mill wrote, comfortingly: "The occasions on which any person (except one in a thousand) has it in his power to . . . be a public benefactor, are but exceptional; and on these occasions alone is he called on to consider public utility; in every other case, private utility, the interest and happiness of some few persons, is all he has to attend to." This was very reasonable, and in accord with the moral intuitions of most people. The only problem was that it wasn't true. And so, a hundred years later, Peter Singer appeared like the ghost of William Godwin to call utilitarianism back to its exigent roots.

To a nonutilitarian, such an extreme morality as Singer's or Godwin's can seem not just oppressively demanding but actually evil, because it violates your duty to yourself. To require a person to think of himself as a tool for the general good could be seen as the equivalent of kidnapping a person off the street and harvesting his organs to save three or four lives. To demand that of somebody else would be wicked, and even to ask it of yourself seems wrong, even perverted. Impartial, universal love seems the antithesis of what we value about deep human attachment.

The British philosopher Bernard Williams despised utilitarianism, but he thought "duties to oneself" were fraudulent—just a clever way of, as he put it, laundering the currency of desire. He thought it was cleaner to put it straightforwardly: morality does not always trump other concerns. Morality likes to make it seem as though outside its kingdom of duty there is only meaningless, selfish impulse, but this is not true. Much of life exists there also. If a person is at every moment required to be attending to his moral duty, then much of what makes life worth living, and people worth loving, will have to be abandoned.

Suppose a man could save either his wife or two strangers from drowning, Williams proposed. A utilitarian might ask: is it permissible for the man to save his wife? But even to *ask* that question in such a situation was to have, as Williams dryly put it, "one thought too many." A loving husband would save his wife spontaneously, without consulting moral rules at all. To grant morality the power to adjudicate impartially in situations like that would be to abandon what gives human life its meaning. Without selfish partiality—to people you are deeply attached to, your family and friends, to place—we are nothing. We are creatures of kinship and loyalty, not blind servants of the world.

Not surprisingly, utilitarians are rare, even among do-gooders. Very few people believe they owe as much to strangers as to family. And most do-gooders, like most people, think about morality in terms of rules and principles—what they ought and ought not to do—rather than quantities of well-being. On the other hand, even a nonutilitarian will start to think about quantity if the numbers are big enough. It might seem repellent for a person to question whether he's permitted to save his wife from drowning rather than two strangers—but what if it were five strangers, or fifty, or five thousand? And what if his wife were a demented serial killer on the lam? At a certain point, even the most emotional anti-utilitarian with no do-gooder tendencies at all would start to feel guilty.

What do-gooders and utilitarians do have in common is the belief that most ordinary ideas about how much you owe to strangers, and how much duty can demand of you, are wrong. A do-gooder might believe, like any ordinary person, that you should save your wife rather than two strangers from drowning; but as the number of drowning strangers increases, the do-gooder will worry far sooner than the ordinary person whether it's immoral not to change his mind. And the number of hours in the do-gooder's life when he feels free to do entirely as he likes—when he owes nothing to the world, when he has done his duty, and what remains of his day and his money and his energy are his alone—are very few.

So is there a limit to what morality can demand of us? To believe that everyone is duty-bound to bring about as much good as possible is to suggest that there is no difference between basic duties, like telling the truth, and the most saintly acts of self-abnegation. Not only is this idea at odds with the way most people think about morality; it threatens to destroy the idea of duty altogether. If sacrificing your life for a stranger is as much a duty as not lying or not stealing; if buying a pair of shoes is as bad as failing to rescue a child drowning in a pond; then it can seem that not lying or not stealing is no *more* required than sacrificing your life for a stranger. Duty must be a law that everyone is bound to obey, no matter what, or it isn't duty. To demand too much can be as corrupting as demanding too little. And to demand too much crushes aspiration. If every good act is required, then none is praiseworthy. There is no more virtue—only duty and vice.

Singer's conclusions strike many people as so extreme as to be almost crazy. Nowadays, a moral theory according to which nearly everyone appears immoral to the point of depravity seems ridiculous. In the past, however, it's worth remembering, the idea that nearly everybody was a wretched sinner seemed perfectly normal.

The do-gooder belief that one is obliged to take care of strangers as well as one's family can seem like a violation of human instinct; but human instincts do not all tend toward comfort and love. Sacrifice is a human instinct, too. There is an instinct to hoard for one's family against future disaster; but there is, too, an instinct to send gifts out into the unknown. There is a sublime austerity about giving to unseen, unknown strangers, like the belief in an unseen and mysterious deity. If it's unnatural to adopt, as Henry Sidgwick put it, "the point of view of the universe," as do-gooders try to do, then it is equally unnatural to imagine the point of view of God.

AT ONCE RATIONAL AND ARDENT

Something she yearned for by which her life might be filled with
action at once rational and ardent; and since the time was gone by
for guiding visions and spiritual directors, since prayer heightened
yearning, but not instruction, what lamp was there but knowledge?

—GEORGE ELIOT, *Middlemarch*

For many years, Julia Wise wondered if she would ever meet another person who thought as she did. Everyone she knew thought her ideas about morality, and what she was duty-bound to do, were strange. Most people just thought she was weird. Some people told her they thought she might be right but they weren't willing to make the sacrifices she made; other people thought her ideas were not only misguided but actually bad. All this made her worry that she might be wrong. How likely was it that everyone else was wrong and she was right? But she was also suspicious of that worry: after all, it would be quite convenient to be wrong—she wouldn't have to give so much. Although her beliefs seemed to her not only reasonable but clearly true, and she could argue for them in a rational way, they were not entirely the result of conscious thinking: the essential impulse that gave rise to all the rest was simply a part of her. She couldn't help it, she had always been this way, since she was a child.

Julia believed that because each person was equally valuable she was not entitled to care more for her own well-being than for anyone else's; she believed that she was therefore obliged to spend much of her life working for the benefit of others. That was the core of it; as she grew older, she worked out the implications of this principle in greater detail. In college, she thought she might want to work in development abroad somewhere, but then she realized that probably the most useful thing she could do was not become a white aid worker telling people in other countries what to do, but, instead, earn a First World salary and give it to NGOs that could use it to pay for several local workers who knew what their countries needed better than she did.

She became a social worker in Boston, and she loved her work. She had never been good at small talk, but the conversations she had with her clients were often deeply felt and about real things, and she hoped that at least sometimes they were of use. It felt good to extend sympathy and help to someone who wanted it, and who was sitting right there in front of her. But she knew that people in other parts of the world were worse off than even the people she worked with in prisons and mental hospitals—they were dying young from preventable diseases, they didn't have enough food or clean water—so she concluded that her donations to charities, which helped people far away whom she would never meet, were more important than her social work. She believed that, if she was to be as helpful as possible, she had to think about what people most needed rather than what gave her pleasure to give. What was important was that people were helped, not that it was she who was doing the helping.

She reduced her expenses to the absolute minimum so she could give away most of what she earned. She gave to whichever charity seemed to her (after researching the matter) to relieve the most suffering for the least money, which usually meant medical interventions in the Third World. Because she earned the salary of a social worker, she could not give very much, but year after year and over her lifetime she knew it would add up to quite a lot—hundreds of thousands of dollars—which meant that many children who might have died young from some easily cured disease might instead survive and live a normal span of life.

Julia has experienced depression in the past, and even now that she has been happy for several years, and is often funny, the dregs of her sadness still cling to her. She is cautious and reserved, and you can imagine the doors of her self closing very tightly, to the point where no light at all can enter. Suffering can cause a person to turn inward, to become so preoccupied with his own pain that he loses sight of other people, but it did not have this effect on Julia. Her depression has made her viscerally conscious of suffering in others in a way that most naturally happy people are not. She is young—thirty—but not so young that her youth accounts for any of her beliefs; she is long past the age when most people forget or distort or reject the terrible simplicity of the rules they learned as children.

Despite her extreme frugality, Julia is not an ascetic. She loves material things as much as anyone. She loves fireworks and ice cream, she loves to cook. She loves to sew clothes and to make elaborate old-fashioned hats out of scraps. She gets pleasure out of things like that; she doesn't get pleasure out of giving money. To her, giving is simply a duty, like not stealing, so it doesn't beget a feeling of virtue. If all were well with the world, she would like to live on a farm somewhere, and keep animals, and grow pumpkins and runner beans and sunflowers in the garden. She would sew curtains and read and bake pies and have children. But all is not well with the world.

It occurred to Julia when she was quite young that she would be hellish to be married to. She was unwilling to compromise on moral questions, which meant, for instance, that she was unwilling to spend money on things that it was normal for married people to spend money on. And yet, when she was twenty-two, having fallen in love with a young man named Jeff Kaufman, she proposed to him and they became engaged. Jeff knew about her principles, but money questions did not come up much while they were still in college, because their food and shelter were taken care of. And so it happened that the first real moral test of their life together did not arise until after graduation.

It was a sunny day in September, and they were at an apple orchard outside Boston with Julia's Morris-dancing troupe. There were candy apples for sale, and Julia wanted one. Normally she would have told herself that she couldn't justify spending her money that way, but Jeff had told her that if she wanted anything he would buy it for her with his money. He had found a job as a computer programmer; Julia was still unemployed, and didn't have any savings, because she had given everything she'd earned in the summer to Oxfam. Jeff bought the apple.

> JULIA: It was, like, maybe four dollars?
> JEFF (Shocked): No!
> JULIA: It was one of those orchards.
> JEFF: *A four-dollar candy apple?*
> JULIA: I don't know.
> JEFF: *I* would feel bad about that.
> JULIA: Maybe it was three?
> JEFF: I don't think it was that much.
> JULIA: I'm sure it's in the spreadsheet.

That night they lay in bed and talked about money. Jeff told Julia that, inspired by her example, he was thinking of giving some percentage of his salary to charity. And Julia realized that, if Jeff was going to start giving away his earnings, then, by asking him to buy her the apple, she had spent money that might have been given. With her selfish, ridiculous desire for a candy apple, she might have deprived a family of an anti-malarial bed net or deworming medicine that might have saved the life of one of its children. The more she thought about this, the more horrific and unbearable it seemed to her, and she started to cry. She cried for a long time, and it got so bad that Jeff started to cry, too, which he almost never did. He cried because, more than anything, he wanted Julia to be happy, but how could she be happy if she went through life seeing malarial children everywhere, dying before her eyes for want of a bed net? He knew that he wanted to marry her, but he wasn't sure how he could cope with a life that was going to be this difficult and this sad, with no conceivable way out.

Then they stopped crying and talked about budgets. They realized that Julia was going to lose her mind if she spent the rest of her life weighing each purchase in terms of bed nets, so, after much discussion and fine tuning, they came up with a system. In the weeks and months that followed, they refined it, adjusting its incentives and allowances, addressing its inequities. The first and most crucial element of the system was that henceforth Jeff's money and Julia's money would be considered entirely separate. Once that was established, they could decide to do with their own money what they wished. Jeff decided he would give away 50 percent of his salary and keep the rest for spending and saving; Julia would give away 100 percent of hers. Out of the remainder of Jeff's salary, he allotted an allowance to each of them of thirty-eight dollars a week, which they would use to pay for everything other than rent and food—things such as clothes, shoes, transportation, and treats like candy apples. Jeff decreed that this allowance had to be spent on these things: it could not be given away, and it could not be saved, or he would donate a matching amount to the Republican Party. That way, if Julia wanted to spend money on something, she would not be taking that money away from someone who was dying. (Julia realized, of course, that this wall they had set up between his money and hers existed only in their heads, but since its only function was to preserve her sanity, that didn't matter.)

Having figured out a system, they stuck to it with rigor. They kept track of every purchase, however tiny, and entered it into a spreadsheet. After a year, they realized that giving away 50 percent of Jeff's salary, before taxes (they had forgotten taxes), while paying rent and student loans, and giving away 100 percent of Julia's salary, was basically impossible, so they adjusted the amount to 30 percent. In 2009, they spent $15,688 on themselves and donated $28,309. In 2010, they spent $20,591 and donated $36,056. In 2011, they spent $17,959 and donated nothing, because Julia was paying for social-work school and Jeff was taking much of his salary in stock options. In 2012, they spent $12,107 (their rent was less, because they moved in with Jeff's parents) and donated $49,933. At some point they decided to merge their finances and donate 50 percent of their joint pretax income; they also realized that it made sense to buy a house and rent part of it out, rather than pay rent themselves. Because they earned more, they were now giving away more than ever before, both proportionally and in absolute terms, despite buying the house: in 2014, they donated $127,556.

Once their financial system was in place, they spent some time looking into various organizations, with the goal of finding the most effective charity, which they defined as the one that relieved the most suffering for the fewest dollars. At first, they settled on Oxfam. They liked that it employed a lot of local workers rather than just NGO types from abroad; they liked that it focused on long-term development rather than splashy but inefficient disaster relief. Later, they heard about an organization called GiveWell, which evaluated charities in terms not of how little they spent on overhead—a silly measure, since overhead costs, such as efficacy research, might be money well spent—but of how effective they were at saving and improving lives. GiveWell promoted groups like the Against Malaria Foundation, which distributed bed nets, and the Schistosomiasis Control Initiative, which administered cheap deworming treatments. People were always telling Julia and Jeff that they ought to help those in their own community first, before sending money abroad, but they thought that was wrong. For one thing, money went so much further in other countries, so it could help many more people. And, then, why were strangers in Somerville or some other nearby town any more their own than strangers in Malawi? they wondered. It made no sense.

All their donations and self-imposed frugality meant that Julia and Jeff thought about money quite a lot, and some people found this off-putting, especially since the amounts involved were relatively small. There was a grandeur to extremely large donations, and to the high aims that those sums made possible, so that the money-ness of the money tended to fade into invisibility beside the dazzling ambition of the idea. But smaller sums seemed petty: they remained *only* money, defined by the ordinariness of what the amount could buy in the First World (a pair of shoes, a car) rather than the value of what it could buy somewhere else (food, medicine). Small renunciations could make a person seem small rather than good.

And what could those small sums actually do? It was true that nothing could really change without the action of governments. Julia and Jeff knew that development alone was limited at best, and at its worst could be actively harmful. But they thought that, if they worked hard to find the charities that were doing the most effective work, and gave them as much money as they possibly could, then over the years that would be worth it. Enabling some lives to be less stunted was as much as a regular person could hope to do, they thought, even if larger, systemic evils persisted.

The point was to try to make sure the money did something useful, and not to become all pure and martyrish about it and start thinking about self-deprivation as an end in itself. They had read about a man named Charles Gray who had decided to restrict himself to what he called the World Equity Budget. His budget was much smaller than theirs, and that impressed them, but they thought it was silly that Charles Gray seemed to think it was more important that he be poor than that other people be less so. They felt sad that a strong moral impulse should have been squandered in such a useless manner. It was not, after all, the thought that counted when it came to doing good in the world.

It was a dull way of giving—writing checks rather than, say, becoming an aid worker in a distant country. There was a moral glamour in throwing over everything and leaving home and going somewhere dangerous that compensated for all sorts of privations. There was no glamour in staying behind, earning money, and donating it. It certainly wasn't soul-stirring, to be thinking about money all the time. But so much depended on money, they knew—it took a callous kind of sentimentality to forget that. Money well spent could mean years of life, and money spent badly meant years of life lost.

>JULIA: People are really bad at thinking of money and lives as interchangeable, but they are. Like, today, at work, we were talking about the teenager who decided to sail around the world and then had to be airlifted out of the Indian Ocean. How much money was spent on saving that one life? And there are other situations where we spend huge amounts on some expensive medical procedure, and we're willing to think of that life as infinitely precious, but we're also willing to stand by while lots of people die for stupid and preventable reasons. I think we should think about how things would be if we had to treat sick people equally, rather than keeping a lot of them hidden in Haiti. I heard on the news that a second person died in Arizona after being denied an organ transplant because the state cut $1.4 million from its transplant program. All I could think was: *That much money, and only two people died?*

The summer after Jeff graduated from college—the summer before the candy-apple incident—he and Julia worked at Pinewoods, a folk-dance-and-music camp; Jeff washed dishes, Julia was a cook. Together they saved about five thousand dollars, which they donated to Oxfam. While they were working at the camp, it seemed to them that this was a good way to spend the summer: they were living simply, spending nothing, helping other people with hard menial work, and saving the money they earned to give away. But after the summer was over and Jeff started donating, it occurred to him that they could have earned considerably more by doing something else, which would have enabled them to give more. Had that summer, then, been a self-indulgence? Did they have the right to spend three months of their expensively educated lives playing peasants by the seaside, earning almost nothing? Was there really any difference between choosing not to earn more money and spending their money on a new sofa or fancy clothes? Had they, in effect, been paying with the suffering of other people for the privilege of feeling wholesomely poor?

It was bad enough to worry about these questions in retrospect, but they became far more pressing when Julia had to think about a career. She wanted to be a social worker—she had wanted to for years—but she could earn far more money doing something else. Was it okay for her to be a social worker anyway? How much was she entitled to consider her own happiness? She could justify not going for the absolute maximum she could earn on the grounds that she would be so crushingly miserable in finance or law that she would have a breakdown within a few years, and then she'd be out the cost of law school or business school or whatever it took to get into the field in the first place. She knew that pushing herself past what she could endure wasn't going to help anyone. A career had to be sustainable over the long haul. But obviously there were lots of jobs that paid less than finance but more than social work. How could she justify going into a field that paid so little? She struggled with this question for a long time, and though she never did come up with a satisfactory answer, she enrolled in social-work school anyway.

All of this was much less of a problem for Jeff. If he had married someone other than Julia, he thought, he probably would not be spending much more than he was now, he would just be saving the extra rather than giving it away. He wanted to have a pot of money in reserve so he would have more options in the future, and so that, if anything bad happened to his family, he would be able to help. If he hadn't married Julia, he would have spent a bit more on nicer musical instruments—he especially coveted a new fiddle—and he would have felt freer to quit his job and do something else that paid less. Maybe he would have become a full-time musician or a folk-dance caller. But other than that, his life would be basically the same. He figured he would enjoy any number of different jobs, so he felt free to pick the highest-paid one. He liked working as a programmer, and he imagined that if he had no charitable duties he would probably be doing something pretty similar. It wasn't hard to make him happy.

While Julia was working on her social-work degree, it occurred to her that she might have enjoyed being a psychiatrist, and psychiatrists earned much more than social workers. That was what she should have done with her life, she realized. But the thought of investing vast sums of money and many years of her life on premed courses and then medical school—years in which, she had reason to believe, she would be utterly miserable and wouldn't be able to donate anything at all—was too awful to contemplate. Later still, it occurred to her that she could earn more money within social work by becoming one of the despised subspecies that adjudicated claims for insurance companies—those who spent their time denying sick people coverage. The work would be awful, but it would enable her to give a lot more without requiring any additional training, so did she have the right to turn away from it?

The trouble was, she loved her job. Her first position was as a counselor in a prison. Much of the time she couldn't do very much for the people she talked with—they were in prison, after all—but many of them were so miserable there, and so desperate for kindness, that she saw that just listening to them and being supportive meant quite a bit. And once in a while she felt that something she had said had really helped. One woman in the prison was the daughter of an alcoholic father who had died from the effects of drinking; the father had always told his daughter that her bad behavior had driven him to drink, and the daughter felt dreadful guilt about this, believing that she had effectively killed him. Julia said, What if your father had told his AA group that he drank because of you, that it was all your fault? The daughter at once saw how wrong that would sound to other people, and felt her guilt ease. Moments like that made Julia happy, but she was careful not to let herself get carried away. She was there to think about what her clients needed, not what made her feel good. She wrote in her blog:

This is an ad for a food bank that appears on buses all over Boston. Here we have a pretty young white woman hugging an older white woman. I guess the young woman is supposed to represent the food bank, since she looks happy, whereas the faceless older woman is presumably hungry and therefore in need of comfort. Oh, wait. Except she doesn't need a hug. She needs groceries. I have a rescue fantasy—what social worker doesn't? Somewhere inside, we love to believe that we could just hug our clients and make everything better. If we took them home and gave them a good meal and enough sympathy, we believe we could fix everything and earn their undying gratitude. But that is an *inside thought*. You do not tell your clients about that thought. The point is to help, not to feel helpful. . . . If I needed groceries, would I really want to go someplace where I might get hugged by some misty-eyed young lady with a savior complex? No way.

Julia had always wanted to keep chickens, and she realized that, though it would not be practical to keep chickens in her and Jeff's tiny studio apartment, it might just work to keep quail. Quail were smaller and quieter than chickens, and you could keep them in a cage in the bedroom. She and Jeff could eat their eggs, and when the birds were done laying, they could eat the birds themselves. She looked into this and discovered that you could order fertilized quail eggs to be delivered to you through the mail; all you needed was an incubator, which Jeff could make. Her birthday was coming up; when her mother asked her what she wanted for a birthday present, she asked for a quail feeder. Her mother, rather than buying one and sending it in the mail, sent her a check with "quail feeder" written on it. But once Julia got the money in her hands, she felt she had to give it away, and did. It was, she realized, like dealing with an addict.

This had been an issue between Julia and her family for a long time. Even when she was tiny, she gave away what she had. When she was five or so, the older sister of a friend of hers lost a ten-dollar bill, and this seemed to Julia such rotten luck that she wanted to give the sister her allowance to make up for it. Julia's mother said no, it was better for the sister to learn to be responsible for her own money; Julia didn't say anything, but she went upstairs and, sometime later, her socks bulging with coins, emerged and told her mother she was going out.

Julia grew up in a suburb of Richmond, Virginia. Her father was a property manager; her mother taught in a preschool. Years later, she would think of the place and way she had grown up as a decline from what had been before. Her parents met at a clog-dancing class while her father was working as a carpenter; when Julia was born, they were living in a little house in the country with a duck pond and a wood stove and no air conditioning. Her mother canned vegetables and sewed clothes. But the schools weren't very good there, so they moved to a big house in the suburbs, with a modern stove and air conditioning, and her father started managing properties. Julia sometimes thought about that little house in the country and wondered how her parents could have given up that ideal life, and how she could someday get it back.

When she was a little older, she stopped giving to friends and started putting her allowance in the collection plate at church, thinking the money would go to the poor. She agonized over whether to go to birthday parties, because she felt she couldn't show up without bringing a present, but she believed it would be wrong to spend five dollars on a present when that five dollars could be given to someone who needed it more. Once, she desperately coveted a particular stuffed animal, but she felt it would be sinful to spend the money on it. She called up her best friend, Bridget, and put the problem to her. Bridget suggested that she put all her money in the collection plate and tell her parents that she'd done so; her parents would be so moved by her virtue that they'd give her more money, which she could use to buy the stuffed animal. (Bridget grew up to be a lawyer.) Julia was so shocked that she slammed down the phone without saying good-bye.

Until she was eleven, Julia was fervently religious. She believed that, since God had given her life, she owed Him a debt so enormous that she could never repay it, but it was her duty to try as hard as she could. She prayed for hours at a time, apologizing for her imperfections. She read the Bible and tried to follow it literally. She read that it was forbidden to mix wool and flax, so she refused to wear clothing that blended different fibers. She stopped working on Saturdays. She kept kosher, although she was Protestant. Then, one weekend, it occurred to her that other people in the world believed in their holy books just as strongly as she believed in the Bible, so what reason did she have to believe that hers was true? She had never seen or felt any evidence of God's presence. Quite suddenly, she lost her faith.

After she stopped believing in God, she stopped giving money to the church, and for a couple of years she just spent her allowance on herself: if God didn't exist, there was no one she owed it to. Then she began to learn about poverty in the world, and how rich she was compared with other people, and when she was thirteen she began giving her allowance away again, mostly to the Heifer Project. Around this time, a boy who went to her family's church developed a serious illness that required major surgery for which his family didn't have insurance. The church took up a collection for them, and Julia's mother told her that here was someone she knew whom she could help—why not give her money to him? Julia said, Why is the life of someone I happen to know worth more than the lives of many more people I don't know, whom I could help with the same amount?

Although she was no longer a believer, she missed the community and the rituals of religion. She continued to celebrate Christmas and Easter and observe the liturgical calendar—she liked the way it gave shape to the year. One day she went online and filled out a religion quiz; the results told her that her beliefs lined up with those of secular humanists and Unitarians. She decided to check out a

Unitarian service, but she couldn't find the church and got lost and ended up at the dump. She thought the story would make a good country song—"I Went Lookin' for Religion, but I Found the County Dump"—except she thought that you probably weren't allowed to mention Unitarianism in country songs. Eventually, she found her way to a Unitarian service, but she thought the hymn lyrics were tacky, so she ended up joining a Quaker meeting instead. The Quaker meeting satisfied her craving for ritual, but she still wished that there was a community she could join that would bring together more of the strands of her moral and emotional life. She liked to think about what to her were utopias—the Middle-earth of *Lord of the Rings*, the nineteenth-century New England of *Little Women*—although she didn't believe in them. She knew that communism didn't work, but she longed for some smaller-scale, less ambitious utopia that might work, like a kibbutz, or a Shaker community, or a cooperative where people shared their stuff and gave things up for the benefit of others.

She went to college at Bryn Mawr, a small women's school near Philadelphia. It was in the spring of her senior year that she met Jeff, who went to Swarthmore, another college nearby. Julia looked at Jeff's Facebook page, and noticed that it didn't have the usual photos of drunken parties and making stupid faces for the camera—instead, there were pictures of Jeff with his family, playing folk music, playing cards, cooking. On one of the walls, she spotted a Quaker wedding certificate. The absence of drunken photographs was not a matter of discretion: Jeff had decided in high school that he would never drink alcohol, because he didn't like the idea of changing the way he thought. Though he had never actually been drunk, the thought of it disturbed him. What if drunk Jeff disagreed on some point with sober Jeff? How would he decide which Jeff was right? The whole thing was confusing and better avoided. Because of this, even though he was an atheist, he ended up making friends with Evangelicals and Mormons.

Jeff grew up in a big Victorian house in Medford, a suburb of

Boston; his father, Rick, was a therapist; his mother, Suzie, was a midwife. Jeff's mother's family had been Quaker for several generations; his grandfather had been a conscientious objector in World War II and had been subjected to harsh military experiments in a CO camp. Jeff had spent even less money than Julia had as a child, but for a different reason. When he was eight, he longed for the instruments he saw at folk festivals, so he started saving his allowance with the idea of buying one. He got a dollar a week; he saved his allowance for five weeks and was very excited to be able to trade the one-dollar bills for a five. He kept saving until he could trade four fives for a twenty. By the time he could afford one of the instruments he had wanted, it had taken him so long to save the money that the instrument no longer seemed worth it, so he kept on saving instead. Once he acquired the habit of frugality, it detached itself from its original purpose and became a fixed part of his character.

Jeff brought Julia home to the family she had seen on Facebook, and the moment she walked into their house she knew she wanted to live there. There were places to be with people and places to be alone; there were lots of books. There was a big kitchen with a table where you could sit and chat while you chopped things. There was always music in the house: Jeff's father played violin, guitar, bass, mandolin, and viola. Jeff played the piano, and played the fiddle with such exuberance that he broke strings. Not long after this visit, Julia sat Jeff down under a tree and told him she wanted to marry him.

Julia and Jeff rarely talked to other people about their giving. It was awkward. People didn't like to talk about money in general, but they *really* didn't want to feel they were being judged for keeping too much of their money for themselves. When Julia had, several times, tried to talk about giving, one person told her she was crazy and was just going to make herself miserable; another person made fun of her. She couldn't decide how to feel about this. On the one hand, she felt that one of the most useful things she could do was encourage other people to give more, and she worried that if she were braver and cared less about social niceties she would be more aggressive about it. She had read in the journals of John Woolman, an eighteenth-century Quaker leader, that Woolman found preaching about righteousness extremely embarrassing; he begged God not to ask him to do it, but since God insisted, he did it anyway. If she were a better person, surely she would preach more, too. On the other hand, she knew that it was important for the cause not to be off-putting, and if anything was off-putting it was preachiness. Or was that just her way of rationalizing what she wanted to do anyway? She wasn't sure. She realized that it was important for her not to seem too puritanical or constrained: people would think that she had some kind of martyr complex, or that it was impossible to give a lot of money without making yourself miserable, whereas in fact most of the time she found it easy to live an enjoyable life without spending much.

The need of the world was like death, she thought—everyone knew about it, but the thought was so annihilating that they had to push it out of consciousness or it would crush them. She understood, and yet she did not understand, why other people didn't give more than they did. How did they allow themselves such permission? She gave, and she was human, just as they were. How could people ignore the misery and unfairness in the world? How could they not help? She was not one of those blithe souls who didn't judge others—she judged. She held her fellow humans to account. But she didn't judge because she believed herself superior—quite the opposite. She didn't believe there was anything special about herself that she should be held to these duties while other people were let off the hook. Anyone could do what she did if they wanted to, she thought. Nick Carraway in *The Great Gatsby* said, "Reserving judgment is a matter of infinite hope," but the opposite is also true: to judge is to believe that a person is capable of doing better; it's to know that people can change their behavior, even quite radically, in response to what is expected of them. To judge is to hope that people are selfish in part because they believe it's the human condition. Julia wrote on her blog:

> One thing I almost never talk about is anger. When I'm happy with my life I don't have any reason to feel angry, but when I'm feeling deprived I sometimes do. I feel like I'm pulling at something heavy that I can't possibly lift by myself, maybe pulling a car out of a mud pit. And everyone is standing around saying, "Boy, it's too bad that car is in that mud pit," or "That looks like hard work you're doing," or, more often, "Did you hear the Italian team just lost out to Slovakia?" I really think there's enough material stuff and human ingenuity that nobody needs to be horribly poor. If everyone who could, pulled a little more weight, I wouldn't need to pull so much.

One thing that was clear to her was the importance of targeting. The average person might not be receptive to her ideas, but there had to be some people out there just waiting for encouragement. How could she find them? She decided to start a new blog, called *Giving Gladly*, in the hope that the explicit title and honed subject matter would attract likely prospects. At some point she had discovered that there was a philosopher at Princeton, Peter Singer, who advocated a moral worldview very similar to her own; she took Singer's book *The Life You Can Save* out of the library and, with the thrill of committing her first criminal act, wrote notes in the book inviting people who had been moved by its message to contact her.

She did these things partly because she felt it was her duty to encourage other people to give, but partly out of loneliness. She didn't know anyone other than Jeff who shared her beliefs about money and duty, certainly not strongly enough to live by them. Coming across Peter Singer's work had been exciting—to find out that there was a philosopher who thought as she did was heartening, though it wasn't the same as having a friend.

This sense of isolation lasted for a long time; but then Julia and Jeff discovered Giving What We Can. This was an organization that had been founded a little while before by Toby Ord, a young professor of moral philosophy at Oxford, to spread the idea that it was incumbent upon everyone to give more to help the worst off. Members had to sign a pledge to donate at least 10 percent of their yearly income until they retired. Some were already giving more than that, but Toby picked 10 percent because it seemed substantial yet not too intimidating, and it resonated with religious norms about tithing.

Julia and Jeff had always felt shy talking to people about giving, but Toby wasn't shy about it at all; in a very short time, he had started something of a public debate. Reporters heard about his organization, and a spate of articles appeared; students started chapters at universities; other people began to find the group over the Internet. Within a year or two after its founding, in 2009, Giving What We Can had become a focal point for what became known to its members as the effective-altruism movement. The "altruism" component was about giving more; the "effective" component was about seeking out research—ideally, randomized controlled trials, but at least reliable data—in order to find the charities whose programs improved the most lives for the least money.

Toby was a cheerful, unconflicted person. He lived the way he believed he ought to live, so he never felt guilty. He gave away a lot of his money, but he didn't experience it as much of a sacrifice. He already had everything he wanted—a wife he loved, friends, interesting and prestigious work. He donated money to relieve human suffering but he wasn't troubled by thoughts of that suffering because he was doing his part to alleviate it. He reckoned it was better not to be too empathetic anyway, because if he were feeling people's pain all the time he wouldn't get anything done. Once, a group of Giving What We Can members were talking about what got them out of bed in the morning; several of them said that they were in-spired by the thought of spreading the movement's ideas around the world, but Toby said that nothing in particular got him out of bed in the morning, he just got out of bed and went to work.

Toby was thin and pale, his skin stretched tightly over his skull, his expression tenacious. He grew up in Melbourne, Australia; his parents were architects. Years ago, when he was a student, he used to think to himself that he should be doing something about world pov-erty. He would see posters of starving children and think, Arggh, I should be doing something about that. Eventually, he thought, Well, why don't you just do something, then? At the time he was earning about eight thousand pounds a year on his graduate-student stipend and his life was perfectly fine, so he reckoned it would be pretty easy later on, when he was earning a professor's salary, to give away ev-erything he earned above eighteen thousand. He sat down and worked out how much he would likely earn in the course of his work-ing life. He calculated that he would earn about a million and a half pounds, and he would need to spend about half a million of that on himself—including savings, probably a mortgage, and funds for emergencies—which left a million pounds to donate to charity.

That was a pleasant surprise—a million pounds was a lot of money! He did some more calculations and arrived at the conclusion that with a million pounds he could save about a hundred thousand years of healthy life. That was *really* exciting. He thought: I could either save a hundred thousand years of healthy life, or I could gar-nish my own already happy life with some extra bells and whistles. The second didn't seem like a very good option, so he went for op-tion one. He then thought about whether he ought to pursue a career other than philosophy, in order to earn even more money to donate; he could probably earn quite a bit as a computer programmer, and he'd like the work. But then he figured that if he taught at Oxford there was a good chance he'd be able to influence students who would go on to be powerful in the world. Once he started Giving What We Can, he realized that that probably was the most effective thing he could have done, since in its first four years it had collected pledges that, he estimated, amounted to about a hundred million dollars, which was a lot more than he could have earned no matter what he did.

In the spring of 2013, Toby was in Boston for work, and Julia and Jeff invited him to dinner. They were holding an effective-altruist gathering that evening: thanks in part to Toby, they had discovered a small network of people who thought as they did about moral matters, and they liked to host dinner discussions from time to time, mostly in order to spread the word, but also because Julia loved to cook for lots of people. Effective altruists were often vegetarians or vegans, she knew, so she had made an enormous pot of pasta with vegetables, and chocolate cake and ice cream for dessert. The effective altruists filled plates and gathered in a circle on chairs and the floor.

The regular attendees of these gatherings tended to be well-educated young white men of technological background and rational disposition who considered themselves part of the effective-altruism community; Julia always wished there were more women. But usually a few new people would turn up, too—friends of friends; people who had found out about the dinner online—and these outsiders would enter the discussions unfamiliar with the norms and principles of the movement. The evening Toby came to dinner, three young Israelis—Barak and Yuval, both medical students, and Netta, a law student and Yuval's wife—had come at the suggestion of a friend.

> BARAK: You mentioned the surgeon who goes for a week to do surgery in Africa instead of continuing his high-paying job and donating money. I know a lot of surgeons who do that, and they derive so much personal gratification from going to Africa that it has an amazing impact for them. And I know we're supposed to be talking about how to help others, but I think there's a lot to be said for fulfilling your

own life. This is going to sound sappy, but I chose my profession because this is my way of helping others; I have chosen to dedicate my life to it, and I think the reason I'll be doing it effectively is because I love it so much.

Barak had close-cropped dark hair and wore a long silver spike through two holes in the upper part of his right ear. The previous year, he had spent time in Kenya starting up a children's health clinic, and he had been startled and bewildered to discover that this effort was not much valued by the effective altruists.

> NETTA: I would even make a stronger argument. I would say that it also helps the people that you come to help in Africa—that they have human contact, not just money being poured on them.
>
> TOBY: But we don't literally pour money on them. What we do is pay other people to do the work—I would be funding a local surgeon. There are nice aspects to going over there and meeting people and so on. But then you think, How important would it be to see a different person in my life, versus *not dying*?
>
> BARAK: But one of the reasons I chose to go into medicine is to say, I don't want to ignore sickness and illness and death anymore—I want to stand where the shit hits the fan. And for me Africa was an incredibly humbling and devastating experience.
>
> BEN K.: I completely agree that doing things firsthand can be very useful in terms of motivating yourself—just not if your goal is solely to do the most good for other people.

Ben K. was a math major at Harvard. He had very thick dark hair and Groucho Marx eyebrows and smiled a lot. He, like other effective altruists, felt it was not important *who* relieved suffering—it was important only that it be relieved. Barak found it astonishing, this casual dismissal of the significance of how a human being—in this case himself—spent his time on earth.

> BEN L.: One thing I've found valuable in my own decision making is to distinguish between the things I'm doing because I'm trying to help as many people as possible, and the things I'm doing to feel good as a person. These are two different problems, and they often have two different solutions. I give away a lot of money, but that doesn't feel fulfilling: clicking a button and having a number in a bank statement be different doesn't get into my monkey brain. So when I want to feel that kind of human connection, I give blood. I'm sure there's a more efficient use of my time in terms of helping as many people as possible, but that's not what I'm trying to do with that time; what I'm trying to do is feel like a good person.

Ben L. was a young software engineer in a purple shirt who had recently shaved off a mustache, on Julia's advice.

> BEN K.: There's a saying in utilitarian circles that you should purchase your fuzzies and your utilons separately. If you try to find one charity that both makes you feel good and contributes to the quality of life of other people, you're going to find a charity that is pretty bad at doing one of those things.

Toby had initially assumed that the altruism part of his message would be harder to push than the effective part: he thought it would be difficult to convince people to give more money, because that involved sacrifice, but easy to convince them to redirect their money to better charities, because who wouldn't want to do more good with their money? It turned out that people were not so rational, and in fact the reverse was true: it was quite easy to persuade people to give more money if you moved them emotionally, but persuading them to abandon causes that they'd believed in for years was very hard. It was easier for him to convert logical types who had never thought much about charity than it was to change the minds of longtime do-gooders. Effective-altruist converts tended to be the sort of people for whom, if emotion or instinct conflicted with a good argument, the argument would win.

The effective altruists had read a lot about aid, and they knew about the many catastrophic mistakes that NGOs had made in the past and continued to make. They knew that disaster relief could bring more disaster, and aid to wartime refugees more war. That was why it was so important never to assume that something that seemed to be an obviously good thing to do—feeding the hungry, for instance—would not have side effects that made everything worse. The previous year, GiveWell had ranked as one of its top three recommended charities an organization called GiveDirectly, whose method was to identify the poorest families in a given area and simply give them cash, with which they could do whatever they liked. (Often families spent it on a metal roof.) GiveWell's recommendations were closely watched by effective altruists, and this one had caused a considerable stir.

> CHRIS: I hope that GiveDirectly is not the best aid intervention we can think of, because that would be kind of sad. It would mean that, when you apply intelligence and really think about how to help people, you can't do any better than they can individually. It would mean that people's own preferences are the best way for them to become happier, and that's not a very well-supported hypothesis.

Chris was older than most of the effective altruists, and was married and had a baby. He worked for the education nonprofit One Laptop per Child.

BEN K.: I can sympathize, in that we have all of this awesome stuff that doesn't exist for the people we're trying to help, and it would be a shame if none of the awesome stuff was really helpful and it turns out that throwing money at them is the best way. I guess it makes it seem pretty futile that we have this cool stuff in the first place.

TOBY: But I don't think it's the most effective way to help people. There's a whole lot of community benefits, like sewage systems, which won't get done through this kind of scheme, even if people knew what was best for themselves, which they generally don't. Experts have done randomized controlled trials, which cost millions of dollars, to work out whether a thing is effective, and ordinary people in these countries just do not have this information.

MIKE: I feel like I should play devil's advocate. I want to support consumerism a little bit. The money you're giving to charity is not money that otherwise disappears—it's being diverted from the larger economy, or from a more effective economy, and Third World outcomes have been improving massively not because of charity but because of general economic growth in the world.

Mike was a bald young transhumanist with a soul patch who had recently quit a job at the phone company.

BEN K.: Yes, we spend all this money on charity, and it turns out that one of the biggest forces helping to improve quality of life is corporations being globalized. In a lot of cases, the things that have large effects are completely unpredictable. If you were sitting around in 1900 wondering how best to help people, you would not say, Coca-Cola globalizing. So it might be more reasonable to just do whatever you're best at, and hope that, whatever the best thing is, it will come more quickly because you're doing stuff that you're good at, rather than something you think will be more helpful but you're relatively bad at.

TOBY: But we have achieved a *lot* through aid. A ridiculous amount. The question is: if I spend my money going to see a movie, does that help people in poor countries as much as if I provide them with bed nets? I just have no idea how the economic argument would work that would make that true.

When Toby talked about his ideas in public, he tried to avoid imposing guilt—he believed that making people feel guilty didn't get you anywhere. He told people instead that giving away money was an exciting opportunity. "We look at people like Oskar Schindler, who saved about one thousand two hundred lives, and we think, That's an amazing kind of moral heroism. But we could make fewer sacrifices than he did and save more lives if we wanted to!" he says. Sometimes people told Toby that his principles were too demanding—that it wasn't reasonable to require people to give most of their money to help strangers. When this happened, he dropped the Oskar Schindler talk. "I think that's a very bad argument," he says. "Morality can demand a lot. Let's say you've been falsely accused of murder, you've been sentenced to death, and you realize that you can escape if you kill one of your guards. Morality says you can't kill him, even though it means you're going to lose your life. That's just how it is. Well, it turns out that we can save a thousand people's lives. If you don't do that, then you have to say that it's permissible to value yourself more than a thousand times as much as you value strangers. Does that sound plausible? I don't think that sounds very plausible. If you think that, your theory's just stupid."

As the effective-altruism movement continued to grow, Toby's Giving What We Can cofounder, another philosopher named Will MacAskill, founded a brother organization, 80,000 Hours, to help the altruistically minded think about how they could do the most good with the hours of their working lives. Will wanted to spread the idea that an altruistic type shouldn't necessarily follow one of the traditional do-gooder paths—becoming an aid worker or a doctor in the Third World, say—but should consider a career that would earn a lot of money which he could then donate. Will called this "earning to give." The idea began to catch on. A student of Peter Singer's went to work in finance; his first year out of college, he donated a hundred thousand dollars to anti-poverty organizations. Another student graduated with an engineering degree; though he initially planned to move to Africa and build dams, he went to work for an investment bank in London instead, figuring that any number of people could build dams in Africa, but very few would do what he was doing. "I decided to be Superman," he told an interviewer. "I saw this ad, [saying] that a polio injection can be bought for 30p. That's three people for a pound. So I thought . . . if I can get a job, give away sixty thousand [pounds], that's 180,000 people a year. Superman couldn't even hope to do that."

Some people found this sort of numbers talk distasteful, like a Don Juan of altruism cutting notches in his bedpost. (Toby did it, too: in talks, he told people that he expected to save three hundred centuries of life with his personal donations, and that all the Giving What We Can pledges added up to between two and eleven million healthy years—and since it had only been five million years since humans diverged from chimpanzees, that was quite a lot.) Julia worried that it would put people off. But most effective altruists weren't concerned about such social niceties. They believed that, if keeping track of your number helped to motivate you and others to give more money away, it was a good thing. They always talked about "having an impact" and "making a difference"—the language not of charity but of ambition.

Julia had always wanted children. Even in high school she had thought about her future children, making plans—the games they would play together, the toys she would make for them.

I want daughters and sons. I want to sing Gilbert and Sullivan in the kitchen with them. I want to teach them to waltz and to grow broccoli. I want to tell them stories and take them on picnics in the woods.

She had always thought that if she gave up children that would be the point at which she felt her life would be not just constrained but blighted. When she thought about a future in which her parents and Jeff's parents had died and there was no younger generation to replace them, just her and Jeff, living by themselves in some small rented apartment, that future looked desolate.

But then she began to question this. Many people had told her that once you had children you became a different person—you thought about the world differently, your views changed. It was a strange thing to contemplate. Obviously, the world was affecting you all the time, whether you wanted it to or not, but to make a decision that she knew in advance would change her in large and unpredictable ways, probably ones that would tend to undermine her convictions about obligations to strangers, that was something else. Jeff had never had a problem with valuing family more than strangers, but Julia was conflicted about it, and she knew that children were the ultimate test.

Q: So, if two children were drowning over there and Jeff were drowning over here, would you feel you were allowed to save Jeff?

JEFF: Jeff probably gives away more money than they do.

JULIA: I would feel justified with either decision, and I would also feel horrible about either decision. Because almost everyone I know thinks that you should take care of yourself and your family and people close to you first, and so few people share my ideas about this sort of thing—

JEFF: And one of them would have just died.

Q: Who?

JEFF: Me!

JULIA: Part of my decision would have to do with the knowledge that other people will judge me for taking care of
strangers on a par with taking care of my own people. I'm
sure that if we have children people will judge us harshly
for not giving them every advantage, and for considering
other people's children as much as our own.

JEFF: I'm okay valuing Julia more than other people. I'm not
okay valuing her infinitely more. So, if it was, like, Julia or
ten thousand other people, I would have to save the ten
thousand.

Q: So how many is she worth? Ten? Twenty?

JEFF: The actual number is really hard. You could attempt to
derive it from how much money I'm okay going to Julia
versus donating, but I don't think that would really work.

While working at the summer camp, Julia encountered some
children who behaved so dreadfully that she realized that the
picture she'd had when she was younger of being a mother and having a family was not only not based on any family she had been a part
of, but not based on anything whatever. Her imaginary children existed only in books about children. She began to wonder whether she
really needed children after all. Part of her suspected that the emotional place she had meant to fill with children was now being filled
by Jeff.

Once Julia opened herself up to the thought that children might
not be necessary—once she moved them, as it were, to a different
column in her moral spreadsheet, from essential to discretionary—
she realized just how enormous a line item a child would be. Children would be the most expensive nonessential thing she could
possibly possess, so by having children of her own she would be in
effect killing other people's children. Besides this, adding a new person to the population of a First World country was a terrible thing

to do from an environmental point of view: compared with that damage, anything you might do to try to repair it—recycling, composting, avoiding packaging, not using hot water—was completely insignificant. Jeff believed that the average person had a net positive impact on the world, at least from the point of view of human happiness, but she wasn't sure that was true.

Julia talked about this with Jeff and she grew very upset. Once the prospect of giving up children felt real to her, it felt terrifying and painful. They started to think about halfway options. They dismissed the idea of international adoption—it was way too expensive—but they thought they could justify raising a child they had adopted from foster care in the United States. She knew that outcomes for kids who stayed in the foster system without being adopted were awful—homelessness, suicide, drug abuse. For that very reason, of course, it was risky to adopt a kid like that—you had really no idea what sort of person it would turn out to be or what kind of life it would lead. Julia had wanted to adopt since she was twelve, but when she began to look into it seriously and realized how high was the potential for utter catastrophe, she wavered. Then again, you never knew what you were going to end up with, even with biological children; having any kind of child meant opening yourself to chance and devastation.

Julia told her parents that she was thinking of not having children. Her father said, "It doesn't sound like that would make you happy," and Julia told him that her happiness wasn't the only issue. This notion was so foreign to the way that he and her mother thought that there was not much more to say about it and the conversation ended pretty quickly.

Jeff reasoned that any child of theirs would be likely to grow up thinking that giving money away was a good and necessary thing to do. They could not assume that the child would be as extreme on this issue as they were—undoubtedly it would regress to the mean to some extent, but probably not all the way. He calculated that if the child gave away around 10 percent of its income, then they would likely break even—that is, the money their child would donate would be equal to the money they didn't donate because they spent it instead on raising the child. Of course, this didn't take into account that it was better to give money now rather than later, especially to urgent causes such as global warming and AIDS, so some discounting would have to be factored into the calculation. All this made Julia feel better for a while, and even though she realized that it would be pretty weird to tell a child that they expected it to pay for its existence in the world with a certain percentage of its income, she figured she was going to be a weird mother anyway, and her child would probably be weird, too, and so perhaps to a child of hers all this would seem perfectly sensible.

Finally, Julia decided, sometime before her twenty-eighth birthday, that she would try to get pregnant. Their baby, Lily, was born in the early spring of 2014. Afterward, Julia began to observe her own reactions, to see if, indeed, parenthood had changed her.

> JULIA: I've noticed that any mention of a young child being hurt makes me feel sick to my stomach. I can't always stay in the room if people are talking about that sort of thing. I wasn't expecting it. Some of my coworkers who are parents had talked about how they found it too painful to work with children who had been hurt in some way, so I knew it was a thing that happened to people, but I didn't think it was going to happen to me.

The thought of leaving Lily in order to go back to work upset her, but she knew that she had to start earning again so she could keep donating. She felt that there were people in the world who needed her money as much as Lily needed her presence, even if their need didn't move her as Lily's did.

Not long before Julia became pregnant, Jeff's mother, Suzie, was diagnosed with ovarian cancer. On the day Julia went into labor, Suzie was very sick, but she was well enough to be able to deliver Lily, her first grandchild, who became the last of the eleven hundred and eighty-nine babies she had helped, as a midwife, to bring into the world. The next day, she was hospitalized herself. She did not expect to live much longer. Through all of that miserable time, people in the family would take turns carrying Lily, and the feeling of holding her small body was one of the few ways they could feel joy and relief.

When Julia found out that Suzie had cancer, she was as sad as if it were her own mother, and she almost was—Julia had lived in Jeff's parents' house for more than two years. After the initial shock, Julia summoned her beliefs about family and strangers, prodding and testing them to see whether, in this terrible new time, she felt any differently. When Peter Singer's mother developed advanced Alzheimer's, Julia knew, Singer, in violation of his theories about both giving and personhood, had spent a lot of money paying nurses to take care of her. "Perhaps it is more difficult than I thought before," he said, "because it is different when it's your mother." Perhaps spending money on your sick mother was the right thing to do for the same reason that it was right for her to have children: if you didn't, there was too great a risk of terrible and embittering regret that would sour you on giving to others later on. But when she thought about giving, she found that her beliefs had not changed.

JULIA: In talking with people who say, "I fund XYZ research, even though I know it's not cost-effective, because my sister is sick with XYZ," I'd always felt kind of bad that I had never been in their shoes. I wondered if I would feel differently if someone I loved were sick. But it really doesn't change my thinking about giving or cost-effectiveness at all. I love Suzie, and I hate that she's sick; and other people love their mothers and hate that they're sick. And if ten families or one family can be spared that experience, even if the one family is mine, I'll go with the ten families every time. If their mothers (or whoever) are cheaper to cure, we should cure them first. I don't want to go through this, but neither do they.

She knew this would be difficult to explain. People even more than before would divide over whether this sounded to them like generosity, or justice, or a failure of love. Julia knew how it felt to her. But, ideas about love being what they were, she didn't expect much understanding.

AN ACCIDENTAL CAPABILITY PRODUCED, IN ITS BOUNDLESS STUPIDITY, BY A BIOLOGICAL PROCESS THAT IS NORMALLY OPPOSED TO THE EXPRESSION OF SUCH A CAPABILITY

THE UNDERMINING OF DO-GOODERS, PART ONE

The idea that there is something unappealing, something suspect, and something destructive about do-gooders has a history. Or, rather, it has many histories, and this is one of them. This is the story of the idea as it spread in the West over the last three centuries, not as a single notion, but as a cluster of related arguments and theories and beliefs that reinforced each other and inflected ideas elsewhere, gathering strength and influence. This is not the whole story, but a linking together of some of the landmarks, the large ideas that began in esoteric form and then spread.

It was never a new idea that people are selfish. Nor was it ever new to suggest that when people appeared to be doing good things they were either secret hypocrites, or else doing those good things for selfish reasons (to appear virtuous, to ascend to heaven, to relieve the discomfort caused by seeing suffering, because they believed that a virtuous life was a happy life, etc.). The idea that took longer to emerge was that even when people were genuinely doing good things, and doing them for impeccable reasons, there was still a problem.

We will begin the story in the summer of 1724, when a middle-aged London doctor with polemical inclinations named Bernard

Mandeville was brought before the Court of the King's Bench to be prosecuted as a public nuisance. His offense was the publication of a book titled *The Fable of the Bees: or Private Vices, Publick Benefits.* Sometime later, upon the appearance of a French translation, the book was set on fire by Paris's public executioner. Naturally, all this, in combination with denunciations from clergy and philosophers alike, considerably increased the book's appeal, and Mandeville and his *Fable* became internationally notorious. Dr. Johnson remarked that every young man had a copy on his shelf.

The inflammatory idea that so outraged Mandeville's readers was that, in a flourishing market economy such as England's, virtue had become an anachronism. What had formerly been considered vices, he claimed—particularly avarice and pride—were now beneficial, indeed crucial, to the public welfare. If an economy was to prosper, it needed people to buy things, and not just the bare necessities but stupid, extravagant, frivolous things. If people were frugal and self-abnegating now, the market would suffer, and that would be a disaster for everyone—worse than a terrible plague!

> . . . Luxury
> Employ'd a Million of the Poor,
> And odious Pride a Million more:
> Envy it self, and Vanity,
> Were Ministers of Industry. . . .

In the past, he surmised, virtues such as frugality and self-abnegation, along with the promise of heaven, had been promoted by the powerful as a means of keeping the masses docile. Man was naturally selfish, but virtue was an excellent way of setting yourself apart from your fellows, so you behaved virtuously out of pride, in order to excite admiration and avoid trouble. But in the affluent new market society, pride could be more easily satisfied through ostentatious spending, and that spending in turn ensured the perpetuation of affluence. And that was not all: a society of contented, honest, virtuous people, Mandeville insisted, would be a slothful, barren place with no art, science, or material comforts. Man must be roused to invention by greed and pride. Thus:

> . . . every Part was full of Vice,
> Yet the whole Mass a Paradise . . .
> Such were the Blessings of that State;
> Their Crimes conspir'd to make them Great: . . .
> The worst of all the Multitude
> Did something for the Common Good.

What was shocking in 1724 did not stay shocking for long. One of Mandeville's admirers, oddly enough, was the German philosopher Immanuel Kant. This was odd because Kant became known, decades later (at the time Mandeville was declared a public nuisance, Kant had just been born), for an exceptionally rigorous and demanding theory of morality. Nonetheless, forty years after the publication of the *Fable*, Kant observed that it was fortunate that so few men acted according to moral principle, because it was so easy to get principles wrong, and a determined person acting on mistaken principles could really do some damage. Most men, he wrote, "seek to turn everything around *self-interest* as around the great axis," and this was all to the good; "for these are the most diligent, orderly, and prudent; they give support and solidity to the whole, while without intending to do so they serve the common good, provide the necessary requirements, and supply the foundation over which finer souls can spread beauty and harmony."

In 1776, a book was published that would establish an idea similar to Mandeville's as one of the founding tenets of capitalism: *The Wealth of Nations*, by the Scottish economist Adam Smith. Smith argued that a man pursuing his own self-interested ends, in combination with many others doing the same thing, could end up working more effectively for the public good than if he had been doing so on purpose. "He intends only his own gain," Smith wrote, "and he is in this, as in many other cases, led by an invisible hand to promote an end which was no part of his intention."

Smith used the term "invisible hand" only once in his book, in making the narrow argument that individuals were likely to invest in domestic rather than foreign industry not for patriotic reasons but because doing so would contribute to their own security. Smith was a moral philosopher as well as an economist, and he found Mandeville's *Fable* repellent. But his "invisible hand" metaphor proved so resonant, and so enduringly popular, that it came to stand for something much larger. It implanted deep in Western culture the idea that individual self-interestedness could be beneficial for society as a whole; which in turn suggested that, if the moral goal was helping others (as opposed to self-perfection), a selfish man might do better than a selfless one.

Not long after *The Wealth of Nations* was published came the French Revolution, and after that came the Terror. The revolutionary leader Robespierre, nicknamed "the Incorruptible," was known both for his ascetic purity and for his extraordinary violence, and through him the two became indissolubly associated. In the past, it might have seemed that saintly figures who had their enemies killed—people like Saint Thomas More, for instance—did so because they believed they were compelled to by God. But Robespierre was a fierce do-gooder who killed his enemies for moral reasons, for justice; and there seemed something more sinister, and more powerful, about a morally passionate killer like him than there was about an ordinary revolutionary like Danton. After Robespierre, extreme moral conviction carried with it the shadow of violence; and after the Communist revolution in Russia reinforced the association, it was no longer possible to see a man who was convinced that he knew how to bring about a better world, and who was prepared to sacrifice himself for it, without thinking of death.

In the century following *The Wealth of Nations* and Robespierre's be-heading, do-gooders suffered a number of further insults. Darwin's *On the Origin of Species* introduced the distasteful idea that the selfish struggle for survival was the basis for life itself. This produced a peculiar paradox: if selfishness was the means by which mankind had come to exist in the first place, then selfishness was also the means by which man had achieved the very moral nature that was supposed to direct him away from self. It didn't make much sense. Virtue came to look less like an endowment from God, the most important part of man's self, and more like a peculiar historical appendage—an alien graft that had, for the most part, failed to take. Darwin himself did not believe this. He believed that self-sacrificing behavior was a basic part of human nature that had come about through natural selec-tion, because human survival was better ensured by a group of peo-ple prepared to sacrifice for one another than by selfish individuals. Groups that cooperated could defeat groups that did not. But to many who believed in the Darwinian scheme, this rationale sounded contrived and unconvincing. If selfishness was the basic mechanism of evolution, then how could true altruism possibly survive?

At the same time that these doubts were circulating, religious faith appeared to be growing weaker; and it was feared that, if belief in God and the afterlife were to wither, man would have no reason to behave morally, and bestial mayhem would ensue. Rallying to the defense of virtue came secular humanists, who believed that human goodness could survive even without God—humanists such as the French philosopher Auguste Comte, with his "religion of humanity." Comte invented the word "altruism" in the 1850s as a secular term for human goodness. He believed that altruism was as much a part of human nature as selfishness. He had even located the seat of benevolence—in the median portion of the frontal division of the brain, with veneration right behind it. He believed that the purpose of society was to foster love. Comte's term was taken up and made enormously popular in the latter part of the century by Herbert Spencer, the British theorist of evolution who coined the phrase "survival of the fittest." Spencer believed in human perfectibility, and that egotism would eventually succumb to altruism in the character of mankind. To Spencer, "altruism" was a nicely scientific, futuristic term without religious connotations, suitable for discussion in contexts from politics to biology. A theory of altruism could compete intellectually with the reigning theories of human selfishness in a way that a theory of "virtue" or "goodness" could not.

Thanks to Spencer's skillful advocacy, altruism became briefly fashionable. A faddish enthusiasm for the idea reached its apogee in Britain and America in the 1890s. Several hopeful periodicals were started up—the *Altruist*, the *Altruistic Review*, the *Altruistic Interchange*, the *Altrurian*. William Dean Howells's 1894 novel *A Traveler from Altruria* spawned a number of short-lived utopian communities from California to New Jersey. The term "altruism" was adopted by those who wished philanthropy to become more pragmatic and rational, less a hostage to sentiment. It was also the term of choice for those disturbed by poverty but frightened by radical solutions. The charisma of altruism was such that it even penetrated economics: in 1885, the well-known economist John Bates Clark predicted a surge of "economic altruism" and a decline in competition thanks to self-sacrificing behavior.

But soon the passion for altruism grew cold. Even at the height of its success, would-be do-gooders were mocked for their modish adventures among the poor. ("'You must have been doing some especially good deed,' said Janet"—a character in a satirical novel of 1895, *An Experiment in Altruism*—"'You are so disagreeable. There isn't any soil that philanthropy thrives in so well as in the ruins of the social and domestic virtues.'") Many people quickly realized that organized politics was a more effective vehicle for human progress than the full hearts of the leisured bourgeois. Paradoxically, altruism became more suspect as it became more altruistic. When everyone believed in God and an afterlife, doing good was simply prudent: you gave up a bit of comfort now to avoid eternal hellfire later. But now that even many of those who still had faith no longer believed in hell, the motive for living a moral life appeared more dubious. But these mockeries were gentle compared to what was to come.

Even as altruism was enjoying its brief vogue in the Anglo-American world, the German philosopher Friedrich Nietzsche was doing his best to destroy it. To him, the Christian idea of goodness—humility, compassion, devotion to others at the expense of oneself—was a morality for the insignificant and the weak. It was unfortunate that such a despicable creed should have become so widely believed, he thought; but that most people believed it wasn't so important. No, its most pernicious effect was that, because its reach was so insidious and so pervasive, it had emasculated even the strong, by teaching them to think humbly, to live for others rather than themselves, and to repress the instincts of their nature. Greatness could thrive only if it was selfish, Nietzsche believed—only if it worshipped itself, and was utterly indifferent to the needs of others. Nietzsche despised the well-being that seemed to his utilitarian contemporaries the proper goal of moral action. "Wretched contentment," he wrote—"happiness as peace of soul, virtue, comfort, Anglo-angelic shopkeeperdom à la Spencer"—was for the masses, for the ordinary people, who didn't matter. The pursuit of happiness, either for oneself or for others, was a contemptible way to spend one's time, because nobility could be achieved only through suffering. Happiness was not interesting: human greatness should be the goal of life.

Nietzsche's contempt for selflessness was total, but for Freud, born not long after, the matter was more complicated. To him, a certain amount of moral feeling was normal—the ordinary consequence of parental authority, internalized as an inhibition of instinct. Such inhibition was necessary to civilization: men without inhibitions would create not a prelapsarian paradise but a violent hell. But only a certain amount of inhibition was good—the right amount. An excess of virtue, Freud thought, might indicate a moral masochism, and a particularly twisted form of masochism because it was disconnected from its sexual origins. "The true masochist," he observed, "always turns his cheek whenever he has a chance of receiving a blow." But for the *moral* masochist, a competent sadist was no longer necessary: suffering alone was enough.

Selflessness was, in Freud's view, usually suspect. The devoted, self-sacrificing mother, for instance, he found to be part masochist, part tyrant, enslaving her child with chains of guilt. But the devoted, self-sacrificing child was equally dubious. In an essay on love, he observed that in the common fantasy of rescuing one's parents from danger there was not only love but also defiance—the desire to close out a debt, to balance one's account with the people who gave you life, to escape from the burden of gratitude. (In a later essay by another analyst, this defiance escalated to violent aggression: after all, to imagine rescue was to imagine the rescuee in danger and probably pain as well.)

Freud's daughter Anna Freud was even more suspicious of selflessness than her father had been. She coined the term "altruistic surrender" to describe the perverse mental state of a person unable to gratify his wishes except through a proxy. All altruism was based in this, she believed; selflessness was always conflicted, always pathological, always twisted away from its original intention.

ANNA FREUD: You don't think anyone is born altruistic.

JOSEPH SANDLER [Another analyst]: Or even *becomes* altruistic, out of the goodness of his heart.

ANNA FREUD: No, it's out of the badness of his heart.

JOSEPH SANDLER: I often wonder about people who dedicate themselves in their work for others—the excellent secretary we are always looking for. Some of the qualities involve so much dedication that one wonders what the difference is between that sort of application to one's work and masochism.

ANNA FREUD: I think that in the end there is a very close link to masochism.

When altruism wasn't masochism, it could be an unconscious inducing of guilt and obligation that could, especially between a parent and a child, become poisonous. But even when it wasn't entangled in the complications of family, altruism was never what it seemed.

ANNA FREUD: Altruists are bossy, because the urge that is usually behind the fulfillment of one's own wishes is now placed behind the fulfillment of the wishes of the other person. And the wishes have to be fulfilled in a certain way, namely in the way the altruist would like to fulfill them for himself or herself. And, after all, the bossiness of so-called do-gooders is proverbial. . . . Originally the individual wants to pursue his or her instinctual aims aggressively. "I want it, I'll have it, I'll fight anybody who won't give it to me." This aggression becomes impossible and forbidden when fulfillment of the wish becomes impossible and forbidden, but now with the altruism, you can fight for somebody else's fulfillment of the wish with the same aggression, with the same energy. So you have both your libidinal vicarious pleasure, and you have the outlet for your aggression. It's surprising that not more people are altruists!

The French psychoanalyst André Green published an essay on "moral narcissism," detailing the louche displacements of the ego that delighted in renunciation. "If it was Freud who said that masochism resexualizes morality," he wrote, "we would like to add: *narcissism turns morality into an autoerotic pleasure in which the pleasure itself will be suppressed.*" The body of the moral man was an enemy, a shame; straightforward enjoyments were forbidden; so his only source of pleasure was giving things up. These feelings were prompted by guilt, but not only guilt—it was more complicated than that, because the moral narcissist's extreme humility masked a dreadful pride. Ordinary people could accept that they had faults; the moral narcissist could not. To Green, this moral straining was not admirable but sinister, for the moral narcissist would do anything to preserve his purity, even when doing so carried a terrible price. Men, he wrote, identify with Christ the innocent lamb. "This is not simply a matter of being crucified or of having one's throat cut; it implies being innocent as a lamb when the holocaust arrives," he wrote. "We know that the innocent have often been accused by history of crimes they allowed in order to remain pure."

More psychoanalysts took up this theme, and new qualifiers appeared: there was "pseudo-altruism," a defensive cloak for hidden sadomasochism; and there was "psychotic altruism," bizarre caretaking behavior and self-denial based in delusion. Suspicious theories abounded. The loss of a loved parent during childhood might produce pathological salvation fantasies—the grown child trying to be for all helpless creatures in the world the loving protector that his parent was for him. This might appear to be a benign adaptation to unfortunate circumstance, but it was not: the overt compassion and empathy masked unconscious fear and hostility, which came out in the form of anger and hatred toward those who were perceived as the cause of the woes he was trying to alleviate. Excessive altruism tended to preclude real intimacy with another person, because intimacy was a business of giving and receiving, but the overly moral person could not receive, only give. And real intimacy meant knowing the other; but for a person preoccupied with rescue, others could be seen only as manifestations of his own suffering.

Even if a do-gooder wasn't actively sinister or sadistic, his behavior still appeared to psychoanalysts to be unhealthy. An article about the "Psychology of the Altruist" examined five do-gooders, including an advocate for leprosy patients, an adopter of handicapped children, and an aspiring doctor; it found them helpful, modest, and attractively sociable, but also compulsive, apt to identify with the victims they sought to help, and liable to feel that the presence of a person in need meant that they were required to come to his assistance. They tended to downplay their own misfortunes ("these altruists were always counting their blessings and reminding themselves about the Starving Armenians") in a way that struck the article's author as overly defensive. They were uncomfortable with being helped themselves, which the analyst suspected was because they sensed the latent hostility in the helping act. Indeed, she surmised that the masking of their own hostility and greed from themselves might be one of altruism's functions for people of this type.

Darwin and Freud led the way. For much of the twentieth century, altruism would be regarded in the human sciences with deep suspicion, usually taken to be a form of selfishness in disguise—that is, when it was regarded at all. There were a few exceptions. An early psychologist, William McDougall, attempted to argue for the existence of a human instinct to help—a "tender emotion"—but by the 1930s he was regarded as a joke. Pitirim Sorokin founded the Harvard Research Center in Altruistic Integration and Creativity. He believed that an increase in altruistic love was necessary if humanity was to survive, and to this end he embraced research of all kinds, from the conventional to the bizarre, from psychology to biology to parapsychology (investigating possible connections between love and extrasensory perception), mathematics (a mathematical theory of egoistic and altruistic behavior), and insights into psychopathy made possible by use of the electroencephalogram. But these theorists of morality were unusual. One early psychoanalyst believed that there was, in the social sciences, a "flight from tenderness," brought on, perhaps, by an overreaction to theology. It seemed more tough-minded to study aggression than to study love; if a social scientist believed in altruism, he might be thought sentimental, or a sucker.

In anthropology, altruism was reconceived by the French anthropologist Marcel Mauss, who in 1925 published *The Gift*, an analysis of gift exchanges, which added a primitivist slant to the story that giving was never quite what it purported to be. In the archaic societies that Mauss studied, giving was always reciprocal: exchange was what bound society together. The point of giving was not generosity—the point was the merging of families and clans, some part of which remained in their belongings and circulated with them. Giving without expectation of return was not thought to be a higher, more selfless act; quite the contrary, it was aggressive, it set the giver up as superior to the recipient, causing the recipient to lose face; it imposed a burden of gratitude without permitting the relief of reciprocation. Because a gift contained in itself something of the essence of the giver, a gift gave him power over the beneficiary. In some societies a gift retained, rather than passed along, could cause serious harm to the recipient—even death. In some ancient languages, the word "gift" had a second meaning: poison.

Darwin had attempted to incorporate altruism into his theory of evolution, but by the 1960s, the mechanism by which he accounted for it, group selection—the idea that a group of people who cooperate with one another is more likely to thrive than a group of people who do not—had been banished from respectable biological discourse. An American biologist, George C. Williams, proved mathematically, so he claimed, that even though cooperation had its benefits, in the end, selfishness would always win, because it always made sense to be a free rider. Morality, he concluded, was not an adaptation but "an accidental capability produced, in its boundless stupidity, by a biological process that is normally opposed to the expression of such a capability." Altruism was explained by biologists with the theories of kin selection (helping your relatives is a good way to propagate your own genes) and reciprocal altruism (helping others, even nonrelatives, is beneficial, because people are more likely to help you if you have helped them, or if they know you to be a helpful sort). Altruism at the biological level, in other words, was just another form of selfishness—a more sophisticated means of ensuring your own survival.

In 1964, the famous Kitty Genovese incident took place. A young woman screamed as she was raped and murdered near her apartment in New York City, while—or so it was believed at the time; incorrectly, as it turned out—thirty-eight bystanders who could hear her did nothing to help. This horrifying story gave rise to many social-scientific experiments in an attempt to explain how such a thing could happen. Human beings, evidently, were even worse than had been supposed. Countless pseudo–electric shocks were administered to countless pseudo-victims in a variety of peculiar and unlikely situations, in order to discern whether any of the experimental subjects would come to their assistance. Most did not; and these experiments contributed to a sense that altruism was not a significant part of the human character. "Bystander research" found that people were more willing to help if there was no one else available to do so; but willingness to help under any circumstances appeared weak, subject to the most trivial disincentives. A famous experiment had seminary students prepare a lecture on the parable of the Good Samaritan, and then encounter a person in need of help on their way to their next appointment; those who had been told that they were late for the appointment were far less likely to stop and help than those who believed they had a few minutes to spare.

But then, toward the end of the twentieth century, the tide began to turn, and attitudes toward altruism began once again to change. In 1990, an article published in the *Annual Review of Sociology* observed that there appeared to have been a paradigm shift in the social sciences since the early 1980s, away from the conviction that apparently altruistic behavior must always spring from ulterior egoistic motives. One of the paradigm shifters was the work of the sociologists Oliners, Samuel and Pearl, who wrote about righteous Gentiles—non-Jews who had helped to save the lives of Jews during the Second World War.

Samuel Oliner's family had been killed in the Holocaust, but Samuel himself had survived because, at his stepmother's urging, he left his family at twelve and found a Polish peasant woman who, risking her own life, took him into her house and taught him to pass as a Gentile: she gave him a new name, different clothes, taught him how to read in Polish and how to recite the catechism. The Oliners estimated that something like fifty thousand Gentiles had risked their lives—and often those of their families as well—without any compensation, in order to save the lives of Jews. Why had they done this when so many others had not—when the risk was so great, and, unlike a more ordinary case of altruism, was not even compensated for by social approval? Was it primarily a matter of circumstance, or of character?

Rejecting the situationist hypothesis, the Oliners concluded that it was a matter of character. They found that rescuers had been taught by their parents to care for others, whereas nonrescuers had been taught to work hard or be obedient. Nonrescuers felt impotent and helpless in the face of what was happening; rescuers felt that they had a degree of control over their lives and the situations they found themselves in, and they were willing to risk failure. Rescuers and nonrescuers alike were susceptible to other people's moods, but whereas nonrescuers were more affected by happiness, rescuers were moved by pain.

In psychology, too, things were shifting. The social psychologist C. Daniel Batson, in the hope of overturning the selfishness consensus, set out to investigate whether altruism was really always pseudo-altruism, or whether it might be caused by genuine empathy and a desire to relieve the suffering of another. "If we are capable of altruism, then virtually all of our current ideas about individual psychology, social relations, economics, and politics are, in an important respect, wrong," he wrote in 1991. "The assumption of universal egoism is so fundamental and widespread in our culture that it is hard to recognize, like water for a fish." Determining whether or not true altruism existed was not just a matter of scientific interest: the assumption of selfishness was self-reinforcing. After all, what was more likely to discourage altruism than the suspicion that it was all really selfishness? If doing the difficult altruistic thing was just another form of selfishness, just another way to make yourself feel good, well, there were many easier and more pleasant ways to do that.

In biology and evolutionary psychology, group selection was revived and reinstated as an explanation for genuine altruism. Even though altruism might be a bad strategy for an individual, since natural selection operated between groups as well as between individuals, evolution ensured that altruism would continue to flourish. In economics, too, the assumption of rational selfishness began to bend. In 1989, an economist concluded that people gave money to public goods not only out of concern for the people who would benefit, but also for the "warm glow" of self-satisfaction that giving gave them. Economists had long assumed that there would be a free-rider problem with respect to public goods: if people could partake in public goods without paying for them, they would. But then a number of studies conclusively demonstrated that this hypothesis held true only when the subjects were economists.

Finally, even in psychoanalysis, something began to shift. A paper by two analysts tried to establish that, in addition to the old pathological altruism, there was also a normal kind. Yes, there were the "many joyless and self-denying martyrs with severe masochistic and narcissistic pathology [whose] compulsive caretaking and self-sacrifice cloaks and defends against their aggression, their envy, and their need to control the object." But there were also people for whom helping others was a source of genuine and unconflicted pleasure. These types helped others and felt good about doing so, and became happier as a result. Psychoanalysis had failed to recognize the existence of people like this, the two analysts suggested, because they so rarely sought out analytic treatment. Moreover, with the help of a skillful analyst, even a joyless martyr could be transformed into a happy do-gooder. For example: after some good therapeutic work, a joyless-martyr patient of one of the analysts found a boyfriend, had an orgasm, and bought a subscription to the opera.

THE HUMILIATION OF STRANGERS

He delivers the afflicted by their affliction, and opens their ear by adversity.

—JOB 36:15

BABA

This is the story of a man who founded a leper colony in a wilderness in the center of India, and who passed on this flourishing and celebrated enterprise to his children and their children as another man might a shipping business or a newspaper. The man had two sons: the younger started a clinic in a remote jungle and won fame and prizes like his father; the elder built on his father's work, but his achievements were not so recognized. The story began with a chance encounter one night in the rain that caused the man to change the course of his life, and everything that happened for the generations that followed was due to that decision. But things could so easily have been different. One can imagine this man, in a different place and time, pursuing any number of ambitions with equal passion and tenacity: he might have been Henry Ford; he might have been Napoleon. If there are such things as congenital saints, he was not one of them.

Here is what he started with. He was chronically restless. He craved novelty and delighted in obstruction. He despised comfort; he needed life to be difficult. He needed to be thrown about and battered; he needed to be agitated, he needed to be in danger. He could tolerate a lot of pain and he was fearless, and he valued those qualities in himself more than any others.

One rainy night, the man passed a body lying on the side of

the road. It was scarcely human—it was a leper in the last stages of the disease, naked, barely alive, his hands and feet stumps, his nose caved in, his flesh decayed and crawling with maggots. The man was repelled by this ghastly sight, and, terrified that he might catch the disease, he ran. But then he realized that he had run in fear— he, who was not afraid of anything. The thought of himself as fearful was more dreadful to him than the thought of catching leprosy, so he went back to the leper and covered him with a piece of cloth to shield him from the rain. The leper was past help and soon died; but for weeks afterward, the man was profoundly shaken by this experience. He had been scared, he had *run away*: he could not tolerate this thought, but it wouldn't leave him alone. Gandhi himself had called him fearless—that was the sort of man he had been! For the first time in his life, he hated himself. He decided that the only thing that would restore his serenity was to steer directly into his fear until he was rid of it: he would make leprosy his work.

He began with the idea of treating the disease, but later, after he had lived in his colony for many years, he realized that it was not just the alleviation of suffering that excited him but the suffering itself. He believed that a person who had not felt pain, mental or physical, was incapable of strong attachments, and that shared suffering was the mortar of community. Pain broke a man open and let other people in; suffering was at the core of what it meant to be human. His colony was held together by the suffering of the lepers, Baba believed, and because he, too, had been in pain for much of his adult life—he had severely degenerative arthritis, and was forced to spend time in traction, and months in bed—he felt himself part of that fellowship. "To me the kinship of pain / Has always been the strongest bond," he wrote in a poem. "I could forget those with whom I laughed / But I will never forget those with whom I shed tears." His wife wrote: "A greater affiliation with pain is what is required and is capable of transforming this world. We need no other religion."

He began life as a princeling. His father owned four hundred and fifty acres in his ancestral village, Goraja, in the dead center of India, five hundred miles east of Bombay; his father also held a good government job in the city of Nagpur, working in the finance department for the British. The young patriarch, Murlidhar Amte, was born in December 1914; his mother nicknamed him Baba. From childhood he displayed what was either an indifference to pain and the approval of his father, or else a taste for pain and the disapproval of his father. For instance: he was a Brahmin, so he was not supposed to be touched by even the shadow of a Dalit (untouchable), much less a Dalit body, because a Dalit was unclean and contact was tainting; this was not snobbery, it was piety. But though his father beat him for it, he played with Dalit children and, more shockingly still, ate with their families. He was attracted to outcasts before he thought to pity them.

By the time he was a teenager, it had become apparent that there was something wrong with his mother. At night, she screamed and sang. One day she put on seven saris, one on top of another, and then began to strip them off in the town square. She ended up in the mental hospital for many months. For the rest of his life, Baba called himself the mad son of a mad mother.

As a young man, he owned a green Singer sports car whose seats were upholstered in animal skins; he had a panther cub as a pet. He wore suits made for him by the tailor who made suits for the British governor; he played bridge; he drank. He did nothing by halves: because he admired a famous popular singer, Mumtaz, he drove eight hundred kilometers to see her perform in Calcutta. He loved Rabindranath Tagore's poetry, so he learned Bengali in order to read *Gitanjali* in the original, and he drove a thousand kilometers to visit Tagore in his ashram. He wrote poetry, too—gushing, romantic verses. He loved movies, so he went to three a day sometimes; he ordered meals to be delivered to him in the theater between shows, and if he loved a particular movie he saw it twenty times, until he knew it by heart. He bought two tickets, so he could put his feet up on the seat in front of him. He wrote movie reviews for *Picturegoer* magazine; he wrote fan letters to Norma Shearer and Greta Garbo, and they wrote back. He toyed with the idea of becoming an actor.

He was not a simple hedonist, however. It was not pleasure he was after so much as adventure. He was always fighting—he boxed and wrestled. His friends were all hoodlums. As a teenager, he smuggled weapons for the underground armed resistance, the anti-British revolutionaries who thought Gandhi's ideas about nonviolence were naïve. He rushed to disasters—earthquakes, famines—and plunged in, trying to help. He went hunting in the forest, and he went on foot; he killed not safely from a platform up in a tree, but face to face with the animal.

While hunting, he wandered deep into the Gadchiroli forest and encountered a remote tribal people, the Madia Gonds. He saw that they were hungry and diseased, but he felt that their community was closer and more loyal than the one he came from. When he stayed in his country estate, he liked to wander about and meet farmers and villagers. They were merely poor, not isolated and strange like the Madia Gonds, but he liked them more than the people he met in his parents' house. As he grew older, these impressions hardened, and he came to believe that rich people were callous and willfully unaware of the desolation around them, whereas poor people, of necessity, were able to see. He began to read books that confirmed such thoughts—Marx, Prince Kropotkin, Ruskin, Pandurang Sane. He had resented being forced, in his Christian college, to attend scripture classes, and had done so with cotton wool stuffed in his ears; but on his own he read about the life of Christ and resolved to live his own life that way.

After some time, he rejected the armed revolutionaries—he saw they had no ideas beyond getting rid of the British—and began to visit Gandhi's ashram, Sevagram, which was not far from his father's house. One day, while traveling on a train, Baba saw British soldiers lewdly taunting a young bride; her groom, terrified, had locked himself in the bathroom. Baba fought the soldiers, and at the station he demanded an inquiry from the commanding officer. Gandhi heard about this incident and called Baba an *abhay sadhak*—"fearless seeker of truth."

During Gandhi's Quit India movement of 1942—his campaign to compel the British to grant India independence—Baba recruited lawyers to defend rebels, and was himself briefly jailed. His zeal attracted the attention of Vinoba Bhave, an ascetic and scholarly Gandhian acolyte living in an ashram nearby. Years later, Bhave walked across India, calling on landowners to give land to the poor— a mad idea that he pursued for several years with astonishing success, thanks partly to post-independence patriotism but mostly to his own saintly charisma. Asceticism was, in India, a source of considerable power—Bhave knew this, and so did Baba. In the course of that walk Bhave visited Baba's leper colony in its desolate early days, in the early 1950s, and compared Baba's story to the *Ramayana*, the Hindu epic in which a prince is exiled to live among wild beasts in the forest.

When Baba finished school, he wanted to train as a doctor, but his father consulted an astrologer who told him that Baba's horoscope suggested the law would be a more auspicious choice. Unwillingly, he trained as a lawyer. He went to work as a criminal defender, but hated it—he hated defending people he knew were guilty, he hated earning fifty rupees for fifteen minutes' work when a laborer earned less than one rupee in a day. He left his firm and the city and set up a cooperative practice in a small town, Warora, with a lawyer from a lower caste. He began organizing low-caste and Dalit workers—sweepers, scavengers, weavers—into unions. The scavengers he was organizing told him that he couldn't possibly understand their lives—they cleaned latrines, collected the waste, and carried it away in baskets on their heads. He took this as a challenge, and for nine months he got up at three in the morning to scavenge for four hours before continuing to his law office.

Despite this repellently un-Brahmin behavior, he was still a reasonably eligible young man, and potential in-laws pressed him with
proposals. He decided that he couldn't live the life he wanted to live
if he was married, and so, for practical more than spiritual reasons,
he became a sadhu: he swore an oath of celibacy and traveled north
to the Himalayas to visit saints in their ashrams. He wore saffron
robes, allowed his hair and beard to grow long and matted, smeared
his body with ashes, begged for food, ate very little, and at three
every morning walked barefoot over thorns to the river for a bath.
He wasn't good at meditation—he found serenity difficult—but discomfort came naturally.

After he returned from the Himalayas, however, he visited the
home of a family friend and noticed one of the daughters of the house
helping a maid with the housework. This being just the sort of eccentric, caste-defying thing that he himself might do, he was intrigued: he
not only felt himself strongly drawn to her but, more important, with
an acute instinct he had for assessing a person's capacity to endure
hardship, he sensed that with her he could live his life the way he
wanted to. He did not rely on instinct, however: he conducted a de-
tailed but secretive investigation into her habits, asking family members about her concern for the poor, about her participation in
domestic chores (her helping the maid might have been an aberration,
after all), her way with the family cows. Having satisfied himself that
she would make him a fit wife, he abandoned his idea of being a sadhu.

The girl, Indu, came from an aristocratic family of Sanskrit
scholars; they traced their lineage back to Gagabhatta, who was
present at the coronation of King Shivaji in 1674. Her family was
devoutly orthodox, and puritanical about caste rules, so her breach
of these rules to help a servant was particularly remarkable. After
Baba left, he sent her a love letter, very flowery—a violation of so
many taboos at once (not only a love letter from a celibate sadhu, but
a love letter without a proposal of marriage!) that her family was
scandalized, and censored her reply. More love letters followed, filled
with poetry, and then a proposal. Indu had been very sheltered, even

for a Brahmin girl, and had no idea what to expect from life with this strange person with whom she'd never even had a conversation, but she knew that it would not be the ordinary housewifely life her sisters were leading. She was ready to follow him, though she didn't know where. She had grown up reading about the women of the *Ramayana* and the *Mahabharata*, who worshipped their husbands and followed them everywhere, no matter the hardships; these were her models for the ideal womanly life. Her family, which had hoped for a good match with somebody normal, was not at all pleased, and her relatives were contemptuous, but she insisted on marrying him and finally prevailed. Shortly before the wedding, Baba fought off a knife-wielding thief who had broken into Indu's family's silk shop and was stabbed in several places; he refused to postpone the ceremony, however, and was married in bandages in the winter of 1946.

By the time he married, Baba had nearly given up his law practice and had become a full-time organizer and social worker for Dalits. This was strange at first for Indu. In her mother's house, if she had touched a Dalit inadvertently, she changed her clothes. But for her, the first principle was obedience to her husband; since everything else was secondary to that, she soon overcame her scruples, even knowing that this taint meant that she and he, too, would become outcasts. No one from her family or his would visit them in their home—to their families, their behavior was disgusting. Baba fought with his father and gave up all his rights to the family's ancestral property. Indu willingly followed him to the bottom of the social order: when she was pregnant with her first son, Vikas, she contracted typhoid and was urged to go to the hospital, but she refused, because low-caste people would not have been able to afford it.

I t was at this point that Baba encountered the leper in the rain and decided to change his life. He started reading about leprosy, and at the same time began working at a Gandhian leprosy clinic in a nearby town. He gave injections, cleaned out ulcers, dressed wounds, removed decomposing bones. The effect on him was immediate: his self-hatred vanished, and suddenly he was full of joy and confidence. He knew that he had found his life's work, and he set about it with a passion. In the middle of his frenzy, Indu caught tuberculosis and had to go away for a cure. She left Vikas with Baba and took their younger son, Prakash, with her, because he was less than a year old; he was also very sick, but because she was so ill, she was unable to take care of him. It was difficult for her to cope on her own, but Baba was busy with the lepers. He wrote:

> Dear Indu,
>
> The pleasure I have experienced while working for the lepers is incomparable. I have never experienced this joy before. . . . They have an unshakable faith in me and even if I just stand under a tree with a sprinkler in hand, I am sure, they will throng to me. I wish you were here to see all that in the clinic last Sunday. You would have never asked me to come home early. Sixty-five patients waiting for their turn in a long queue! Can you imagine? What does it all foretell? What a joy to see their eyes sparkling with hope! . . . Isn't that enough for you, me and the children? It will definitely see us through. Indu, they pray to God for our health and happiness. I know I should have been with you at such a difficult hour at Urali Kanchan but you would not have liked me to leave them uncared for. I would have had my pleasure of your company only at the cost of hopes and aspirations of these poor, helpless, disabled lepers. In fact, the sense of guilt for having forsaken them would have spoilt our joy too. Tell me, do you really think it is right to have me by your side in these circumstances?

She did not think it was right. She thought: "The evil in this world is the creation of those, who make a distinction between the self and other."

For a man who read the life of Christ not as an account of perfection but as a practical template, leprosy was a wise choice of vocation. The cleansing of lepers was said to be one of Christ's miracles, and in the two thousand years before a more ordinary cure was found, the embracing of lepers had become a hallmark of saintliness. The disease's uniquely repulsive symptoms—the sight and stench of decaying flesh—and its contagiousness, combined with the belief that the bodily deformities marked even more horrible deformities of soul, made lepers a dreadful trial of love. Saint Francis wrote in his *Testament* that it was an encounter with lepers that transformed his life most deeply. Father Damien, a Belgian monk born in 1840 who sought out the most punishing austerities, begged to be sent by his order to Molokai, a leper colony on a Hawaiian island. Albert Schweitzer, three decades later, feeling it his duty to share in the pain of the world, went to work among lepers in Gabon. Baba wrote: "It is strange that man seeks sublime inspiration in the ruins of an old temple or church, but sees none in the ruins of man."

Baba realized that there was a limit to what he could do for leprosy patients as a lawyer, and decided to spend a year studying at the Calcutta School of Tropical Medicine. A professor there told him that there was no cure for the disease, in part because it appeared impossible to transmit it to animals for the purpose of experiments. Baba thought about this for several days, and then offered himself as a human experimental subject. He was injected with the leprosy bacillus, and waited for his fate to be decided; he did not catch the disease. From then on, he knew he was immune (as are, it was later discovered, the vast majority of humans) and had nothing to fear.

As it happened, a cure for leprosy was developed shortly thereafter, in 1950—the drug dapsone. After his training in Calcutta, Baba moved back to Warora and started traveling around the area, dispensing doses. He soon realized that, even though the drug could cure most patients medically, it couldn't change their lives. A leprosy patient taking medicine was soon no longer contagious, but whatever awful damage the disease had already done—fingers and toes disfigured, eyebrows gone, collapsed nose, strange patches on the skin—marked him forever. Fear of leprosy was so great, and the signs of the disease so unmistakable, that even cured lepers were rejected by their families. Relatives of lepers were ostracized and unmarriageable, so to keep a leprosy patient at home was to sacrifice normal life for everyone else. In many villages, lepers were burned alive. Even a cured leprosy patient faced a ruined existence: he couldn't work, he couldn't live with his family or even in his village, he had no choice but to beg. Thus, even after a cure for leprosy had been found, leper colonies were still necessary.

At the time, Christian missionaries ran a number of leprosariums in India. But dependence upon charity was death, Baba believed. This was what Baba was trying to get away from—treating lepers like charity cases with nothing to offer but their beggared souls for sale in return for medical assistance. He defined himself against the canon of Christian leprosy saints like Schweitzer and Father Damien. Schweitzer put leprosy patients to bed, Baba said; he would put them to work. If a person had lost seven fingers, after all, he had three left, and there was a lot you could do with three fingers. A man could live without fingers, but not without self-respect.

He applied to the state of Madhya Pradesh for land, and in 1951 was given fifty acres of wilderness—rocky scrub, with no water. He and Indu went to live there with their two tiny sons, six lepers, a cow, four dogs to protect them from wild animals, and fourteen rupees—nearly nothing. They built two shelters—four wooden sticks and a grass roof, no walls—one for Baba's family, one for the lepers. Later, they built huts out of sticks and mud.

There were deadly snakes and scorpions and rats everywhere; when it rained, the rats and the snakes came into the houses. Lepers would wake to discover that rats had eaten their insensate flesh while they slept. There were leopards and tigers and wild boars nearby in the forest. Tigers came in the night and snatched the dogs from the huts, one by one, but did not take the two human babies. In monsoon season, the huts flooded; sometimes in heavy rain the roof would fall in. There was almost no food; the nearest source of water was more than a mile away. The first thing to do was to dig a well. This took six weeks, digging every day. It was May, and 115 degrees out—hotter than that in the sun. They had to dig down thirty feet before they found water. Baba named the place Anandwan, Forest of Joy.

It was a measure of how terrible life outside was for lepers that they flocked to this hellish place—more than fifty came in the next two years. They dug more wells and cleared the land and grew crops for sale in the market. Most were desolate when they arrived, having been thrown out by their families and rejected by their friends, but work revived them. The leprosy patients called Indu "Tai," older sister. Tai was still weak, recovering from her tuberculosis, but she worked all day, cooking and serving meals, milking cows, cleaning. Baba's doctors had advised him to rest in bed for a year, but instead he worked maniacally, day and night, cleaning and bandaging leprous wounds, cutting wood, digging in the fields, building houses. He drove his lepers to astonishing feats. Their crops were superb—chilies as big as fists, eggplants the size of pumpkins—Baba was an enthusiastic agricultural experimentalist—but the villagers nearby were afraid of catching leprosy and wouldn't buy them.

It was one thing for Baba and Tai to impose poverty on themselves, but their children had not chosen this life. They were so poor that Vikas and Prakash had barely enough food to stave off hunger. Because the local people were afraid of leprosy, they wouldn't allow their children to play with the Amte children, so the boys had no friends. They had no toys; Prakash took to playing with poisonous scorpions. They had no warm clothes. They didn't even have parents, most of the time, because Baba and Tai worked from before dawn until late at night; the boys spent their days wandering around the jungle. Baba was not distressed by this: he thought it would make his sons tough. But Tai felt guilty, since she and Baba had been pampered as children.

The boys were nearly the same age: Vikas had been born in October 1947, Prakash in December 1948. Vikas loved to talk; Prakash was usually silent. Vikas did better in school. The understanding in the family was that Vikas had inherited Baba's way with words, whereas Prakash had inherited his courage; of these two qualities, there was no doubt which Baba and Tai valued more. Once, when Prakash was six, Baba heard a tiger roar close to the well; as a test, he asked Prakash to draw a bucket of water. Prakash did not hesitate. When he returned with the bucket, Baba, overcome with love, gave him a pat on the back.

A few months into the Anandwan experiment, a contingent of international volunteers came from Sevagram, Gandhi's nearby ashram, to help construct a clinic and other buildings. The sight of dozens of Europeans living among the lepers in strikingly hygienic conditions persuaded the local villagers that Anandwan vegetables were safe to eat. The acceptance of their vegetables transformed Anandwan's economy: now it could generate income. Baba started a dairy, a spinning factory, and other workshops. He was determined that Anandwan should become self-sufficient, and after two years, apart from sugar, oil, and salt, it was.

Baba kept track of everyone and everything. He tried but failed to find a doctor willing to work at Anandwan, so he did everything himself—picking maggots out of wounds, dressing and bandaging every patient each day, cleaning bedpans. In the evening, he served dinner. Everything had to be impeccably organized, everything had to be clean, everything had to be perfectly efficient and exactly as he wanted it; if it wasn't, he would rage. His temper was terrible. When he felt that Tai had made his food too salty, he would refuse to eat. He was a zealot about precise bookkeeping, and would spend hours making sure that every rupee had been accounted for. Alcohol was forbidden.

Although the rules by which Baba lived were of his own devising, he was as rigid in their observance as if they were mandates from God. This was not puritanism—he was never an ascetic like Gandhi or Bhave—but a matter of personal discipline. He had decided not to eat sugar, chili, or milk when he was a sadhu, and he stuck to that, even if it meant hurting the feelings of people who had prepared a meal for him. Nothing could shake his faith in the rightness of his own ideas.

Tai was as obstinate and uncompromising in her own rituals, which included both the required Hindu devotions and additional rites of her own invention. If fasting for a certain span of time was required, she would fast longer; and if scripture reading was required, she would read more. Once, for no particular reason, she vowed to offer 108,000 betel leaves to Lord Shankara, which meant making a thousand sheaves of 108 leaves each. She ignored the pleas of her unbelieving husband to be more rational in her worship.

As soon as Anandwan was no longer desperately poor, Baba became restless. His ambitions for Anandwan extended beyond industry: it was not enough for lepers to be physically cured and economically self-sufficient, he thought; they must also be culturally stimulated. Anandwan was to be the Forest of Joy, a model community, not a workhouse. He started a yearly cultural festival, to which he invited musicians, artists, philosophers, politicians, and intellectuals. He built a theater and staged plays that went on until four in the morning. It was important to him that the place be beautiful—he believed that beauty was essential to human happiness. He built a rose garden and planted flowers everywhere.

And it was not enough that Anandwan do without charity: it would *dispense* charity. A school for blind children was needed in the area; Baba started one, a boarding school so that children could come from far away. Later, he started a school for the deaf, and after he and Tai found a tiny abandoned girl on the road, they built an orphanage. They built a home for the aged. One of the most pressing needs of the area surrounding Anandwan was higher schooling; there was no college anywhere nearby, and sending children to board in a distant town was prohibitively expensive. Well, Baba said, they would build a college right there, on the grounds of Anandwan, and every student who attended that college would live among the leprosy patients and know that he owed them his education. The Anand Niketan College opened in 1964.

Stories about Anandwan began to spread. By the late 1950s, it had became a place that well-known people were curious about—playwrights, poets, actors, politicians. Baba had become famous. Later, Prime Minister Indira Gandhi paid a visit, and the Dalai Lama planted a tree.

Vikas and Prakash graduated from high school in the mid-1960s and took their undergraduate degrees at the college at Anandwan. Afterward, Vikas wanted to study engineering, but since Anandwan needed doctors, not engineers, Baba told him to study medicine. Prakash had always wanted to be a doctor. For medical school, the brothers moved to Nagpur. They lived there for four and a half years, but they never liked it. They felt self-conscious about being the sons of Baba Amte—they were always careful to avoid doing anything frivolous that might taint his reputation.

By this time, there were more than six hundred people living in Anandwan, but it wasn't enough. Baba could not tolerate a steady progression—that felt like stasis, it was death to him. He needed to start new projects—he felt there were always more people who needed his help. He started Ashokwan, a farm for leprosy patients to work in, in an area just south of Nagpur that was known to be inhabited by bandits. One night, robbers came to this farm and stole food, plates, and cooking pots; then they learned, to their horror, that the food and pots were used by leprosy patients. "They came running back!" Baba told people delightedly. "They returned everything, down to the last plate!" Such dangers thrilled him. He started a second farm that lay near the haunt of a fearsome tiger and spent many nights camped out in the forest, waiting to catch sight of it.

He wanted his projects to last beyond his lifetime, for a hundred years. He had two sons; they would continue his work. But that wasn't enough, he needed more than two sons, he wanted to start a movement in which young people from all over the country would be inspired to work with him and start projects like his. He decided to run weeklong summer camps for students: during the heat of the day, they would work in the fields or construct buildings (it was essential, he felt, that they learn to respect manual labor and know how tough it was), and in the evenings, there would be lectures and discussions and music. He would rouse the young people to work hard; he would give impassioned speeches about leprosy and poverty and the future of India. The purpose of the camps was to persuade people to follow him into good work, but he didn't take on just anyone—he tested them first, to see what they were made of. Baba didn't want do-gooder types, people who thought they were sacrificing themselves for the helpless lepers: they would be taking up this work for their own reasons, because they wanted to, and if they didn't understand that, it was better that they not come. A man with a good government position saw Baba speak at a youth camp and volunteered to leave his job and his home to work in the as-yet-nonexistent school at one of the projects. Baba told him, "Don't expect an appointment letter. Your appointment is with yourself. Come when you are ready."

People began to call Baba a saint. Sometimes he rejected such talk; sometimes he did not. He had taken up leprosy work, he said, "not to help anyone but to overcome that fear in my life. That it worked out well for others is a byproduct." He knew that the idea of saintliness was an alibi: to call him a saint was to suggest that he was a different order of creature, so ordinary people need not try to emulate his work. He didn't believe in God and he couldn't bear organized religion—he refused to let priests into his house. But his ambition was too large to be captured by secular categories such as "social worker," or "activist." "I wanted to be a contemporary of those 'Lords of Conspicuous Scars'—Christ, Damien, Gandhi," he wrote. "Everytime I stand in the company of a leprosy patient I see the imprint of Christ's kiss on his forehead."

Some people accused Baba of being an autocrat, the Emperor of Leprosy, using the labor of deformed patients to increase his own glory. One man, proposing to work at one of Baba's farms, asked about the blueprint for the project's future. Baba, annoyed, said, "Did the disciples of Jesus Christ ask for a blueprint when they followed him?"

Baba made people angry, but those who loved him didn't care. People wanted to follow him. The people who left their work and their families to join him weren't drawn to leprosy—they were drawn to Baba. They sensed that a life spent near him would be more exciting, more risky, more deeply felt, and more significant than the life they were living. Even people he only met for a short time felt known by him, and fiercely loved.

VIKAS

When Vikas came back to Anandwan from medical school, he was full of ideas for improving the hospital facilities. He loved cleanliness and he loved systems and procedures. People began to come to him with ideas or complaints. Many people were terrified of Baba—they never knew when he would fly into a rage and shout at them—but nobody was frightened of Vikas. Vikas was an enthusiast, an encourager of new projects. Vikas was unlike Baba in a number of ways. He was big—taller than his father and brother, broad in the shoulders, and capacious in the stomach. His features were bigger, his hair thicker. He loved food, he loved nice clothes, and he ironed his shirts so they were perfectly smooth; he was not, like Baba and Prakash, a wiry, barely clothed Gandhian figure in white khadi. Baba never had an office, but Vikas wanted an office, a proper one with a desk and file drawers for paperwork.

Though he had not been permitted to study engineering, he made himself into an amateur engineer of extraordinary inventiveness. He wanted Anandwan to be a model village—efficient, harmonious, and beautiful. He had a passion for machines, for industry, for architecture. He was obsessed with recycling and conservation. He rebuilt Anandwan's toilets so they consumed less water and generated biogas. He raised emus and sold their eggs. He wanted to build a lake, but there was no water. He persuaded a group excavating a nearby coal field to lend him their excavator at night, and he dug and dug, looking for water. Everyone told him he was a fool. Finally, he found water two miles away, installed tube wells and ducts, and brought the water to Anandwan and built his lake. Over the years, he dug other, smaller ponds to conserve every drop of rainwater, and around their edges he planted tall, protein-rich grasses for cattle feed.

He worked like a demon. He chewed raw green chilies and raw onions all day. He liked to work late into the night, when everyone else was asleep—he felt freer then, without his parents watching him, without people criticizing his ideas before he'd had a chance to work them out. He thought about new things he'd like to build, and read the newspapers; anytime he saw something that interested him, he clipped it and filed it away. A cousin of Vikas's, Dr. Pol, had worked at Anandwan since 1984 with relentless devotion—thirty years later he had never taken a vacation; Vikas began to leave more and more of the medical work to him, and continued his building.

Vikas thought of himself as an emotional engineer as well. A couple of leprosy patients had arrived at Anandwan in such a state of despair that they drowned themselves in a well just after they got there; Vikas built the well wall higher, and planted a ring of bright flowers around it in the hope that these alterations would deter more suicides. One day, he heard that a blind girl returning home from Anandwan's school for the blind had felt so useless that she had tried to kill herself; he decided to start an Anandwan orchestra, in which blind students and other Anandwan residents could sing and play instruments and dance. Later, hearing of a spate of suicides by bankrupt farmers in the region, Vikas devised a campaign to help them: he traveled around in a bus, telling farmers how Anandwan had improved its yield by managing the watershed and diversifying its crops, showing them how they, too, could work themselves out of debt.

Vikas started a vocational training center for people with disabilities other than leprosy—people who were accepted outside but had trouble finding work. They were trained to become tailors, or machine repairmen, or printers, or weavers, or caners; people who were unable to use their hands could be trained as teachers or administrators. He appointed as manager of the center one of his closest friends, Sadashiv Tajne, an immense, booming man whose legs were crippled by polio; he had heard about Anandwan as a schoolboy and made his way there, dragging himself over the ground for several miles with his hands. At the time Anandwan was only for lepers, but Tajne persuaded Tai to make an exception for him. Under Tajne's supervision, the training center was so productive that it began to turn a profit.

Anandwan had a few handlooms to weave cloth; Vikas installed power looms, whole rooms of deafening, clattering power looms, and Anandwan began to export sheets and carpets. Responding to the needs of lepers who lacked working legs, Anandwan began to manufacture tricycles that could be operated by hand. Eventually, Anandwan sold so many goods that the government began imposing taxes. "My father felt very proud that the leprosy patients had become the object of tax!" Vikas exulted. He built new buildings and repaired the old ones.

Tai observed these developments with ambivalence. To her, Anandwan was a place where people were bound together by pain and embraced a necessary austerity. They came because they were outcasts, and its people were the only family they had. The introduction of too many comforts threatened its purpose, she thought. Tai's wariness was not just puritanism; visitors from Israel sometimes said that Anandwan reminded them of kibbutzes in the difficult early days; the kibbutzes' sense of purpose had dissipated as they prospered. Vikas was a modern man—he wanted to alleviate suffering.

Perhaps he did not understand that suffering was necessary, she thought. Tai wrote in her memoir, *Samidha*:

> Between the two brothers, Vikas is more extravagant than Prakash. He wants the best in everything, and for everyone. . . . I have often taken him to task for these simple luxuries. I keep telling him, our journey began with "nothing"; but he is out for "everything", everything for all. Prakash is the opposite. He luxuriates in hardships, not for its own sake of course. If he finds someone denied of something, he would deny it to himself too. His life at Bhamragad, has been a long chain of denials. He lives with the bare minimum and would like other people too to do so, rather than aspire for material comforts. The projects, that Vikas completed, dazzle the eyes of the onlookers, those of Prakash, open their eyes. Vikas complains that he is always criticised for everything he does. That is not true. That Prakash has been admired more, does not mean that Vikas doesn't possess excellence. His strength lies somewhere else. Vikas has a versatile brain, a sharp memory and excellent aesthetic sense.

Vikas had no wife. His parents told him that he could marry a girl of any caste, but she must be a doctor, because that was what Anandwan needed. One day, a young pediatrician named Bharati visited Anandwan in the hope of meeting Baba, whom she had read about; Tai and Vikas met her and talked for an hour, and shortly thereafter Tai arranged the marriage. Vikas and Bharati had two children—a boy, Kaustubh, born in 1979, and a girl, Sheetal, born in 1981. Baba told Sheetal and Kaustubh that they ought to be doctors, but Bharati told them they should do whatever they wanted. Neither was inclined toward medicine. Kaustubh loved mathematics, and became an accountant—he would run Anandwan's finances.

Sheetal wanted to be an architect or an interior decorator, but Baba told her it was his dying wish that she become a doctor, so she went to medical school, then returned to Anandwan and began working in the hospital. She discovered later that he was not actually dying, and that over the years he had confided a variety of dying wishes to a large number of people, but by then it was done.

One day, a group of business students visited Anandwan, and Sheetal talked to them about how she wanted to transform Anandwan from an extended family into a modern NGO. One student asked her why there were no professionals there other than the Amtes. She told him that professionals wanted things that Anandwan could not provide: they wanted a good salary and nice housing, they wanted to be able to go to a restaurant or a movie in the evening, they wanted a community of people like themselves. She told him that when you found the meaning of your life you no longer needed these things—you were happy to spend your time with leprosy patients and go to bed at seven o'clock. That night, the student, Gautham, telephoned his parents and told them he had met his bride.

Meanwhile, Kaustubh had also gotten married, to a girl from Nasik named Pallavi. Pallavi had read about Baba in school, and her older brother suggested that she go to one of Baba's youth camps. She arrived during a terrifying storm and found herself in the middle of a jungle; there were insects everywhere, and she was to sleep on the floor. She resolved that the next day she would run back home. But the next morning, Vikas gave a speech to all the young people who had come. He said to them, If you quit everything that you are involved in outside, who will notice? Who will care? But here, there are many people who need you, and you can change their lives. By the end of the speech, she had decided that she would spend her life working for him.

By the time Pallavi and Gautham moved to Anandwan, it was a pleasant place to live, very clean and groomed. Outside its gates the vegetation turned dry and dead in the winter, but inside there were always flowers, planted in neat rows behind stone borders or lined up in pots. Its different parts—it now spread over nearly five hundred acres—were connected by wide dirt paths lit with streetlamps, and there were many trees for shade. There were a few large, several-story concrete structures—the hospital, the main office building, the guesthouse, the college—but most of the buildings were bungalows surrounded by trees. There was a formal French-style garden, neatly clipped concentric circles of hedge interspersed with gravel. Vikas's lake had become a sanctuary for birds, and there was a path around it that was a nice place to walk at sunset or in the cooler hours of the morning.

A little hut café in the center of Anandwan sold yogurt and other products from the dairy; a gift shop sold craft items made in the workshops. The gift shop catered to visitors. There was such a demand now for tours of Baba's empire that several nonprofit operators made it their business to organize multi-day trips: these would leave from Mumbai or Pune or Nasik or Goa, and would drive around Anandwan and to Prakash's clinic, a few hours away—twenty people one day, fifty the next, tens of thousands a year. When groups of visitors turned up, Vikas would talk to them. There were many people who had wrong ideas about Baba, or wrong ideas about leprosy, and he felt he must correct them. Sometimes he spoke for hours without stopping.

Several thousand people now lived in Anandwan, only about fifteen hundred of them leprosy patients. Many of the others were temporary residents—the blind children, the deaf children, students at the college, handicapped students at the training center. Anandwan was no longer isolated. The local town, Warora, which had been several miles' walk away when Baba and Tai first set out to live in the wilderness, had sprawled, and now backed right up against Anandwan's gates. Local people were no longer afraid to come inside. Every year there were several surgical camps, in which surgeons came from far away and spent a few days at Anandwan, performing staggering numbers of operations, on outsiders as well as on the residents of Anandwan. Two eye surgeons from Mumbai corrected seventeen hundred cataracts in a few days; plastic surgeons from England corrected the various deformities that came with leprosy—the claw hands, the dropped eyelids; other surgeons fixed cleft palates and treated gynecological ailments. A prosthetist from Nagpur manufactured artificial limbs.

The thing that was hard for Pallavi and Gautham to get used to was the total absence of family life. Sheetal and Kaustubh felt that they had a family of several thousand people—everyone at Anandwan was part of it. That was how it had always been—Baba and Tai had never made a distinction between the leprosy patients and their family. None of the Amtes had ever had a place at Anandwan that was private, that was not part of their work. People were always dropping by; there were people everywhere. Pallavi was startled to discover that people would walk unannounced into her bedroom, until she asked Kaustubh to put up a sign asking them to knock. The Amtes ate at the canteen. Other people at Anandwan had family homes where they lived and took meals together, but the Amtes were different.

PRAKASH

In 1971, Baba proposed that his family have a picnic. It was to be a distant picnic: to get to the place Baba had in mind, they traveled for three days, 150 miles, deep into the jungle. When they reached the spot, a convergence of three rivers into a wide open space in the middle of the forest, they stopped and built a fire. They ate their picnic and slept on the ground. The next day, they walked in the forest. The trees grew so close together that little sunlight penetrated through the leaves. It was nearly silent: they could hear no birds, only the occasional footfall of a boar or a deer, and the distant sound of the river. They walked until they came upon a small group of huts. The people who lived in the huts scattered like frightened animals at their approach; the few they caught sight of were emaciated and barely covered. These were the Madia Gonds, the tribal people that Baba had encountered in the forest when he was a boy.

The Madia Gonds lived wretched lives. They were attacked by bears and leopards and bitten by snakes. They ate leaves—they barely farmed—and ants, and animals that they hunted, but these sources of food were uncertain, and they often starved. They looked much older than they were. They wore few clothes or went naked, although it was cold in the winter. They had no doctors. If someone was disabled or wounded past help, he was left to die—there was no food to spare for someone who couldn't work. Even those who survived childbirth and weren't gored by bears or bitten by snakes or scorpions died by forty. They were preyed upon by corrupt forest guards who induced them to harvest bamboo and honey and paid them nearly nothing.

As the Amtes set out for home, Baba announced that he wanted to start a project there. When he had encountered the Madia Gond tribals as a teenager, he had noticed their misery but thought that, overall, their society was preferable to the one he lived in. He had always meant to go back and help them, and now he was going to do that. It was not clear how: his back prevented him from doing much physical work, and he was nearly sixty. Prakash had just finished medical school. He said to Baba, If you start it, I will join you.

Baba applied to the government for land in the Madia Gond area, but such requests took some time to come through; while they were waiting, Prakash took up postgraduate training in surgery, and during that time he met a young woman named Manda—she was training in anesthesia, and because of that they found themselves working together often. She was the first person he had really spoken to other than Vikas in all the years he had been in Nagpur. They decided to marry, and she agreed to follow him to work in the forest, even though she had never seen it and had very little idea of what it would be like. They were married at Anandwan, and the next day they left for Hemalkasa—as Baba had named the project—to begin their work.

They began as Baba had begun at Anandwan, by building a few crude huts. Until they dug a well, they carried water from the river, which was a mile away, in a bullock cart. Then they set about cutting down trees to clear some land, and breaking stones for crude roads. There were ten or so people living at the project in the early days: besides Prakash and Manda, there was Renuka, Prakash's adoptive sister; a couple of men who had been inspired by Baba at one of his youth camps; and a few leprosy patients from Anandwan. It was hard. Prakash was used to living with scorpions and snakes in the jungle, but he was not used to living without people. They were completely isolated. The jungle around them was enormous, and still, and very quiet. Sometimes they would play the radio even when the only station it received was in Telugu, a language they didn't understand, just to hear a human voice interrupt the silence.

There were no real roads to Hemalkasa. The route required fording several rivers, and often the jeep would get stuck and have to be pushed out. Sometimes, after enormous effort, the jeep would strain free, only to get stuck again a few yards on. Vikas made this journey countless times, bringing supplies from Anandwan, but for as much as six months a year—from June to December, during the rainy season—the rivers would run so high that it was not possible to ford them at all, and Hemalkasa was completely cut off. During those months, they had no vegetables or fruit to eat, and no flour, all things that rotted too quickly to store. They ate potatoes and rice. Fungus grew on everything. The first year, everyone caught malaria.

Soon they were ready to begin medical work, but they had no patients: the tribals wouldn't come near them. They knew they had to learn the tribal language, but how were they to learn if nobody would talk to them? Prakash walked around to the villages, urging the tribals to come for treatment, but because he couldn't speak their language, he had no success. The local shamans, sensing rivals, forbade the villagers to go to the clinic, telling them that the gods would curse them if they did. A string of headless cockerels was hung up to reinforce this point. To pass the time, Prakash chopped wood, or carried bricks. He walked in the forest. A year passed, and still they had treated only a handful of patients. Prakash had expected hardship but he had not expected that the whole venture would be a failure. He told himself that he had come to Hemalkasa for his own reasons, the tribals hadn't asked for his help; if it turned out they didn't want it, he would have to accept that.

At last, their luck changed. A boy was brought to them with burns over 40 percent of his body—he had epilepsy and during a seizure had fallen into a bonfire. Since the shamans had failed to cure him, and he was clearly going to die if he was not treated, his family decided to take their chances with the clinic. Several days had already passed since the accident, and his wounds were crawling with worms. Prakash was used to this, having seen such wounds on leprosy patients; the difference was that leprosy patients couldn't feel their wounds, whereas this boy was in agony. Prakash cleaned the wounds and gave the boy antibiotics—which were unusually effective on him, since he'd never taken them before—and a month later, he was healed. The story of this miraculous recovery spread around, and more patients began to come. One man arrived unconscious, late at night, having been carried on a stretcher through many villages; a few days later, completely cured, the man made the return journey back through the same villages, carrying the stretcher himself. This dramatic change, visible to everyone on the man's route home, persuaded still more people to trust them. A third turning point came when the daughter of a shaman fell ill, and he failed to cure her. Fearing for her life, he brought her to the clinic, and she was cured. From then on, even the shamans' resistance was diminished.

Once the tribals decided to trust the clinic, they came by the thousands. They traveled for days through the forest to get there, from as much as fifty miles away, about a hundred people each day. When a patient arrived, he was usually accompanied by eight or ten relatives, who would camp out around the clinic for the duration of the treatment. Patients came with malaria, diarrhea, snake and scorpion bites, and wounds from bear attacks. They came with terrible burns from falling into their fires while asleep (this was very common). They came in the middle of dangerous childbirths. They came with swollen limbs that were sometimes broken and sometimes not; because the clinic had no X-ray machine, Prakash would determine whether a limb was broken by twisting it above and below the swelling in opposite directions; if he could hear the scratch of bone, he knew it was broken, and twisted it back into its place for setting in plaster. If a patient turned up with a toothache, Prakash couldn't fill the tooth, but he could at least extract it and stop the pain.

The tribals' capacity for enduring pain astonished him. One day, a girl about ten years old arrived holding her own intestine, which protruded from a hole that a bamboo shred had slit in her abdomen; she had walked many miles to the clinic, and she did not complain as Prakash pushed the intestine back in through the hole and stitched it up. He often had to put in stitches without anesthetic, and his patients never cried out. He wondered how he himself would tolerate such a thing; and so when his hand was torn by the teeth of a leopard, he took no anesthetic as Manda stitched him up.

Prakash had had only a little surgical training, so at first he operated while reading instructions from a book. There was no electricity, so if he needed to operate at night, someone would hold up a lantern for him; in the hot months, someone would stand by to wipe the sweat off his face so it didn't drip into the wound. They couldn't afford trained nurses, so Prakash and Manda taught local helpers how to give injections, how to set up a saline drip, how to stitch up a wound. They made their own bandages, they made their own gowns. In the beginning, nearly every day required some nerve-racking guesswork or surgical improvisation. If an operation had been new to Prakash, he might lie awake all night afterward, too anxious to sleep, waiting to see if the patient would be okay in the morning. It was disturbing to think about the mistakes he could make, and had made, but at the same time it was thrilling always to be forced to push himself past what he thought he could possibly do.

Gradually, Prakash and the others learned the tribal language. It bore no resemblance to Marathi, the official language of their state. Patients explained what was wrong with them, first in sign language and then in words; Prakash wrote these words down, and slowly he began to compile a dictionary. When he wasn't working at the clinic, he went into the villages and tried to speak. Once he spoke the language, diagnosis became easier, but misunderstandings still happened often. The distinction between the medicine and its packaging had to be explained, as did the concept of dosage, or a patient might swallow an entire course of drugs at once. The tribals had no clocks, so timing dosages was difficult. There were other problems, too, impossible to foresee. One patient, given a cake of soap, swallowed it whole. Sometimes a corpse would be brought to the clinic, and the corpse's relatives would ask Prakash to breathe life into it.

Confronted by this forbidding distance between the tribals and himself, Prakash tried to reduce it. He saw that the tribals were cold in winter because they wore so few clothes, so he stopped wearing sweaters and trousers and long-sleeved shirts and took to wearing a white cotton vest and white shorts, no matter the weather. Manda and some others decided to follow him and stopped wearing sweaters too. Prakash wasn't a missionary type—he didn't like talking, he wasn't a preacher like Baba, and he wasn't spiritually ambitious, as Baba was. He had no notion of changing the tribals' way of life; he was a doctor, that was all. If, as sometimes happened, a patient decided to abandon his treatment and go home, Prakash accepted that decision.

One night, a man appeared at the clinic with half a face. A bear had attacked him, clawing off the top of his face, crushing his eyes, and smashing his skull. Astonishingly, the man was conscious. Prakash had no anesthetic, so he cleaned the wound of dirt and then tried putting in a stitch to see if the man could take it. The man told him to continue. Prakash put in 150 stitches to hold together what remained of the man's face, and the man suffered the pain without a sound. After a week, the man was able to go home: he was blind, but he was alive and out of danger. However, being blind, he was unable to hunt. His family started feeding him less, and two years later he died of starvation. Prakash heard of this death and tried to see it from the tribals' point of view. He understood that to feed this man would be to take food away from other people; perhaps it would be a choice between their lives and his.

Another day, a woman came to the clinic in labor that had stalled; the child's head was turned sideways and already partly out. Prakash could not safely perform a Cesarian section at the clinic, and he didn't then have a vehicle to transport the mother to a hospital. The only thing he could do was to cut the infant into pieces, in order to pull it out and save the life of the mother. He braced himself and did it; but he discovered that the mother and her relatives weren't nearly as disturbed by it as he was. They told him that many babies died in their first year of life from malnutrition or illness or snake bites; if a mother died in childbirth, the father usually didn't take care of the infant—it was left to die. This death was just a little earlier, that was all.

The year after they came to Hemalkasa, Manda found that she was pregnant. This presented them with a distressing dilemma. On the one hand, she and Prakash felt that it would be immoral for her to travel to Nagpur and take advantage of medical resources they couldn't offer their patients; on the other hand, Prakash knew that if Manda's labor stalled he might be forced to cut his own child into pieces in order to save his wife. Could he face that? They talked about this question for a long time. Finally, they decided that Manda should stay. But then Tai heard about their decision. She still felt guilty about giving birth to her own children without good medical care, endangering all of their lives, and she wasn't going to let Manda do the same thing. She traveled to Hemalkasa and forced Manda to return with her to Nagpur; soon after, she gave birth to their first son, Digant.

It seemed to Prakash that the Madias had no particular notion of improving their lives. Survival alone was challenge enough. But their territory had been increasingly encroached upon by logging companies that wanted trees for paper. The logging companies and forest-department officials told the tribals that the forest belonged to them, so when the tribals took honey, plants, and animals from the forest they were stealing; therefore, they were obliged to work for nothing to repay their debt. Government schemes were launched to help tribal people, but often the aid money was stolen by middlemen, and the tribals saw very little of it. Prakash thought that if the tribals were literate they would be better able to resist these various sorts of thievery. There were already a few government schools in the district, but the teachers didn't speak the tribal language and didn't show up most of the time, so in effect these schools existed only on paper.

Prakash decided to start an elementary school. Because the tribal villages were so far apart, it had to be a boarding school, but it was difficult to persuade the parents to send their children so far away: they needed them at home, to work. In trying to persuade them, Prakash didn't talk much about literacy—he thought that would be too remote a goal. He told them he would feed their children and teach them how to farm and how to administer rudimentary medicine. This worked. The children found it hard to be at school; they wet their beds and ran away into the forest. But the school fed them better than they would eat at home, and the Amtes had acquired credibility through their clinic, so their parents sent them back. As the years passed, some of the tribal students learned not only Marathi but also English, and went on to become doctors, but none of them came back to Hemalkasa to work. Doctors at Hemalkasa were paid six thousand rupees a month; an ordinary government doctor elsewhere might make twenty times as much.

The salary was one of the reasons it was impossible to retain doctors who weren't Amtes; the other reason was the Madias themselves. At the clinic, they didn't show gratitude, or emotion of any kind—you never saw shock or relief on the faces of the patients or their families, as you did in hospitals elsewhere; when someone died, nobody wept, and when a healthy baby was born, nobody seemed particularly happy. The Madias didn't seem to place much value on their lives, or else were fatalistic to the point of nonchalance. Often they missed their operations at the yearly surgical camps because they didn't turn up. Once, a baby was born prematurely, weighing not much over two pounds; it was a hot summer, and the clinic procured a generator to keep the baby cool, and tended it day and night. One morning, the baby disappeared: its parents needed to rethatch their hut and had taken it home, ignoring the pleas of the clinic to leave it behind until it was well enough to travel; the baby died the next day. People who felt that they had nobly sacrificed comfortable lives outside to move to Hemalkasa found all this difficult to take; sooner or later, they all left. Prakash reminded himself that he had chosen this work himself, for his own reasons; nobody had asked him to come.

Malnutrition among the Madias was a bigger problem than sickness, so Prakash decided to teach them to farm. Farming was pushing against a belief that many Madias held, that digging into the earth was like cutting into your mother's body, but Prakash's demonstrations with high-yield seeds on his own land so impressed the Madias that they adopted his techniques. For Prakash, this intervention was only partly in the service of human health. He thought that if the Madias were able to grow crops they wouldn't need to hunt so much, and this mattered to him a great deal. When Baba had hunted in these forests as a teenager, fifty years before, they had been full of birds and monkeys and all kinds of small creatures. Now the birds were gone, and most of the smaller animals, too. Prakash had grown up playing with scorpions; he had always loved all animals, no matter how ugly or dangerous. If there was any way to get the Madias to kill fewer animals, he was going to find it.

One day not long after the clinic first opened, a group of Madias passed by carrying a female monkey that they'd killed, with a live baby still clinging to her fur. They were planning to eat both, but

Prakash persuaded them to give the baby to him in exchange for a bag of rice. He fed the baby monkey milk in a bottle, and let her live in the house. She sat on Prakash's shoulder as he walked about; she also took to riding on the back of Prakash's dog. News of this exchange spread around, and more baby animals were offered. Prakash and his brother-in-law, Vilas Manohar, took care of them. Later, they adopted an orphaned bear named Rani, who accompanied them on walks to the river, growling if anybody else came near. They had deer, antelope, foxes, hyenas, peacocks, snakes, and squirrels. After their school started, they gave the tribal students the responsibility for feeding the animals, hoping that the children would come to think of them as pets rather than food.

At first they fed their animals vegetarian meals, but after two leopard cubs died on this diet, the next time a leopard arrived they fed it meat. They didn't kill for meat—they sent the word out to the villages that if an animal died they would buy it. The leopard cub, like the bear cub, roamed freely around the grounds of the clinic and played with the children. Another leopard cub accompanied Aarti, Prakash's adopted daughter, to school, until it grew so large that it scared the other children.

Prakash had unlimited faith in his way with animals—even new animals, who didn't know him. He inherited an angry adult leopard who had been kept on a chain by the forest department. The man who had been in charge of him begged him to be careful and not let him off the chain just yet; instead, Prakash let the leopard off his chain at once and shut himself in his cage. Something about him seemed to disarm even the fiercest animals: his lack of fear, his natural authority, but also a kind of motherly charisma, an intimate, nurturing, patient, magnetic quality. He befriended even snakes— even banded kraits, whose bite would kill a man in minutes. His faith was not always justified. Once, he nearly died from the bite of a viper he was handling; he was charged by a bear. His second son, Aniket, inherited his fearless love of animals; when Aniket was ten, he approached a leopard with which he had played when it was a cub, and was attacked—the leopard didn't recognize him. Prakash had to pry Aniket out of the leopard's jaws.

Little by little, life at Hemalkasa improved. Baba brought several SwissAid volunteers, who helped to build proper houses and a dispensary and bored wells. At one point, they acquired a refrigerator that ran on kerosene, a dinosaur left over from the time of the British. One aspect of life grew worse rather than better as time went on: gangs of Maoist insurgents who lived in the surrounding jungle grew more and more violent; they attacked vehicles and set off bombs, they killed and raped, and they stormed into villages demanding food. Around 1990, electricity finally came to Hemalkasa. A few years later, Hemalkasa got a phone.

Over the years, various people heard about the project and helped out with funding, but Prakash never made any effort to raise money. He didn't see the need. He would do his work and make do with what he had; it was enough.

In 1990, Baba made a dramatic announcement: he was leaving Anandwan for good, to move four hundred miles west to a tiny village on the banks of the Narmada River, as a protest against a giant dam project that would displace several hundred thousand people. An anti-dam movement already existed, but he would not be active in it—he was seventy-five and could barely walk. He would simply live next to the Narmada as a gesture of resistance.

Everyone was shocked. Many were angry. How could he have made this decision without consulting anyone? How could he simply abandon all the people who had devoted their lives to working with him? How could he do this to Anandwan, and for what cause? Nehru, the country's first prime minister, had called dams the "temples of modern India": dams weren't just construction projects, they were symbols of patriotism. Many donors stopped giving money to Baba's projects. People who didn't like Baba anyway took the opportunity to presume the worst motives: he wanted attention, he was bored. Baba ignored them.

Baba spent ten years living at Narmada, but then he came back. He had been content there, lying on his bed, looking out at the river and being the emotional center of the Narmada movement, but Tai was miserable. She missed her family; she missed the orphans and blind children and elderly people she had visited every day. At Anandwan, she had been constantly busy, always in demand; now she had nothing to do, she was useless. It began to affect her mind. She began to sleep much of the day; she was always crying. Eventually, Baba agreed to go back to Anandwan. He hated to go back on his promise to die on the banks of the Narmada, but Tai had sacrificed everything for him her whole life, and he knew that now he must do this one thing for her.

He was now nearly ninety. He grew sicker and sicker and required more time in the hospital. He was diagnosed with leukemia. He couldn't move. It became difficult to hear what he said, and he talked less and less. He died at ninety-three. For Vikas, Baba's death changed everything. "I was hooked to my father for thirty-five years," he said. "I never had a family life. I was hooked to my father, twenty-four hours, in thoughts and action and spirit."

Around the time of Baba's death, news of Prakash's project began to reach the outside world. Prakash had barely left Hemalkasa in seventeen years. He had not taken a single vacation. This had suited him—he liked burying himself in his work, not having to go out and talk to people. But now he was awarded one prize, then another, and another. He was asked to make speeches at Marathi conferences abroad. Prakash disliked speaking, even in private. He didn't care what anyone thought of him—he didn't care if people criticized Baba, either. Let them—what did it matter? He never talked about Baba, as Vikas did. But he was persuaded that speaking would bring needed money to the project, so he did it.

By the time the larger world took notice of their work, Prakash and Manda had mostly retired. Digant and his wife, Anagha, ran the hospital. Aniket had decided that the project needed publicity for fund-raising purposes, so he worked on spreading the word through social media and traveling exhibitions. His wife, Samiksha, worked at the school. When visitors came, Prakash would take them around the animal orphanage and show them what they had come to see: he played with the leopards and put his hand in their mouths; he fed bears; he picked up deadly snakes and wound them around the necks of his grandsons. But mostly he sat in a plastic chair in the dirt yard outside his house, tending the small bonfire that he lit on cold mornings and chatting with whoever stopped by. In the evenings, the family sometimes biked to the river.

Prakash was still strong and could have gone on working, but it was customary in India to retire in one's sixties, and he wanted Digant to run the hospital without his interference. He did not feel the passion that drove Baba and Vikas, to be always fixing the world. He had started a clinic in the jungle and he had worked there for thirty years. It was enough.

THE LEGACY OF DRUNKS

THE UNDERMINING OF DO-GOODERS,
PART TWO

Always, if he had a little money, a man could get drunk. The hard
edges gone, and the warmth. Then there was no loneliness, for a
man could people his brain with friends, and he could find his
enemies and destroy them. . . . Like to stay drunk all the time. Who
says it's bad? Who dares to say it's bad? Preachers—but they got
their own kinda drunkenness. Thin, barren women, but they're too
miserable to know. Reformers—but they don't bite deep enough
into living to know. No—the stars are close and dear and I have
joined the brotherhood of the worlds. And everything's holy—
everything, even me.

—JOHN STEINBECK, *The Grapes of Wrath*

The recent history of do-gooders, at least in the West, is insepa-
rable from the history of alcohol. In centuries past, saints re-
nounced sex: sex was the pleasure that humans had always
indulged in, involving a loss of self-control, the renunciation of
which marked the renouncer as different and separate from other
people. Chastity was a higher path, a saintly path, preserving the
strength and the purity of the saint for his service. But in the course
of time, chastity lost its allure—came to seem more like pathology
than virtue—and was replaced by sobriety. Giving up alcohol is an
asceticism for the modern do-gooder, drinking being, like sex, a
pleasure that humans have always indulged in, involving a loss of
self-control, the renunciation of which marks the renouncer as different and separate from other people.

To drink, to get drunk, is to lower yourself on purpose for the sake of good fellowship. You abandon yourself, for a time, to life and fate. You allow yourself to become stupider and less distinct. Your boundaries become blurry: you open your self and feel connected to people around you. You throw off your moral scruples, and suspect it was those scruples that prevented the feeling of connection before. You feel more empathy for your fellow, but at the same time, because you are drunk, you render yourself unable to help him; so, to drink is to say, I am a sinner, I have chosen not to help.

In America, Prohibition—that brief, doomed attempt to ban the manufacturing and sale of alcohol—came to seem like an emblematic lesson in the limits of morality. You could expect only so much of people, America realized after Prohibition failed. You could restrict human pleasure only up to a point. To attempt to push a country too far in the direction of saintliness could backfire, turning its citizens into cynical hypocrites with no respect for the law. Try to force an excess of virtue on a people and you merely pushed the sin underground, with worse consequences. Prohibition was a landmark; but alcohol had another, more enduring effect on do-gooders, which began subtly, around the same time, and then sprouted and strained and twisted over decades until it wasn't subtle at all.

Around the time Prohibition went into effect in America, an American Lutheran missionary in England founded a Christian fellowship that became known as the Oxford Group. It set high moral standards for its members, who strove to achieve what it called the Four Absolutes: absolute truth, absolute unselfishness, absolute purity, and absolute love. The group believed in rigorous self-examination; in making restitution to others for any harm one had done them; and in helping each other to stay on the moral path. It believed in surrendering one's life to God, and believed that drunkenness was a sin.

Late in the fall of 1934, Bill Wilson, a sometime investment adviser and full-time alcoholic, was introduced to the New York branch of the Oxford Group by a formerly drunk friend who was convinced that the group could help him get sober. Wilson was an agnostic and an unrepentant smoker, but he attended a meeting (drunk) anyway, and a few days later he had an ecstatic religious vision in a hospital and never drank again. The following year, Wilson founded the group that would become Alcoholics Anonymous with Dr. Bob, another alcoholic, and in crafting the methods of their new society they adopted several of the Oxford Group's ideas: self-examination; making restitution; surrendering your life to a higher power; and helping other drunks in order to stay straight yourself.

But in the transition from the Oxford Group to Alcoholics Anonymous, something peculiar happened. AA grew to be quite different from its parent, and spawned a sister organization, Al-Anon, for the families of alcoholics, that was more different still. First, AA took what had been a sin—drunkenness—and recast it as a disease. And then, some years later, Al-Anon took what had been a virtue—trying to get a drunk to stop drinking—and called that a symptom of the same disease. These were both quite radical innovations, but it was the second that would have further-reaching moral effects. After all, whether alcoholism was a disease or a sin, either way it was undesirable—either way it was a bad and harmful thing that the world would be better off without. But if certain kinds of helping—particularly the entangled, tormented, devoted helping of a drunk's long-suffering spouse—were a manifestation of illness, too, something that ought to be cured, then that made a whole realm of moral behavior look startlingly different.

Al-Anon was cofounded by Bill Wilson's wife, Lois. When Lois first met Bill, Bill didn't drink at all—his father had been an alcoholic, and he was terrified of turning out the same way. Shortly before they married, he started drinking a little, then drinking a lot, but Lois didn't worry about it; Bill loved her, she was charming, she was sure she could get him to stop. As a young girl, Lois had daydreamed of changing bad people into good ones. In one fantasy, she caught a burglar stuffing the family silver into a sack; instead of being angry, she reasoned with him so sweetly, with such radiant moral charisma, that she inspired him with a desire to be good, and he put the silver back.

Bill graduated from law school but got drunk and never picked up his diploma. Lois had three ectopic pregnancies, but Bill was often too drunk to visit her in the hospital, and then, because of his drinking, they were turned down for adoption. Bill decided he wanted to be an investment analyst, traveling around the country evaluating companies; since they had almost no money, this entailed driving around for a year on a motorbike and living in a tent. Through all of this, Lois was a trouper. She worked to help support the family, but when Bill wanted to go on the road, she left her job and home without complaint. When Bill didn't visit her in the hospital, she felt guilty, wondering if her failed pregnancies were driving him to drink. She tried to help him, and when she failed, she wondered what she was doing wrong and how she could do better.

"Was I to blame for his drinking?" she wondered. "He had once told me that when he was a little boy, he was given a small ax for Christmas and immediately tried it out on Susie, his rubber doll. Thereafter, every time he looked into the toy box and saw the doll's head dangling by a thread, he would weep and say, 'Poor Susie! I nearly cut off her head.' As he later sometimes called me Susie, I wondered just where this placed me. Could he hold a subconscious resentment against me for some subtle reason? Or was the reason perhaps something obvious that I was doing wrong? It was highly puzzling and confusing, so I would try hard not to let myself be discouraged and to rivet my attention on the job I was doing." Her job was to stop Bill's drinking, and her weapon was love.

When Bill got sober, Lois was at first ecstatic. But he immediately became as absorbed in sobriety as he had been in drinking—he was always organizing meetings, attending meetings, and talking with other alcoholics. He almost never spent time alone with Lois anymore. For a long time, she couldn't admit to herself that she wasn't as happy as she ought to be. Then, one day, when he told her she needed to hurry or they'd be late for a meeting, she threw a shoe at him and yelled, "Damn your old meetings!" He was shocked, but she was even more shocked; and it was only then, as she tried to understand what had made her so violently angry, that she began to realize what had really been going on.

All those years when Bill was drinking, when she thought she was unhappy, she had also been glad. She had known that he needed her: she was in charge, she was the righteous one in control of herself; he was the bad, weak one, dependent on her for everything. Now that Bill was sober and independent, she had lost her purpose, and she resented that God and alcoholics had been able to help him where she had not. She saw that not only had she not cured him: he had been cured in *spite* of her. By attempting to help him change, she had been preventing him from changing himself. She had not had children, so she had mothered Bill. In the past, the sin of the alcoholic had been that he refused to control himself. Now control had begun to look like the problem—both alcoholics imagining that they could control their disease, and spouses of alcoholics attempting to control it for them.

Lois decided that she needed to do exactly what Bill had done when he got sober: take an inventory of her flaws, turn her life over to a higher power, and stop thinking that she could control others or even herself. He needed AA; she saw that she, too, needed help. She cofounded Al-Anon in 1951, to support the unhappiness and correct the delusions of the families of alcoholics. She decided that self-righteousness was one of the worst sins there was because it was impregnable, sealing a person up inside an armor of smugness, aloof from other people and from God.

At first Al-Anon's primary purpose was to help the families of alcoholics to support the drinker in a constructive way. But as time went on, the focus shifted more and more to the family members themselves—their needs, their flaws, their spiritual mistakes. Over the decades that followed, the behavior of the family member came under increasing scrutiny. Family members began to call themselves co-alcoholics, and in the 1970s a word became increasingly popular—"codependency"—to name the disease from which they now believed themselves to suffer.

By the 1980s, codependency had become bigger than Al-Anon; it had come to describe anyone who was preoccupied with controlling someone else's behavior—typically, though not always, an unreliable romantic partner. The moral culture had changed greatly since Lois married Bill and tried to save him. Lois was born in 1891; Bill fought in the First World War; in their generation, selflessness had been uncomplicatedly virtuous. But half a century after AA's founding, the suspicions of Freud had merged with the teachings of Al-Anon, and selflessness had become tainted and suspect.

One of the first books to cast wifely helping in an unflattering new light—nonfiction books, that is; novels had always been skeptical—was *Women Who Love Too Much*, published in 1985, by Robin Norwood. Norwood was a therapist who had spent years counseling addicts; she had found, to her surprise, that whereas addicts sometimes came from troubled families and sometimes did not, their partners typically did. When they grew up, these partners unconsciously sought out addicted or otherwise grotesquely unreliable mates with whom they could reenact and attempt to master the traumas of their childhood. Having felt unloved and uncared for as children, they attempted to fill their need for love by becoming caretakers to needy men. "We want to be the one to break the spell, to free this man from what we see as his imprisonment," Norwood wrote. "We take his emotional unavailability, his anger or depression or cruelty or indifference or violence or dishonesty or addiction, for signs that he has not been loved enough. We pit our love against his faults, his failings, even his pathology. We are determined to save him through the power of our love."

As long as they were occupied with their turbulent men, these women could avoid confronting themselves. They needed to feel like saviors; they were addicted to that feeling, just as their partners were addicted to alcohol or drugs, and in order to sustain it they were willing to suffer. They expected that their love and slavishness would yield gratitude, but there was only so long even an addict could put up with the feeling of dependency, and sooner or later he would become resentful and leave. But these women would then go and find new and equally horrendous partners. They had no conception of love without pain: love was pain, pain was exciting, and the greater the pain, the deeper the love. If there was no pain, if their partner treated them decently, they felt bored and unconnected and went to look for someone else. But what felt to them like love was really just suffering; what felt like selflessness was really just an obsessive need to control. What these women needed to learn, Norwood concluded, was acceptance: to accept themselves and other people and reality as they were, without helping, without feeling responsible, without needing to change them.

Many of the women who loved too much were children of alcoholics: their personalities were formed early, in response to their addicted parent, and became, in adulthood, the metastasized altruism of the codependent. Because children of alcoholics grew up in households where grown-ups could not be depended upon, they often felt that it was up to them to take care of things. Often they believed that the unhappiness of the family was their own fault, and they tried to become perfect children in order to make things better—doing well in school, cleaning the house, cooking, taking care of as much as they could. When these children grew up, they felt guilty for failing to be perfect, and, not having been well loved as children, they grew up hungry for praise and affection and looked to others for approval. They felt responsible for taking care of other people; having grown up in a chaotic house with no control over their lives, they grew to crave control over themselves and the people around them. At the same time, they had grown used to such extremes of drama and disorder that ordinary life felt empty and dull. They were accustomed to atrocious behavior and terrified of abandonment, and so they put up with appalling abuse from their partners, remaining loyal and vowing to save them in spite of everything.

Women Who Love Too Much reached number one on the *New York Times* best-seller list, but it was superseded in 1986 by a book that would sell over five million copies and make codependency a household word—*Codependent No More*, by a recovering alcoholic named Melody Beattie. During her period of recovery, Beattie was far more hostile to codependents than Norwood had been. At that point, to her, codependency was not just pitiful—it was sinister and repellent. She found codependents hostile, controlling, and manipulative. Instructed by her employer at a Minneapolis treatment center to organize support groups for wives of addicts, she seethed with contempt. "In my group, I saw people who felt responsible for the entire world, but they refused to take responsibility for leading and living their own lives," she wrote. "I saw people who constantly gave to others but didn't know how to receive. I saw people give until they were angry, exhausted, and emptied of everything. . . . I saw mere shells of people, racing mindlessly from one activity to another. I saw people-pleasers, martyrs, stoics, tyrants, withering vines, clinging vines, and, borrowing from H. Sackler's line in his play, *The Great White Hope*, 'pinched up faces giving off the miseries.'"

Beattie's critique of codependents was not only more scathing than Norwood's; it was also broader. Codependency wasn't just about women and their dreadful husbands—it was about anyone who offered advice when it wasn't wanted, anyone who felt responsible for others, anyone who felt pity for other people's problems, anyone who felt obliged to help when he didn't really want to. "We control in the name of love," she wrote. "We do it because we're 'only trying to help.' We do it because we know best how things should go and how people should behave. We do it because we're right and they're wrong." Trying to help was just a recipe for victimhood, because helping was impossible and you'd just end up feeling bitter that you'd done so much and received no gratitude in return. "Some of us become so tired from the enormous burden—total responsibility for all human beings—that we may skip the feelings of pity and concern that accompany the rescue act and move ahead to anger," Beattie wrote. "We're angry all the time; we feel anger and resentment toward potential victims. A person with a need or problem provokes us to feel we have to do something or feel guilty. After a rescue, we make no bones about our hostility toward this uncomfortable predicament." The only person you can change is you, so you must let everyone else be, she concluded. She dedicated the book to herself.

By the 1990s, the codependency critique had become so widespread in America that it was taken up by some Evangelical Christians connected with the Campus Crusade for Christ activist Pat Springle. Codependency was a particular risk for Christians, Springle pointed out, because it looked so much like good Christian behavior—helping others and forgiving their misbehavior; striving to be morally perfect; denying oneself; fearing sin. Springle urged his followers to avoid developing a savior complex, and to realize that they were not required to help others or love cheerfully all the time. Imperfection was okay. Anger was okay. Guilt was okay, too, if it led to acknowledging sin and asking for forgiveness; the problem was bad guilt, when a person felt so profoundly worthless that he ceased to believe in the grace of God. God was not harsh or demanding but loving and affirming, they urged. If a Christian found it difficult to believe this, Springle advised, he might benefit from joining a group called Sinners Anonymous.

Both Norwood and Beattie mentioned, in passing, that codependents and women who loved too much often went into the "helping professions"—social work, therapy, nursing. Too much caring here could lead to violations of the necessary boundary between professional and patient, ensnaring the patient in dependence rather than setting him free. Therapists, like everyone, had hurt people and been hurt in the past, but, unlike other people, they were able to use their patients to try to make this right. Helping was not always generosity: it could also be reparation, or revenge. At best, it was, as the therapist Michael Jacobs put it, quoting Mary Sherrill Durham, "constructive vengeance": what better and more savagely effective way could there be to shame one who has hurt you than by caring tenderly for him? Many people who were abused as children either grew up to become abusers themselves or tried to help others who had been abused, and these responses were not as different as they seemed. There was only so much, Jacobs darkly concluded, that one could do to resist the force of fate.

The problem posed by professional relationships is a complicated one, because in that situation it's a person's job to give help, and the client, at least most of the time, has asked for it. Binding oneself romantically to a brutish addict is one thing; counseling an addict professionally is another. Of course, if a social worker's perception of his alcoholic client is distorted by memories of his alcoholic father, then the encounter may not be too helpful for either of them. But suppose he is good at his job—what then? These are people who sign up for a hard job that pays very little, with the hope, usually, that they are going to change the course of people's lives, and that what they lose in ease and money they will earn back in gratitude and moral satisfaction.

But it's difficult to sustain this hope, especially in a time when helping is suspect. This is one of the stories they tell about themselves. At the beginning, a social worker is often convinced that he is going to change lives dramatically and forever. He feels that he will change not only other people's lives but his own as well: he will feel a sense of recognition and potency that he has never felt before. These prospects are so intoxicating that at first he may work like a maniac, twelve or sixteen hours a day, sacrificing everything else. "I'd go fifteen miles to fix a broken shoelace," one counselor wrote of those heady early days. "I'd throw my wife out of bed to answer the beeper." Everything is urgent, he feels he is needed constantly, his adrenaline is going all the time, he cannot rest, he cannot stop to think. It seems to him that if he isn't working as hard as he can, disaster will ensue. He has no life outside his work, or, if he has, he pays it scant attention. The needs of his clients are overwhelming and critical, and the needs of ordinary people—those of his family members, for instance—seem trivial by comparison; he brushes them off. How can he think about math homework or watching a movie when people are getting shot and thrown out onto the street? How is it that other people don't understand what is going on? He still believes he can change people: he doesn't need anything else.

But people are difficult to change. Most of them change slowly, if at all, and then only slightly. They are not always grateful—some are resentful instead. At first the social worker may become too emotionally involved with his clients, so that when they fail he suffers, both because they are unhappy and because their failure is his failure, too. It's hard to spend his days confronting devastating problems that he cannot fix—the misery and helplessness rub off on him. It may seem to him that to feel happy or spend money on himself is to betray the people he knows who are still suffering; or it may seem that his own unhappiness is a sign of his devotion. Perhaps he becomes angry, blaming systems and society for what he cannot fix himself.

Gradually, he learns to be more detached. He realizes that he needs to be tough, and to develop a thick skin. But if he becomes too detached, he stops caring about his clients at all. Perhaps he withdraws into cynicism and self-defense, as he feels his ideals and his sense of potency wither. Longer-serving people in the office notice the waning of his enthusiasm, and welcome him to their gallows-humor fellowship. He retreats into apathy and jokes and drinks after work. But even with his fellow apathetics to keep him company, the situation is depressing, and he looks for a way out.

It's one thing to try to change the life of a troubled client; it's a much taller order to try to change the life of a village, or an entire country. And so it's no surprise that the doubts that spread from the wives of alcoholics to the counselors of alcoholics should also have come to afflict foreign-aid workers. Perhaps it should have been obvious sooner that it was complicated and potentially disastrous to attempt to help large populations of foreigners of whom one had only a sketchy understanding, than that it was complicated and potentially disastrous to attempt to help one's alcoholic husband. But a husband is close and intimately known, and failure is immediately apparent; detecting failure through thick cultural distortions is harder.

One of the best-known attacks on the moral delusions of the aid worker was a speech given by the Austrian priest and social critic Ivan Illich, delivered to young Americans in Mexico in 1968, in language that could have been taken from Al-Anon:

> If you insist on working with the poor, if this is your vocation, then at least work among the poor who can tell you to go to hell. It is incredibly unfair for you to impose yourselves on a village where you are so linguistically deaf and dumb that you don't even understand what you are doing, or what people think of you. And it is profoundly damaging to yourselves when you define something that you want to do as "good," a "sacrifice" and "help." . . . I am here to challenge you to recognize your inability, your powerlessness and your incapacity to do the "good" which you intended to do.

In 1968, when Illich delivered his speech—titled "To Hell with Good Intentions"—foreign-aid work was not yet the Brobdingnagian moral industry it is now. It took twenty years for the aid workers who came of age in the late sixties and early seventies to grow demoralized and begin to analyze what had gone wrong.

Tony Vaux, one such worker who poured out his doubts in a book titled *The Selfish Altruist*, worked for Oxfam for twenty-seven years. His first road-to-Damascus moment came in university, when he was making the rounds among his fellow students, asking them to donate money for charity. Usually people were polite, but one languid boy ordered him scornfully to get out of his room. Vaux was so startled that he still remembered the moment vividly thirty years later—the bright light coming through the window, the boy lounging over tea with a friend. Vaux did not think that the languid boy was rude, but that he had detected in Vaux a kind of altruistic dilettantism—he, Vaux, was just a student engaged in a pointless conscience-salving exercise—and had correctly concluded that he was not worth his money. Vaux realized that it was not enough to make a vague gesture in the direction of the poor: he must do charity seriously or not at all.

After university he went to work for Oxfam, but at the end of his career he still felt that he and his colleagues did not morally measure up. Selfishly in love with their own ideas and sense of mission, they failed to really *see* the people they were trying to help: they perceived them as hungry or wounded bodies, innocent victims, not as striving humans with political and economic goals that might be either palatable or pernicious. "In order to understand the person in need and his or her full social, economic and political context, we need to obliterate our own self," he wrote.

He was dismayed by the self-regard he saw in his fellow workers: he had gone into aid work believing it to be the antidote to selfishness and ego, but he found that it could be just the opposite. "There is a lot of 'masculinity' in emergency work," he wrote. "The business of 'saving lives', especially in a war zone, has a great deal of attraction for a man, and relief workers often talk of an adrenalin surge when the action gets tough, especially when they are living in danger. Some become addicted to it and are listless without the excitement. An African woman recently told me how appalled she was, after the Rwanda genocide, to find Western aid workers yearning for more and more dire events so that they could prove their prowess." The impulse to become an aid worker allaying the pain of war was not, then, so different from the impulse to become a soldier inflicting pain. For young people of a certain political temper, aid work was what battle used to be—a field of glory.

Several books were published around the same time as Vaux's—most concerned less than he was with the tainted motives of the humanitarians, and more with the ineffectiveness or harmfulness of their work. The authors knew that humanitarian aid could prolong conflicts, thus possibly killing as many people as it saved—that the food the aid workers provided could free up resources for weapons, or be exchanged directly for them on the black market. Michael Maren in his book *The Road to Hell* described how food aid destroyed local markets and forced farmers out of business. The food appeared to benefit donor farmers from the First World, who dumped their excess and received tax benefits, more than it did the recipients. Most NGOs did little to investigate whether their aid was doing any good, and even when they understood that they were actually causing harm, some seemed not to care, and continued to collect government contracts and donor money. Alex de Waal argued in *Famine Crimes* that international relief NGOs, by assuming ownership of hunger, relieved national governments of responsibility for famine prevention. This undermined political attempts by citizens to hold their governments accountable, thus perpetuating the lack of accountability that led to famines in the first place. Moreover, NGOs were themselves unaccountable, to anything but the market for publicity and donations—a market that seemed to take little notice of whether the NGOs vying for attention and money did any good at all. David Rieff, in his book *A Bed for the Night,* maintained that humanitarianism was often a new form of colonialism—a new form of control, only nominally for the benefit of the targeted populations. NGOs were apt, like colonizers, to believe that, because their intentions were good, their institutional interests should be promoted, their methods unquestioned, their results unscrutinized.

Rieff felt that, overall, development aid was a failure, and it required either hypocrisy or self-delusion to believe otherwise. "The truth is, anyone who is not disillusioned has not heard the bad news," he wrote. "Is optimism really the only legitimate moral stance?" But he could not bring himself to denounce aid workers completely.

"They are the last of the just, these humanitarians," he concluded. "There is nothing small or insufficient about what they do, except, that is, in the tragic human sense that all effort is insufficient, all glory transient, all solutions inadequate to the challenge, all aid insufficient to the need."

Rieff was not alone in this. At the same time that critics pointed out the problems with humanitarian aid, they for the most part clung to the possibility that with better understanding and purer motivations, with less ideology and more economics, it might someday be done better. Doing nothing at all did not seem like a good option. However much postcolonial condescension and racism and machismo there might be mixed up in an aid worker's urge to help suffering foreigners, that seemed less awful than isolation and unrepentant selfishness. Helping was complicated and easy to mess up—that much was now obvious. But this didn't mean it was okay not to try.

Thirty-six years earlier, Rieff's father, Philip Rieff, had published *The Triumph of the Therapeutic*, in which he bemoaned the advent of "psychological man"—the new twentieth-century Everyman who had ceased to worry about morals because his only orthodoxy was to live a fulfilled and healthy life. This horror came about, Rieff believed, as a result of distortions of Freud's legacy that sought to make a religion out of freedom and impulse. (Freud himself had been resigned to a permanent truce between the individual's desire and the rules of the collective: without such a truce, he believed, no civilization was possible.) But Philip Rieff, for all his pessimism, failed to anticipate how much more complex and tangled the critique of selflessness would become than it seemed in 1966: how the precepts of morality would be turned against themselves; how selfless people would come to seem not just old-fashioned and repressed, but vain, twisted, and vengeful, even dangerous. Philip Rieff mourned the abdication of the cultural elite from their age-old moral duty, to exemplify and lead the masses; David Rieff saw that there was still a moral elite, but that they were doing terrible damage.

David Rieff's tone in *A Bed for the Night* is similar to his father's—

the same hectoring combined with resignation—but his message is ambivalent and contradictory. Feeling as concerned about the wounds of foreigners as one is concerned about one's countrymen is "ahuman" and unnatural; but at the same time "no decent person" could fail to become more involved in foreign suffering than merely by giving money to humanitarian causes. Trying to help is at best useless and at worst damaging; but to stop trying to help is to give up on humanity. Humanitarians are condescending hypocrites, but they are the best of us.

So is helping a pernicious disease or not? Even considered in the simpler context of alcohol, the question is complicated. While Al-Anon and its descendants spread the idea that devoting yourself to helping someone in the wrong way can be crippling for both the helper and his victim, AA spread the idea that trying to help someone was the best way to help yourself. Bill Wilson quickly realized that the only way he was going to stay sober was to find other alcoholics to work on: he needed them as desperately as they needed him—thus the AA method of meetings and sponsorships. So what was the difference between Lois's helping, which didn't work, and Bill's helping, which did? Why was one a disease and the other the road to health? The difference seems to be the difference between helping from above and helping someone like yourself—between telling someone what to do and telling someone what you've done. What is a blessing coming from a sinner is malignant coming from a saint.

The logic of codependency suggests that helping is often a disease, because the one who helps is not free. She may believe that she chose to become a therapist, say, because she liked the work, but in fact she *needed* to do the work, had no choice but to do some work of that sort, because she could not see people in trouble without feeling obliged to help them. But then the question becomes: Is she wrong to feel that way? When she feels responsible for helping other people, is she making a mistake? Anyone who acknowledges the force of morality at all feels bound to do *something*. A person who understood herself to be freely choosing a moral life as just one option among others, with no obligation involved—who might with the same sense of freedom have chosen to spend her life throwing pebbles into a bucket—would not be more free but more confused. A person who feels herself wholly unfettered, unbound by duties of any kind, is not free, but a sociopath. And it's not only do-gooders and codependents who crave duty: duty gives meaning and structure to a life. Without it, there can be no home—only the aimless freedom of a tourist.

Moral intuitions, like all intuitions, come from somewhere. Suppose a person grows up feeling responsible for helping others because her good parent taught her to do so. What is the difference between a sense of duty that comes from a good parent and a sense of duty that comes from a bad parent? Is one less free or true than the other? Perhaps evil in sublethal quantities begets its own cure, as antibodies are produced by an injection of poison.

ONE OF THOSE GOD THINGS

After the terrible months in Senegal, Kimberly Brown-Whale was sent by the bishop to be the pastor of a church in Essex, Maryland. Essex was an unbeautiful sprawl across the Back River from the east side of Baltimore. Many of the storefronts on Eastern Avenue, the main drag, were boarded up; among those that were not, there were bars, and bail-bond outfits, and pawnshops, and used-car dealers. But the church was a big white clapboard building, a hundred years old, and this long history, and the parish's sense of itself as a suburb of respectable working people, rather than a place where homeless men froze to death behind the shopping center, turned out to be a problem.

The congregation was divided. There was a traditional United Methodist service early on Sunday mornings, with a choir and an organ, and later there was the contemporary service, with recorded popular music and DVDs and PowerPoint. This division was not without animosity. The older members disliked the contemporary service—they felt it wasn't really church—and they were alarmed to see, year by year, their numbers growing fewer, and the contemporary service growing more populous.

Kimberly had a lot of nervous energy. It was hard for her to sit still. She talked a blue streak. She had a loud and hearty laugh, and she laughed a lot. In church, she was always touching and hugging people, and when music played she swayed and clapped with vigor.

She was the first woman pastor the church had ever had, and some people weren't pleased about it. There were nasty notes dropped in the collection plate or on the pulpit. There were letters sent. There were people who told her to her face that they didn't want her there and they were going to ask the bishop to remove her. But in every church she ever worked in she had been the first woman pastor, so she was used to that. She thought: Can I love them into giving me a chance? Some people left because she was a woman, and other people were annoyed that those people had left and blamed her for it. But she didn't feel too bad about that—she couldn't change her plumbing, she said, and she hadn't asked to work in this church, the bishop had sent her. Besides, conflict wasn't always a bad thing. The church wasn't a social club, it had a mission to win people for Christ, and it was her job to push that mission forward. Doing that was usually uncomfortable, but if she was just a people pleaser, she wasn't doing her job.

She loved the work. She loved officiating at weddings, and even funerals, though the funerals got harder as she stayed longer in the parish and began herself to grieve for the dead. She felt it a privilege to be taken into a family at such profound and intimate moments. Even on ordinary days, every time she entered the church she felt lifted up.

She was always sending out little notes or birthday cards or calling people on the phone; if she hadn't seen someone lately, she would be in touch to find out if he was all right; if someone had asked her about a problem, she would ask him about it. And every now and again she would find that she had called someone just when he most needed it, or said hello to a person whose marriage was falling apart, or sent a birthday card when nobody else had mentioned the birthday. There were a lot of lonely people in her church; maybe they knew some colleagues at work, but they didn't have a family or anyone close, and she felt very grateful for those lucky moments, and believed that God had kicked her in the seat on those days so she would know what to do and when to do it. She couldn't always solve a person's problem, of course, but she could tell him, I am your sister in Christ, and you do not have to bear this burden alone.

She had learned over the years to listen closely, because often the problem that a person brought to her was not the real problem. A person might talk about unemployment, or problems at work, or difficulties in a marriage, when the real problem was alcohol or drugs.

Once, a young family came to her in despair; they had just bought a house, they had had three young kids one after the other, and they were struggling with money problems. She and a few other church members collected money for a fund and paid several of the couple's mortgage payments without telling them. Later, it turned out that the husband was addicted to calling sex telephone lines, and that this—not the house or the three young kids—was the reason they never had any money.

Some of her colleagues felt that too much emotion, too much empathy, was not a good thing in a pastor—it could cloud the judgment, or lead to burnout—but she didn't agree. She couldn't help herself, in fact: detachment wasn't in her nature. If someone told her a story about his life that was so awful it made her cry, she didn't think that was a problem; it showed him she could feel how bad it was. And when someone she knew was betrayed—infidelity in particular horrified her, she couldn't understand it at all, and she saw how it destroyed people—she would feel hurt and angry, too. She grew to love many of her parishioners, and she told them, I love you. A member of her church who was a pastor's child told her he had never heard a pastor say that before. The more she loved, the more she felt capable of loving; she felt that she was surrounded by people to whom she was connected by bonds of love, and that, just as she would share their burdens with them, they would share her burdens with her, and catch her if she fell.

It wasn't just comfort she was offering. Loneliness and unhappiness were bad, but there were worse things. Sin was worse; living a good life wasn't just about feeling happy. So, when she talked to her parishioners, she tried to hold them to the standard of their best selves. That was a more uncomfortable thing to do than just listening, but she believed that if someone could feel that she was saying what she was saying out of love, and that no matter what he did she wouldn't love him any less, then he would listen. If someone was being unfaithful to his spouse, or drinking too much, she felt that it was her job to help him stop. Sometimes a person would tell her it was none of her business, and sometimes her asking him about it caused him to dislike her. This made her sad, because she liked to be liked, but she knew that she had to push people, and that things weren't always going to turn out well. She knew that some pastors needed to be loved by everyone; those pastors were just place markers—you couldn't get anything done if you felt that way.

She didn't think that she, as a pastor, was on any kind of higher plane, spiritually speaking. She was a sinner like everyone else, and she needed a savior just as badly. But for her there was a witness factor: if she didn't act right, people would see that and think, Well, I certainly don't need to worry about anything outside my own family if she doesn't; or, What is the good of being a Christian if even a pastor behaves no better than I do? And maybe she might have a good reason to be short-tempered one day, and maybe there was a good reason why she gave a boring sermon another day, but nobody else would know that—people would only see that she was doing a lousy job for God, and draw their own conclusions.

Once, a girl in her church, barely in high school, got pregnant and decided to keep the baby. The girl's mother threw her out of the house, and until the father's family stepped in sometime later, Kimberly told the girl she was going to be all right and helped her out with various things that she needed. This was not appreciated by the girl's mother, who felt that Kimberly was interfering, and the mother ended up joining another church; this in turn created resentment among church members who liked the mother and felt that Kimberly should not have offended her.

Kimberly found the whole thing bewildering. How could a parent just dispose of a child, throw her away like a piece of trash, especially one still so young and so much in need? It was something you just didn't do. She didn't dislike the mother for it—she never disliked people—but she struggled to understand. She knew that the mother had been a single parent herself, so perhaps her rage and disappointment were greater because she knew how difficult the daughter's life would be, but that still didn't justify her throwing her daughter out of the house. Kimberly decided that there must be something about the situation that she wasn't aware of, some missing key or piece of information that would explain how a mother could reject her daughter in this way. Then the situation repeated itself sometime later, with a different mother and a different but also very young pregnant daughter, both regular churchgoers, and Kimberly was confounded all over again. The daughter was sad and lost, and took to calling Kimberly to ask if she could come over, because she was lonely and just needed to talk to a mother, any mother. Kimberly said to herself, I don't get it, I don't get it, I just don't get it at all.

She wanted to do big things. God was big and He did big things. She was not just serving the church, or the people in the church: she was serving God, and that meant she had to push herself as hard as she could; though, at the same time, she could not think too much about the full size and weight of that responsibility because it would paralyze her. How could anything she did be good enough for God? She also knew that she needed to restrain herself from becoming too exacting or energetic, for fear of exhausting her congregants. If word got around that she would wring you dry because she thought that everybody should give their best to God, then no one would want to work with her and she could do nothing.

Besides services, there was a lot going on in her church. In the evenings there were classes for adults: Bible study or book groups that read religious books by contemporary authors or a popular book from which spiritual themes could be extracted. Sometimes there were more practical classes—on personal finance, on disciplining small children. And then there were the meetings that took place in the church: there were AA and NA, and Boy Scouts and Girl Scouts, which required background checks and fingerprinting of all the adults involved. There was a day-care center during the day and a driving school at night. There were men's and women's ministry groups that discussed problems with family and work.

These things were all very well, but they were only helping certain sorts of people. There were other people who needed more who were not being helped. So Kimberly started a food pantry, and persuaded all kinds of places to give her food to stock it, and soon she was taking in ten to fifteen thousand pounds of food a month, sorting it, storing it, dividing it up into allotments that were the right size for a family. She distributed toiletries and gave away secondhand coats and blankets and tents and tarps for the homeless people who were sleeping outside. Every month she asked herself whether she had the money to keep the food pantry going, whether people would keep donating even though the economy was terrible and people were anxious.

There was a deserted lot next to the church filled with old, broken playground equipment. She hauled off the junk and set up raised beds and planted vegetables and fruit trees—pears and peaches and apples. It made her happy—it felt good to put her hands in the soil and grow something. She thought how wonderful it would be to have fresh, homegrown vegetables and fruit for the food pantry. But then the fruit from the fruit trees was stolen. This wounded her at first—she felt almost maternal toward those fruit trees—but then she figured that anyone who would steal fruit probably needed it more than she did.

She started a hot-food ministry—she thought "soup kitchen" sounded depressing—Wednesdays at lunchtime, which she thought could serve as a gathering place, fulfilling a social need as well as a physical one. Since the church didn't have a budget for it, she raised as much money as she could and paid for the rest herself. She got to know the homeless people who showed up for this each week. Their lives were complicated, and she tried to help them. Most of them had mental or physical disabilities of some sort or another, which meant they always had prescriptions to fill but no money to fill them with. They needed bus fare to the shelter they were sleeping in. Knowing that some of them were addicts, she tried not to give out enough money to get them into trouble, but she didn't check up on people—

she took them at their word when they said they needed something. She knew that some of the time she was being lied to, and that always left her feeling compromised.

As she got to know the homeless men in the neighborhood, she realized they had nowhere to go. There was a shelter for women and children but not for them, and so every winter some of them froze to death. Every couple of weeks in the coldest months, it seemed, she would hear about another person who had died, someone she knew, someone she had cooked for and fed. She couldn't bear it, especially since the church had so much heated space that wasn't being used at night, with a kitchen and bathrooms too. She decided to try to turn the upstairs into a cold-weather shelter. There was considerable resistance to this idea. It involved alterations to the church building, and it meant that there would be homeless men in the church all night. People didn't want change—they wanted the church to remain the church of their childhood. People suspected she would be bussing in homeless people from Baltimore, even though she told them there were already plenty of homeless people right there in Essex.

People were worried about all kinds of things. What if the homeless people set fire to the church and burned it down? What if one of them got injured and sued? What if a homeless man attacked someone, or molested a Girl Scout or Boy Scout? Things got ugly. The people who didn't want a shelter began a movement to get rid of her. She told her congregation: This is your church. You have belonged to this church your whole lives, you have raised your children and your grandchildren here. If anyone has to go, it's going to be me.

Finally she suggested that instead of using the church as a shelter, they could use her home, the parsonage—she and her family would move out and live somewhere else. People didn't like this idea either—they wanted their pastor to live in the parsonage, not a bunch of homeless people—but this sounded less bad than having homeless people in the church, and eventually the congregation voted yes. A number of people threatened to leave, but in the end nobody did.

Kimberly and her husband, Richard, moved out, and the shelter moved in the next day. Moving out was easy because they owned almost nothing: every time they went on a mission they gave everything away, and when they got back, they borrowed things, or people gave them old stuff they didn't want anymore. Every now and then, usually on one of their wedding anniversaries, Kimberly would remark to Richard that they had been married for ten years, or twenty years, or twenty-five years, and had never owned a sofa. Someday, she told him, we will have a sofa of our very own. Then again, if God hadn't arranged for them to own a sofa by now, it was surely a sign that they didn't really need one.

When Kimberly was growing up there were sofas but not much God. Her parents told her they met at a church tea, but it was really a bar. Her father was from Oklahoma. He had finished up his military service in the war and come to Chicago to do graduate work in engineering at the university. Her mother, the youngest child of Czech immigrants, was working in the bar. They married and had five children; Kimberly was the youngest, born in 1955.

Kimberly's father became an aerospace engineer, and, partly because of the requirements of the profession but mostly because he wanted to, he moved constantly, all over the country, uprooting his family once, twice, three times a year so he could work in different places. He was always looking at real-estate ads from other states—Michigan, Arkansas, Illinois, California—thinking about where his next move was going to be. In those days, he was a drinker. The worst days of his drinking were when Kimberly was little. She said she didn't remember them, but there were times still when she was older when he would fall off the wagon and disappear for days, and when he got back, there would be fighting.

Her father eventually began going to AA and stopped drinking, but by that time Kimberly's two oldest brothers had started. By the time she was in high school, her oldest brother, David, was a junkie, always getting arrested, always in and out of jail; there were always policemen pounding on the door in the dead of night. He brought creepy friends to the house, and the creepy friends threatened and stole, and David threatened and stole. Her parents fought about what to do, but there was nothing to do. When Kimberly was in college, someone beat David up nearly to death, and shortly afterward he committed suicide. But he had been so nasty, so incapable of caring about anyone else or doing anything for anyone else, and his life had been so chaotic, just one piece of bad news after another, that his death seemed like just one more piece of bad news. She had seen it coming for so many years; things were never going to end well for him.

She loved her second brother, Tim. He was a drunk, too, but he was kind to his little sister. He was a hippie—he wandered around and met people and brought them home for a meal or a place to stay. Later on, he became homeless. He told Kimberly he wanted to start a sock ministry: people were always giving homeless people coats, but nobody ever thought to give them socks, and they needed socks. He ended up in Las Vegas, where there was free health care and abundant alcohol. Eventually, he got married and managed to start working again, but by then the drinking had destroyed his kidneys and his liver and his heart, and he died.

Despite, or perhaps because of, everything going on with her brothers, Kimberly developed what her father called a Pollyanna personality. She always thought that people were basically good, and that everything would work out for the best. Her father told her she didn't understand the world, and when she grew older she saw what he meant, but she didn't want to change. Before she went abroad on her missions for the church, she worried that seeing so much poverty and desperation—having to turn away people who asked for her help because there were just too many of them—would harden her heart, but it didn't.

She was a happy child, but she noticed suffering. She was always bringing home stray animals, to the disgust of her mother, who kept a clean house. She cried when she watched Jerry Lewis telethons for muscular dystrophy. She walked for miles on sponsored walks. She gave away her babysitting money to people she saw on the street. Her parents thought that was weird; she told them she loved giving stuff away. But she never connected any of these things to God until she was thirteen and living in Arkansas and a friend of hers brought her along to a Southern Baptist church in town. She had scarcely ever been to a church before, but the moment she walked in that day, she felt that she had come home. She thought: I need to find a way that I can always stay here.

It wasn't a small church dominated by families, in which a girl alone would have been conspicuous; it was a big church, well organized, with a youth choir and a youth fellowship and programs for little kids. Soon she was going twice a day. Neither of her parents was religious, and they worried that she was becoming a nut, or that the church was some kind of cult. Her mother asked her if she didn't think she was becoming rather fanatical; Kimberly told her she felt this was what God wanted her to do. She never tried to get anyone in her family to come with her to church, and nobody ever did. In college, she majored in sociology and religious studies and worked in kids' programs at a couple of churches nearby. One day, the pastor of one of these churches asked her if she'd ever considered becoming an ordained minister. She was astonished—she hadn't known that a woman could be a pastor. But the moment the thought was presented to her, she realized that this was what she had been looking for: a way to live in the church for the rest of her life.

In her last year at seminary, she met Richard. Richard came from a family that was as difficult as Kimberly's but for different reasons. He grew up in southwest Baltimore, a pretty rough part of town. His father worked for the army at Fort Meade; he was a disciplinarian of the old school. He expected absolute obedience, and if he didn't get it, he would become very angry. When he came home from work, dinner had to be ready. When he had finished eating, he would get up and watch TV until he went to bed. The children were not allowed to speak at table or have more to eat until he left. They went to church a few times when Richard was a child, on Christmas and Easter, but then, one year, someone stole the battery out of the family car the night before Easter, and Richard's father took that as a sign and never went to church again. The best memory Richard had of his father was of the two of them going out into the rain during Hurricane Agnes in 1972 to help flooded-out families at the bottom of their hill, but that was about it.

Richard thought that neither of his parents had any feelings for their children. When he went to college, he moved five miles away to live nearer campus; for his mother, he was gone. She never contacted him. Later, when he acquired the language to think about this, he decided that his mother lacked human empathy. Perhaps because of the way his parents were with him, or perhaps because he was more like them than he wanted to be, Richard was so reserved he was almost mute. He seemed hard and standoffish and was blunt to the point of rudeness. He saw everything in terms of right and wrong, with no gray area in between. Kimberly's mother so disliked him when they met that at first she refused to come to the wedding. Kimberly had a lot of work to do to help Richard become sociable enough to be a pastor.

Their children came to them in different ways. They adopted their eldest child, a biracial girl named Sarah, from foster care in Maryland when she was six months old. After Sarah they had a biological baby, Peter. Sometime later, when they were posted as missionaries in Grenada, they took in Cassie as a foster baby, and when it became clear that there was no home for her to go back to, they adopted her. Cassie had ended up in foster care after her uncle smashed a liquor bottle onto her head when she was an infant. The blow injured her brain; she spent several months in the hospital, and she was left developmentally disabled.

Kimberly hadn't thought any of this out beforehand—she hadn't planned to adopt, it just sort of happened that way. A lot of people thought they were wrong to adopt a biracial child, and doubly so to adopt a foreign black child and take her away from her birth country, but all that never made any sense to Kimberly. She didn't care what color the children were, as long as they needed a home. When she and Richard were on missions abroad, a lot of people, seeing that they had adopted black children already, asked them to take their children, too, and give them a better life, but Kimberly told them no. She didn't want to take children away from their parents; besides, three was enough, she felt. They weren't an orphanage—they were a family.

Early on, not long after they married, Kimberly and Richard applied for a mission and were posted to Anguilla. This was not the sort of posting they had imagined. They had wanted to see another part of God's church, to see the larger world. But Anguilla was sixteen miles long and three miles wide and contained six thousand people: their world had not expanded but drastically shrunk. Over time, however, they came to love that part of it, the intimacy of the place—the fact that they knew everyone and everyone knew them and it was impossible to take a step outside or transact any business without an extended conversation. On Sundays, they would drive around the island, giving sermons in several different churches. It was so different from America, where the church was marginal: in Anguilla, the church was the center of things, and the place was so small that, almost without effort, she found herself involved in everyone's lives.

They had moved to the island with two toddlers, and this presented some difficulties. Peter was always sick, and when he wasn't sick he was injured, which made it difficult to live in a place without much by way of medical care. Peter had been a failure-to-thrive baby to begin with—he wouldn't eat and had to be force-fed; as an infant he had septicemia, and later, when they were on the mission, he got staph infections and sprouted lesions all over his body. Kimberly was boiling the water and boiling his diapers and soaking greens in chlorine solution, but he got sick anyway. After Anguilla they were posted to another island, Grenada, where Peter fell into a drainage ditch and punctured his abdomen on a sewage pipe. He got stung by a bee and went into anaphylactic shock. Then Richard got sick—he had a stroke, and he got dengue fever. But they made it through.

After their posting in Grenada, they went back to the States so that Richard could get a Ph.D. that would qualify him to teach in a seminary abroad. They were originally supposed to go to Zimbabwe, but relations between the government and the church deteriorated, and they couldn't get a visa; suddenly they were told they were going to be posted to Mozambique instead. Because the posting was last minute, they boarded the plane not speaking a word of Portuguese.

It was then 1993, a year after a fifteen-year civil war had ended, and the country was in rough shape. It was difficult to figure out how to give, the need was so extreme. If Kimberly tried to give food to a child, or a bottle of water, a crowd could form with astonishing speed and violence. Richard was teaching liturgy at an ecumenical seminary outside the city. She was putting together theological texts for rural churches, working in a women's center, giving Bible-study classes, and teaching English.

During the war missionaries had been pulled out or thrown out, and there were places it hadn't been possible to visit since before the fighting. Kimberly didn't know when she arrived in the country how they would be received in those places: would people feel that the church had abandoned them? But she found that in many places people had been waiting, as if they'd known that one day the church would come back. From a missionary point of view, Mozambique was exhilarating. People flocked to church in the thousands, young people, old people, everyone. Kimberly felt as she had never felt in America—that you could offer God's word and people couldn't get enough of it. People in the capital came to churches, and people in the villages held services under trees. It was as if, after decades of war and misery and repression, a kind of spiritual feeling was bursting out and looking for God. She thought: I will probably never see anything like this again.

Not everyone who became a Christian gave up traditional beliefs. But Richard and Kimberly, like many other missionaries at the time, had come to feel that missionaries of the past had been too severe about that: it was better to welcome people into the church and muddle through with a mixture of beliefs than to accept as converts only those who were prepared to reject everything they had ever known. There were ways to make the beliefs fit. A belief that ancestors watched over you, for instance—that fit well with a belief in saints. Of course, some customs presented more of a problem. Polygamy, for instance, was awkward. But what could you do if the marriages had already taken place? You accepted it and hoped for the best.

Despite all the enthusiasm for the church, often people could not understand what Kimberly was doing there. They wanted to know what her motives really were. What did she want from them? Was she going to take something away from them, and if so, what would it be? They saw that Sarah and Cassie were not her biological children, and they assumed that she must have taken them on as servants. When she explained that they were not servants but members of her family, people were baffled.

One day, Richard was attacked on the street and left for dead. The attacker stole his money and his clothes and choked him until he fell. The attack took place on a busy street during the day, but nobody came to help. It was this that made Richard angry afterward—that nobody helped seemed to him even worse than being attacked.

Another day, the whole family drove north out of Maputo in a truck. Kimberly had put together some theological materials, and they were setting out to meet unofficial pastors in rural areas, give them the literature, and organize professional training. Their first stop was a Methodist hospital; they left their truck in the locked hospital lot and had dinner with a local missionary, and when they returned the truck had been broken into and everything stolen—not only their clothes but also all the religious literature that Kimberly had prepared. The police told them that their best bet would be to go to the market in the neighboring town, because it was likely that their things would be on sale there and they could buy them back for not too much money. They drove to the town, and Richard walked off into the market. But their arrival had attracted attention—it was a small town, and they were conspicuous. A large crowd soon gathered around the truck, and when the crowd spotted Cassie, who was then about four, sitting in the back of the truck, they started to point at her and shout. It took Kimberly some time to understand what they were shouting, by which time the crowd had grown larger and more threatening—several hundred people.

They were shouting that Kimberly was Chinese and had kidnapped a Mozambican child, Cassie, to sell her for her organs. They were shouting that they were going to take the child back. People started pounding on the truck, and tearing at the flimsy aluminum shell over the truck bed, under which the three children were cowering, Sarah and Peter protecting Cassie with their bodies. The shell had already been ripped open during the robbery, and started to give way. When Richard returned, he waved Cassie's passport at the crowd to show that she was American, but the crowd shouted that the passport was fake and kept pounding on the truck and trying to grab her. Finally, the police arrived and shot into the air to clear enough space for the family to drive away.

At around the same time, they discovered that Peter had an abnormality in his heart that required treatment, so the church granted Kimberly medical leave to take Peter and Cassie home and assess the damage. Kimberly's parents begged her not to return, and even some people in the church urged them to stay, but in the end they decided to go back. They didn't want to abandon the work they had begun, and they didn't want it to be said that missionaries had been attacked in Mozambique and had to be pulled out; that would make it very difficult to replace them, just when the church was expanding so thrillingly and needed help the most.

Kimberly said: Life is risky. You can get attacked at home, too. You can get sick at home, too. She felt that they had made a promise, and she wanted to keep it. She felt that they were doing good work and she wanted to see it out. People said to her that they could never do what she was doing, serving as a missionary in a dangerous place like Mozambique, but she thought that was nonsense—there was nothing special about her. She said to them, Why not? You pack up some stuff and you go and see, How can I be helpful? We can do more than we think we can. Give it a try!

In 2006, Kimberly and Richard were posted to Senegal. Senegal was truly a mission. The country was nearly 100 percent Muslim, and there was no Methodist church; the outpost there was just a tiny adjunct of the Methodist conference in Ivory Coast. But Dakar, the capital, was the kind of place that people migrated to, and from which people tried to get to Europe, and some of these people were Methodists who needed a pastor, so Kimberly and Richard were there to plant a church for them. The church had set up some health clinics, handing out feeding supplements for babies and testing people for diabetes; they had been distributing microloans. The church had not had much success with conversions, but even when it did, it was complicated. When a Senegalese became a Christian, he exiled himself from his entire world: Muslims would often refuse to do business with converts, and so the convert, and by extension his whole family, was likely to starve. In order to help new converts out and prevent this sort of disaster, the church in the past had taken to hiring them for church jobs. Kimberly could see the reason for this, but at the same time it made her uncomfortable—it felt distressingly close to paying for conversions.

The church sent them to live in a house in a village on the coast. Food was a problem. Bread was subsidized by the government, so they could always buy that, but finding other food was difficult. A man might wander by with six potatoes, and she would want to buy them, but she worried that if she bought them all the next person would go hungry, so she would buy only two or three.

Because the place they were living was conservative regarding women, there wasn't much that Kimberly could do there. Richard could travel around and preach and baptize, but no one was going to accept a woman as a pastor. It was even harder for Cassie. Sarah and Peter were grown up now and living on their own, but Cassie went to Senegal with her parents, and where they were living, girls and young women stayed inside the house. Because Cassie was a young woman and American, and also because of her intellectual disability, any time she left the house people crowded around her and stared; after a while, she stopped going outside. She never spoke to anyone other than her parents. Kimberly felt that it was awful and unnatural to keep an eighteen-year-old indoors all the time, but going out was worse.

Cassie was trying to finish up her senior year of high school online. She was naturally a sunny, smiley sort of child, but as the months passed she became sad. Kimberly hated to see Cassie so miserable, but at the same time it seemed terrible to her to break a commitment to the church, and she hoped they could muddle through. Things would get better somehow, she thought—they always had before. But things did not get better, and Kimberly grew more worried and more confused and didn't know what to do. She began to fear that the experience would damage Cassie for life. She felt that her devotion to the church was absolute—as absolute as her devotion to Cassie—but the church could draw on many people for a mission in Senegal, whereas Cassie had only one mother.

After a long time, she called the bishop and asked if she could come home. In a strange stroke of fortune—"just one of those God things," Kimberly thought, as she often did—shortly before she decided that she couldn't keep Cassie in Senegal any longer, the pastor of the church in Essex suddenly dropped dead, and the bishop offered the position to her. Very soon after that, another position turned out to be open in the same area that was suitable for Richard.

It was all so easy that she felt it was meant to be. She knew there had to have been a reason for the terrible time in Senegal, and there had to have been a reason for that terrible time to end, but what those reasons were she would never know.

You never knew what God's reasons were for doing the things He did, and you never knew how children were going to turn out and whether anything you said to them would stick. Cassie got a job as a lunch lady at the elementary school down the street in Essex, and then she met a man online. He was a white man, older than she was, who lived in East St. Louis, but he was developmentally disabled like her—he had also incurred a brain injury as a child, from being pushed down a flight of stairs—and she felt she had found a kindred spirit. They corresponded for a while and she decided to go out there to meet him. Kimberly was very reluctant to let her go—she worried that the man had bad intentions and would take advantage of her, and she didn't know anyone in St. Louis who could check up on her, but she knew that she could not keep Cassie prisoner, however vulnerable she was.

Cassie ended up moving in with this man. He lived in a very poor neighborhood in which a white man living with a black woman was unusual and met with some resistance. He was on disability, and his whole family was subsisting on government assistance of one kind or another, but Cassie went out and found herself a full-time job with benefits, in the bakery section of a supermarket. They weren't married, and this made Kimberly sad, but overall the situation had turned out so much better than she had feared that she felt she ought to be grateful.

Peter had started riding horses in Mozambique, and when he was older he became a nationally ranked show jumper. He grew too tall to be a flat jockey, so he became a steeplechase jockey, and worked for a fox-hunting family's barn for a while; finally, he became an exercise rider and a horse trainer at the Laurel Park racetrack, southeast of Baltimore. When he wasn't riding horses he was racing dirt bikes. Kimberly worried that he was an adrenaline junkie and that all these very dangerous things he was doing would lead to disaster; indeed, he did get in a couple of very serious accidents, but when the bones healed he went right back to the track. He never went to church, which hurt, but he was always willing to help out in the food pantry, and amid all the drinking and drugs and gambling and corruption at the track he had stayed clean and honorable; even if he wasn't a churchgoer, she felt, the teachings had rubbed off on him and made him a good person.

Sarah graduated from college and took a job with Bread for the World, a Christian lobbying group on hunger issues, where she ended up planning fund-raisers. It always seemed odd to Kimberly that you raised money for hunger relief by throwing a big dinner, but Sarah told her this was the way things worked, and she accepted that. Later on, Sarah went to culinary school and married a lawyer. They settled in Denver, and Sarah became an event planner. They moved into a high-rise building downtown, with valet parking and a concierge. She and her husband were foodies, and they spent a lot of money going out to restaurants. To Kimberly, all this was pretty unfamiliar. She couldn't imagine spending more than fifteen or twenty dollars on a meal, at most—it was just a meal, and in four or five hours you were going to need another one. But Sarah was her only child who still went regularly to church, and she was grateful for that.

One day, when Kimberly had been at the Essex church a year or two, she saw a news report about a local young woman who needed a kidney transplant. Her assistant at her previous church had had a kidney transplant, and so she knew how awful kidney disease was and what a blessing a successful transplant could be, so when she heard the report, she thought, Bless her heart, she is a young person, and a transplant would make such a difference to her. There was a number to call to arrange for a test to see if you were a match, and she thought, Why not? and called it right away.

It turned out she was a bad match for the young woman, but the nurse asked her if she would be willing to donate her kidney to someone else. Since she hadn't known the young woman anyway, she thought, Why wouldn't I give to a different stranger? So she said sure. They asked her if she needed to know who the recipient would be, she said no. She thought it would be neat to meet the person, but only if they wanted to. Then she thought about her children, but since two out of three were adopted, she wasn't any more likely to match them than anybody else. She told her husband that if one of the kids needed a kidney it'd be his turn. She thought: For two or three days of discomfort, who can't do that? I mean, if you're sitting around with a good kidney you're not using, why can't someone else have it?

Part of what appealed to her about donating a kidney was the concreteness of it: she knew that she was helping someone, and she knew exactly how. She thought of herself as being in the helping business, but so much of her work was just talk, talk, talk—her sermons on Sundays, funerals, weddings, visits with parishioners in the hospital—that she often wondered whether anything she did made any difference. When she got home, there were always people sitting on her front steps, asking for food, or money for transport, or a room for the night. She loved that people still thought to come to the church for help, but if she didn't know a person, she worried that if she gave him money he'd spend it on drink or drugs, or that he'd become dependent on her.

And sometimes things went wrong. Like the time she and a group of parishioners cooked up a big meal for a family shelter, but when they arrived there was no one there to eat it, because the shelter had forgotten to put it on the schedule. Or the time they asked seventy kids in a shelter what they wanted for Christmas, and parishioners spent a lot of money buying them those things, and then the presents were stolen. Helping was difficult and complicated. That didn't mean she was not obliged to keep trying to be helpful—she was—but it was hard. Donating a kidney was different She knew it was going to help someone for sure, and that felt like a very precious and rare opportunity. Besides, she was always so frantic and run off her feet that the idea of accomplishing something while asleep, followed by several days of enforced passivity, seemed rather attractive.

Her recovery from the surgery was uneventful. She didn't use the morphine drip in the hospital (she claimed she kept losing the button, though it was attached to her bed), so the nurses sent her home with Tylenol, which she didn't use, either. The hospital gave her a potted plant as a thank-you present, which she named her transplant. She was back at work in a week. "Gosh," she said. "I've had flus that made me feel worse."

KIDNEYS

Before Kimberly Brown-Whale was permitted to donate one of her kidneys, she was required to undergo a psychological examination, in order that the hospital could satisfy itself that she had not been coerced into donating and was not crazy. This hurdle was not a difficult one for her; the examining psychologist seemed to find it understandable that a pastor would be generous in this way. But her experience was unusual. Doctors are often disturbed by the idea of performing surgery on a healthy person who can't benefit from it, can only suffer harm—it seems to violate the Hippocratic oath. Some transplant programs refuse to deal with altruistic donors at all. When kidney donations to nonrelatives first became possible, many people, particularly doctors, found this strange new way to be a do-gooder—the giving of an organ to a stranger, called "altruistic donation"—bizarre, even repellent.

These days kidneys are often extracted laparoscopically, which leaves only tiny scars. A donor usually feels normal again in two to four weeks, the remaining kidney growing to compensate. And the risk of complications is low. If a person gets kidney disease, it affects both kidneys, so as far as that goes a donor is not giving away his spare (though a spare kidney is useful if the other is damaged in an accident, say, or if a person develops kidney cancer). Still, the carnality of it, the violation of the body, stops people. The moral logic of donation seems, to some, inhumanly rational—suicidally so: after all, if we are going to start thinking of bodies as repositories of spare parts for other people, why stop at a kidney? Why not donate all our organs and save several lives? Wasn't that where you ended up when you started thinking of bodies, and their owners, as tools for the common good?

After Kimberly got out of the hospital, her life went on as it had before. She had no contact with the man who had received her kidney—she never even knew his name, although the hospital told her the transplant had been a success and he was doing well. In its simplicity and brevity, her experience was also unusual. When Paul Wagner set out to donate one of his kidneys to a stranger at around the same time and not far away, his experience was completely different.

Paul was a purchasing manager at Peirce-Phelps, in Philadelphia, a wholesale distributor of heating and air-conditioning products. He was forty years old and lived with his partner, Aaron, in a small apartment. His mother had died six months before, in her late fifties, of sarcoidosis. They had not had a good relationship—she'd had a heroin problem while he was growing up, and he attributed his sanity and his values to the school for troubled youths that he'd been placed in as a teenager—but her death had nonetheless affected him quite deeply.

Paul considered himself a "dry person"—curt, moody, sometimes rude. He believed that, to people who didn't know him, he came off as an unsentimental type, possibly even a bit mean, though in fact he was not like that at all. He owned two cats and two elderly cocker spaniels that he had rescued from a shelter. He ran the United Way fund-raising campaign at work for three years and organized food drives for local soup kitchens. He regarded these acts not as virtuous but as duties. He believed that if his needs were met and he found himself in possession of a surplus—of money or time or wherewithal—he was obliged to share it. Share it, not give it all away: he liked nice things, he wasn't going to become Amish. But it was very, very important to him that when he met his Maker (he didn't consider himself religious, but he did believe in God) he could say that he gave more than he took.

Before he was hired at Peirce-Phelps, Paul worked in a bank. He went from a job in a call center to managing a branch in just two years, but he quit because he believed that the incentive structure in the bank was unethical, rewarding him for steering customers to financial products that weren't in their best interest. As a young man, he had worked at a day-care center, but one day he heard an employee senior to him talk nastily about another employee, and he took it upon himself to inform the latter about the former. This intervention made everybody so uncomfortable that he was fired. From this, he concluded that it was sometimes best to mind his own business and not try to do God's work for Him.

It was the day before Thanksgiving, and Paul was on his lunch break, reading the paper. He noticed an article that described a website called MatchingDonors.com, where people who needed a kidney transplant could post a message describing themselves and their situation, perhaps appending a photograph. The hope was that a stranger would see the posting and be moved to donate. He typed the name of the website into his computer. He clicked on the "search patients" box, and typed in "Philadelphia." The first patient he saw was Gail Tomas. He enlarged her photograph on his screen so that he could examine every detail. She was sitting on stairs in what appeared to be her living room. She was a woman of mixed race in her late sixties. He stared at her, searching for clues to her personality in her hairstyle and how she wore makeup. He inspected the stairs behind her, trying to see how clean they were. Almost immediately, he felt that she was the one. He knew that his blood and her blood would match and that he would donate a kidney to her. There was no question of backing out: having seen her picture, he felt himself to be already involved. It was like seeing a car crash—if he didn't help, he thought, he would cheapen himself.

He went home and told his partner, "Aaron, there's this lady I read about that's going to die if she doesn't get a new kidney, and I've decided to give one to her." Aaron said no. Paul told him sorry, but he was going to do it anyway. He told his sister and she said, only half joking, "What if I need a kidney someday?" He thought that was selfish. He told her that she had a husband and two children and she could look to them, but this lady was going to die now. Talking to his father was more difficult. Some years before, his father's second wife had had kidney disease. Paul had offered to donate to her, but she and his father had felt that it was against their principles to ask so much of a person, even a son. So they refused his offer, and, waiting for a cadaver kidney, she died. Now his father got very quiet for a while, and then said he wished Paul wouldn't go through with it.

But once Paul had decided to donate, he felt as though he had a calling. He was not usually brave about medical procedures, but he breezed through all the tests. He was late for work almost every morning, but he was on time for every one of his hospital appointments. He wasn't anxious about pain or complications. For once in his life, he felt that God's instructions to him were absolutely clear. Besides all the tests, there were other hurdles to be overcome. The transplant surgeon was puzzled by Paul. He wasn't sure he was willing to do the surgery. They met and talked for more than an hour, and, near the end of the conversation, Paul was astonished to see that the surgeon was crying.

Paul assumed that he and Gail would not become friends after the surgery. He had given the matter some thought. How could they possibly have a healthy relationship? he reasoned. It would be bad for her to feel beholden to him, and it would be bad for him to have her believing that he was some kind of saint. The whole thing would just be way too freighted and creepy and was better avoided. Gail, however, had other ideas.

Gail Tomas was a retired opera singer who had performed all over Europe, after being discovered in a master class by Licia Albanese, the famous soprano. If Paul was dry, she was the opposite—vivacious, chatty, candidly emotional. She had been looking for a donor for about a year. None of her family members matched her blood type, and she hadn't wanted to ask friends, so her daughter signed her up on MatchingDonors. At first, there were a few obvious no-no's: A man wrote from India to say that he would get all his testing done locally if she would send him five thousand dollars. Then, she says, there was a woman from Texas who seemed legitimate and eager to help, and they corresponded for months, but it turned out that her son, who was seven feet tall, had outgrown his liver and needed a transplant himself; with all that going on, the woman disappeared. "It was like someone had taken you to the altar and then, all of a sudden, new scenery came down and you say, 'But I thought I was getting married,'" Gail says. "I thought, We'll never find another person, because how many people want to do this?"

Shortly before the surgery, Paul and Gail met for the first time. They were both at the hospital, getting tested. Paul had described himself as skinny, so Gail looked around the waiting room, identified the skinniest guy in it, sailed up, and introduced herself. For her, the meeting was wonderful: she felt that they'd known each other all their lives. Paul managed to be friendly, but he was all churned up. He didn't know what to make of this exuberant lady he was giving his kidney to; he couldn't figure out what emotions he should allow himself to experience. His mother had died less than a year before, and now here he was, potentially entangling himself with another very sick older woman, and what did that mean? Donating a kidney to find yourself a new mother—what could be more obviously twisted than that? He was also worried that he'd done a bad thing by allowing himself to meet Gail at all. It made him feel guilty. Did it diminish the value of his deed to accept her gratitude? Wouldn't he be a better person if he hadn't met her and had received no thanks? Had his donation now become just a matter of gratifying his ego? By the time he got home, he felt completely drained.

The surgery itself left him feeling battered and exhausted. Afterward, when he was sitting in his hospital bed, the phone rang. A woman on the other end, who had heard about him on the local news, told him that she hoped his remaining kidney would fail quickly and kill him, because her husband had been next in line to receive a kidney and he, Paul, had given his to someone else. Paul asked the hospital to turn his phone off after that, but then someone wrote an article about him in the Philadelphia *Daily News,* wondering whether it was fair for him to pick his recipient, choosing who lived and who died. He couldn't understand it—he had heard about a sick woman who lived near him, and he had helped her. How could that make people angry?

After he got home from the hospital, he started feeling very sad all the time. He admitted to himself that it was difficult to come down off the high of being a hero. Before the surgery, everyone he knew had made a big fuss about him; there had been a lot of hoopla at the hospital, attention from the local media. He had loved telling people that he was donating a kidney to a stranger, just to see their reactions. Now all that was over. Worse, Gail had suddenly stopped returning his phone calls. Was she angry with him? he wondered.

Looking for advice, he started posting on a website, Living Donors Online, and he discovered that many donors had to deal with peculiar emotions after surgery. He read about one case in which a woman had donated to her sister, but the kidney was rejected and her sister died; after that, the rest of the family stopped speaking to her. One spouse donated to the other; then the recipient spouse left the donor, perhaps because the burden of gratitude had left the marriage irredeemably distorted. That had happened quite a few times, it seemed.

Finally, worried, Paul started calling hospitals, and he found her. She'd been very sick and hadn't wanted to scare him, but now she was better, and she wanted Paul in her life. Still smarting, he wasn't sure. She invited him to her son's wedding. He declined, several times, until finally she got angry and yelled at him, and that, somehow, for Paul, made everything all right. If she could yell at him, it meant he was not always perfect in her eyes, and they could have a normal friendship. She wasn't his mother, he knew that; it would be fine. In fact, Gail did consider herself his mother, more or less. She wanted him at her house on holidays; she hounded him about smoking and taking his blood-pressure medication. But it was fine anyway.

t might seem that Paul Wagner's donation was quite complicated, but in fact, compared with what it would have been, say, twenty years earlier, it was not complicated at all. His experience was the result of four decades in which medicine and morality had transformed each other, with the consequence that a do-gooder act that had once looked obviously pathological had come to seem provisionally sane, and even good. But it was only in retrospect that this change appeared predictable.

In the early days of kidney transplants, in the late sixties and early seventies, doctors tended to see altruistic donation through the lens of psychoanalysis, and, viewed thus, it looked troubling indeed. Altruistic donors, some doctors felt, were "not to be trusted," "screwballs." "These people must be abnormal—to do such a thing," one transplant surgeon said. Donating an organ to a stranger was not just not admirable, doctors felt—it was perverse, it offended the conscience. It was against human nature. (The general public was much less suspicious—many people were even willing to entertain the idea of doing such a thing themselves, once the idea was presented to them.)

In 1967, a long-term study of living, unrelated kidney donors was initiated, with the aim of helping transplant centers form policies on these confounding individuals. The study subjected the donors to free-associative interviews, dream analyses, and Rorschach and Thematic Apperception tests. Published in 1971, it found evidence in the donors of primitive masochism, reaction formation against early sadism, homosexual conflict, pregnancy symbolism, and penis envy. But it noted that, in this, the donors were no different from the rest of mankind, and that, after the operation, each donor reported a deep feeling of increased self-esteem—a feeling "that he had done something wholesome and natural with no indication of regret." ("Only good thing I ever did," said one donor, who, according to the study, suffered from inadequate personality. "I'm better for it.")

Another paper reported: "The act of making such a gift becomes a transcendent experience, akin to a religious one. Many donors testify that giving an organ was the most important, meaningful, and satisfying act of their lives: one that increased their self-knowledge, enhanced their feeling of self-worth, gave them a sense of 'totality,' belief and commitment, and increased their sense of unity with the recipient, people in general and with humanity." A psychologist investigating the subject wrote: "The most puzzling aspect of our investigation has been the striking contrast between the naturalness, relative calm and equanimity of the volunteer donor, and the uncomfortableness of the transplant team." There were no reports of postoperative depression or physical ailments. These studies, however, didn't change anything.

Forty years ago, even donors who were family members were regarded warily. Beginning in the late sixties, two academics, Renée Fox and Judith Swazey, spent years observing transplant centers, and found that surgeons and psychiatrists went to heroic lengths to draw out the conflicts and ambivalence that they believed lay hidden beneath donors' supposed willingness to undergo surgery. If the potential donor's motivation appeared inadequately healthy, they turned him down. Billy Watson (a pseudonym), a ten-year-old boy, needed a kidney transplant in order to live, and his mother wanted to donate. But was Mrs. Watson's motivation acceptable or pathological? the doctors wondered. Mrs. Watson had nine other children—was she showing an unhealthy favoritism toward Billy by wanting to keep him alive, since the surgery would leave her temporarily unable to care properly for the others? And was this a normal family, psychologically? How stable was the Watson marriage? (After two months of debate, the doctors reluctantly decided to permit Mrs. Watson to donate.)

One man wanted to donate a kidney to his brother, but his wife opposed the idea; the renologist suspected that the man was motivated in part in order to break away from his domineering spouse, and rejected the man as a donor. Another case involved Susan

Thompson (also a pseudonym), a twenty-six-year-old unmarried woman. Her mother said that she wanted to save her daughter, but the transplant team noticed that, while undergoing testing, Mrs. Thompson developed gastrointestinal problems and heart palpitations. The team decided that, on an unconscious level, she didn't really want to give up her kidney, so they told her she was "not a good tissue match" and turned her down.

Doctors began to realize that to transplant an organ was to stir up a muck of emotions, with consequences that could not be predicted. Donation tended to bind the donor and the recipient together, sometimes with love, sometimes with guilt, or gratitude, or a feeling of physical union due to the presence of the organ of one in the other's body. The strength of these new bonds could weaken other bonds and leave families strained and distorted. If a person donated to a sibling, for instance, might he not become too close to that sibling, at the expense of his relationship with his spouse? One transplant physician believed that, after a sister donated to her brother, the sister "felt absolute control over her brother, as if she had castrated him." After the surgery, instead of going home to his wife and children, he moved into his sister's house to recover. Another man was so overcome by a feeling of obligation toward his donor sister that he couldn't stand to look at her. A son refused a kidney from his mother because, he told his surgeon, "she's devoured enough of me already."

The force of gratitude could be dreadful with the gift of an organ, when no thanks seemed adequate and reciprocation was impossible. There was, Fox and Swazey observed, following the French anthropologist Marcel Mauss, something tyrannical about a gift. "Why does the benefactor love the recipient more than the recipient loves the benefactor?" the bioethicist Leon Kass mused on the subject of transplants, alluding to a passage in Aristotle's *Nicomachean Ethics*. "Because the benefactor lives in the recipient, the way in which the poet lives in the poem."

Even in the case of cadaver donors, emotions shadowed the

transplant. In fact, the burden of gratitude could be even weightier when the donor was dead, particularly if, as was often the case, the donor was young, and the death was sudden and terrible. Donor families, appreciating the magnitude of their gift, sometimes felt that the recipient had become part of their family, someone they could love and also lay claim to. One father of a dead son said to the father of the girl who had received his boy's heart, "We've always wanted a little girl, so now we're going to have her and share her with you." Many people felt that, in some quasi-animistic way, the dead beloved survived in the body of the recipient. People cared deeply about what happened to the remains of their dead, even when those remains consisted only of ashes; how much more potent this caring became when the remains consisted, instead, of a pulsing kidney, or a beating heart.

All these strong, atavistic emotions made transplant teams uncomfortable, and, over time, protocols were developed to keep transplants anonymous and families apart. A regime of emotional hygiene was put in place. Perhaps in the future, it was thought, when transplants became more ordinary, these precautions would no longer be necessary. Perhaps this attachment to the organs of the dead would come to seem as strange as the belief that a person's hair cuttings or fingernail clippings could be used to place a curse on him. Perhaps the thought of an organ living by itself, separate from its owner, would no longer seem uncanny, Gothic, sinister, something out of Poe. And perhaps this change would also ease the reluctance that so many families felt toward donating the organs of a relative.

To some—to the ethicist Gilbert Meilaender, for instance—this prospect was feared as an encroaching spiritual callousness. To Meilaender, the reluctance that many felt about donating organs, even after death, was not selfishness or superstition but a sign that our sense of the body as something whole, something human, something sacred, had not yet withered. A society in which everyone in cheerful rationality signed his donor card without a qualm would be, to him, a horror. The giving of an organ, by the living or the dead, should not be purged of anguish.

These days, kidney donation to a relative, at least, is more commonplace, no longer grounds for suspicion. Twenty-five years ago, the philosopher Peter Singer was struck by an article about a woman who had donated one of her kidneys to save the life of her son. He felt that this was an extraordinary sacrifice, and he cited the story in one of his books as an example of extreme unselfishness. These days, a mother donating a kidney to save the life of her son would be ordinary; a mother who refused to do so would be more remarkable.

Over time, donations of organs to strangers have also become more normal. Some donors want to pick their recipient; other people feel that it's fairer, and a more elevated moral act, to donate anonymously, leaving it to the transplant center to assign their organ to the next person on the list. To some of these, picking a recipient seems like egotism—playing God by choosing who will live, and encouraging gratefulness by arranging for a relationship with the recipient. But in a certain literal sense, a nondirected donation is not altruistic in the way that picking a recipient is, because there is no *other* there. There is no human story, just a principle; the only thing visible to the donor is his own shining deed.

Much of this change, no doubt, is attributable to improvements in transplant technology: it's far safer and less painful now to donate a kidney than it used to be, and far more likely that the kidney will give the recipient many years of life. But it may be that at least some of this change is a change in moral expectations. Now it no longer seems quite so bizarre that a person would volunteer one of his kidneys to save the life of a stranger. It no longer seems incomprehensibly twisted that such a person might even anticipate his deed joyfully, as a moral consummation.

PLEASE REPLY TO ME
AS SOON AS POSSIBLE

From time to time, Ittetsu Nemoto gets a group of suicidal people together to visit popular suicide spots, of which there are many in Japan. The best known is Aokigahara Forest, the Sea of Trees, at the foot of Mount Fuji. The forest became associated with suicide in the 1960s, after the publication of two novels by Seicho Matsumoto, and even more so after Wataru Tsurumi's 1993 *Complete Manual of Suicide* declared it the perfect place to die. Because its trees grow so closely together that they block the wind, and because there are few animals or birds, the forest is unusually quiet. The Sea of Trees is large, fourteen square miles, so bodies can lie undiscovered for months; tourists photograph corpses and scavenge for abandoned possessions. Another common suicide destination is Tojinbo Cliff, which overlooks the Sea of Japan. Visiting such a place turns out to be very different from picturing it. The sight of the sea from a cliff top can be a terrible thing.

At other times, Nemoto, a Buddhist priest, conducts death workshops for the suicidal at his temple. He tells attendees to imagine they've been given a diagnosis of cancer and have three months to live. He instructs them to write down what they want to do in those three months. Then he tells them to imagine they have one month left; then a week; then ten minutes. Most people start crying in the course of this exercise, Nemoto among them.

One man who came to a workshop had been talking to Nemoto for years about wanting to die. He was thirty-eight years old and had been institutionalized in a mental hospital off and on for a decade. During the writing exercise, he just sat and wept. When Nemoto came around to check on him, his paper was blank. The man explained that he had nothing to say in response to the questions, because he had never considered them. All he had ever thought about was wanting to die; he had never thought about what he might want to do with his life. But if he had never really lived, how could he want to die? This insight proved oddly liberating. The man returned to his job as a machinist in a factory. Previously, he had been so averse to human company that he had been able to function only in certain limited capacities, but now he was able to speak to people, and he got a promotion.

Sometimes Nemoto tells his attendees to put white cloths over their faces, as is customary with corpses in Japan, while he conducts a funeral ceremony. Afterward, he tells each to carry a lighted candle up a hill behind the temple and imagine that he is entering the world of the dead. This exercise, for reasons he doesn't understand, tends to produce not tears but a strange kind of exhilaration, as though the person were experiencing rebirth.

In the past, Nemoto organized outings whose main function was to get *hikikomori*—shut-ins, some of whom have barely left their rooms in years—to go outside. (There are hundreds of thousands of *hikikomori* in Japan, mostly young men; they play video games and surf the Web and are served meals on trays by their parents.) He led camping trips and karaoke evenings; he held soup-making sessions and sat up all night talking. But, on the whole, these outings were unsatisfactory. *Hikikomori* were phobic, and suicidal people were disorganized; you couldn't rely on them to show up.

Nemoto believes in confronting death; he believes in cultivating a concentrated awareness of the functioning and fragility of the body; and he believes in suffering, because it shows you who you really are. When asked whether he believes that happy people are shallower than those who suffer, first he says that there are no such people, and then he thinks for a moment and says that his wife is one. Is she less profound as a consequence of her serenity? Yes, he says, perhaps she is.

n Japan, there has never been a religious prohibition against suicide, as there is in the West—no sense that to take one's own life is to reject God's grace, or to seize a power that belongs only to God. By tradition, suicide can absolve guilt and cancel debt, can restore honor and prove loyalty. In Japan, suicide can be a gesture of moral integrity and freedom, or an act of beauty. When the writer Eto Jun killed himself, in 1999, he was praised by intellectuals, and it was said that his act demonstrated "first-class aesthetics." When a Cabinet minister under investigation for financial impropriety killed himself, in 2007, the governor of Tokyo called him a true samurai for preserving his honor. Many Japanese psychiatrists say that a person with no mental disorder has the right to choose his own death; they have no business intruding on this most weighty and private human decision.

E-mail to Nemoto:

DATE: 10/8/2009

Since I failed to pay my cellphone bill for a while, my cellphone service will be cut off tomorrow, so please reply to me as soon as possible. We are a couple . . . who are currently living in our car. We were living in the H. area . . . but since we couldn't find any jobs there we went to N. . . . We tried looking for jobs . . . while collecting cans, but our applications were always rejected because we were not local. . . . We gradually started feeling like we want to die. When we tried choking ourselves with a belt, we ended up loosening it when it became too painful. We also tried taking a lot of cold medicine at once, but we ended up waking up after a while, so we couldn't even die. That said, it's not that we really want to die. We do have a desire to find a job somehow. In this way, we're really undecided, and we can't find a way out alone.

Often the difference between death and life depends upon the difference between two o'clock and four o'clock—upon tiny infrastructural adjustments and barely perceptible shifts in situation. A suicidal person whose way off a bridge turns out to be blocked will generally not find another bridge; he will go home. Some Tokyo subway stations have installed bright-blue lights on their platforms to deter jumpers, and these, oddly, have proved quite effective. A few years ago, a suicide-prevention group conducted a minute analysis of suicide in Japan: it was necessary to make strategies of prevention more precise, the group believed—to know exactly who was committing suicide, in which streets, in which buildings, by what methods, and at which times of the day—as though, with enough factors in place, you could perhaps catch someone in the act. Home was the most common location for suicide, followed by tall buildings and bodies of water. The largest number of suicides were committed on Mondays, followed by Sundays and Tuesdays, between four and six in the morning. Suicidal women were likely to kill themselves between noon and two in the afternoon, but unlikely to do so between two and four.

DATE: 07/05/2008

Please forgive my rudeness of sending you an e-mail out of the blue. My name is T. . . . I saw your blog on the Internet, and I am writing an e-mail, hoping that you could give me some advice on my current situation. After I graduated from college, I was studying for the bar exam in order to become a lawyer, being supported by my parents. However, even though I tried six times, I couldn't pass. . . . I was diagnosed with "depression" from too much stress and too much work, so I've been taking a leave of absence. . . . As a result, all I have left is debt from student loans.

I felt the limits of my talents, so I decided to give up on becoming a lawyer, and started looking for a job. However, since I'm over thirty, and I only have worked part time before, it's extremely hard to find one. I lost myself, and I don't even have any ideas what I want to do, or in which direction I should proceed. I started being a *hikikomori* . . . and now I cannot go out except for going to see my psychotherapist once a week. I understand that I'm in such an irretrievable situation because of my own fault, and I myself have to solve the problem. However, I'm a weak, dependent person who was financially supported by my parents until after reaching thirty, so I'm too weak to find a way out of this situation myself. . . . Recently, I started thinking about suicide. Currently, my fear of death is so strong that I don't have enough courage to actually commit suicide. However, if this situation continues, I feel scared that I might lose control for some reason and actually kill myself.

Such is the situation I am in. I'm sorry that I rambled incoherently. I feel like I'm at a dead end and there's nothing else I can do. . . . I hope you can give me some advice if you have time. I'm sorry to ask you when you're so busy, but please help me out.

When Nemoto was a child, an uncle he was close to committed suicide. While he was in high school, in the late eighties, a friend from middle school killed herself. He went to her funeral and saw her body in its coffin, and saw that her mouth had been sewn shut to hide her tongue, which protruded, because she had hanged herself. Some years later, he heard that another friend had committed suicide, a

girl he had been in a band with in high school. He went to her funeral, and found it even more disturbing than the previous one: this
girl had also hanged herself, but she had starved herself, too, and her
body was shockingly emaciated.

When he was young, he often drank and got into brawls with kids
from other schools. In high school, he read Nietzsche every day; he
liked the strength and the power of it. After graduating, he took
some philosophy correspondence courses at a university and worked
on boats, testing for pollution in Tokyo Bay. He wasn't interested in
pollution—he just liked boats. He worked as a marine tour guide in
Okinawa for a while. He didn't have any long-term plans; he was just
doing whatever seemed fun. Then, when he was twenty-four, he got
in a terrible motorcycle accident that left him unconscious for six
hours and hospitalized for three months. He came to realize that life
was precious and he had been wasting it. He wasn't going to figure
out the meaning of life by reading. He had to do it through
experience.

One day, his mother saw an advertisement in the newspaper:
Buddhist monks wanted. She pointed it out to him because she
thought it was hilarious to advertise for monks, but his curiosity was
aroused. He already knew a little bit about Zen: he had studied karate after high school, and that had involved some basic austerities,
such as standing under an icy waterfall for an hour while chanting.
His friends thought becoming a monk was a ridiculous idea, and
even he had no very high opinion of monks, but he answered the
advertisement. The job was entry-level monk work for people who
hadn't any training—pet funerals, that sort of thing. After a while, it
was too easy; he wanted to learn more. At the time, in his late twenties, he was living with Yukiko, a nurse-in-training whom he had
met when he was in the hospital, and who later became his wife, but
he decided that he wanted to enter a monastery.

He did his training in a Rinzai Zen monastery on a forested
mountainside in Gifu Prefecture, two hundred miles west of Tokyo.
Long flights of stone steps lead up the mountain and end at a wooden

gateway with a tiled roof. Through the gateway is a courtyard of raked gravel, some larger rocks and stunted pines, and several traditional buildings with curved tile roofs. When a candidate presents himself for training, he must prostrate himself and declare that he is willing to do anything that needs to be done to solve the great matter of life and death. By tradition, he is scowled at by the head monk, who orders him to leave. He persists, he continues to prostrate himself, and after two or three days he is taken in.

Apprentice monks are treated like slaves on a brutal plantation. They must follow orders and never say no. They sleep very little. They rise at four. Most of the time, they eat only a small amount of rice and, occasionally, pickles (fresh vegetables and meat are forbidden). There is no heat in the monastery, even though it can be very cold on the mountain, and the monks wear sandals and cotton robes. Junior monks are not permitted to read.

There are many menial tasks a monk must complete in a day (cooking, cleaning, cutting down trees, chopping wood, making brooms), and he is given very little time to do them. If he does not move fast enough, senior monks scream at him. There is very little talking—only bell ringing (to indicate a change in activity) and screaming. There is a correct way to do everything, which is vigorously enforced. When a monk wakes in the morning, he must not move until a bell is rung. When the bell rings, he must move very fast. He has about four minutes (until the next bell rings) to put up his futon, open a window, run to the toilet, gargle with salt water, wash his face, put on his robes, and run to the meditation hall. At first, it is very hard to do all those things in four minutes, but gradually he develops techniques for increasing his speed. Because he is forced to develop these techniques, and because even with the techniques it is still difficult to move fast enough, he is intensely aware of everything he is doing.

He is always too slow, he is always afraid, and he is always being scrutinized. In the winter, he is cold, but if he looks cold he is screamed at. There is no solitude. The constant screaming and the running, along with chronic exhaustion, produce in him a state of low-level panic, which is also a state of acute focus. It is as if his thinking mind, his doubting and critical and interpreting mind, had shut down and been replaced by a simpler mechanism that serves the body. The idea is to throw away his self and, in so doing, find out who he is. A well-trained monk, it is said, lives as though he were already dead: free from attachment, from indecision, from confusion, he moves with no barrier between his will and his act.

Several times each year, the monks spend eight days walking long distances to beg for food; in the winter, they walk in sandals through snow. When they go begging, they wear broad conical straw hats to cover their faces. They do not talk to anyone, and, if someone asks, they may not say their names. When someone gives them food, they are obliged to eat everything they are given. This forced overeating can be the most physically painful part of the training. Every day, each monk has an audience with his teacher about a koan that he is pondering. These audiences last a few minutes at most, sometimes a few seconds. Occasionally, the teacher will make a comment; usually, he says nothing at all. The koan is a mental version of the bodily brutalities of training: resistant, frustrating, impossible to assimilate, it is meant to shock the monk into sudden insight.

In January, the monks hold a weeklong retreat, during which they are not allowed to lie down or sleep. One January, Nemoto was cook; he had to prepare special pickles for the retreat, and he was driven so hard by the head monk that he did not sleep at all for a week before the retreat began. By the third day of the retreat, he was so exhausted that he could barely stand, but he had to carry a heavy pot full of rice. He stood holding the rice and thought, I cannot carry this pot any longer, I am going to die now. Just as he was on the point of collapse, he felt a great rush of energy: he felt as though everything around him were singing, and that he could do anything he had to do. He felt, too, that the person who had been on the point of collapse a moment before, and, indeed, the person who had been living his life until then, was not really him. That evening, he met with his teacher about his koan, and for the first time the teacher accepted his answer. This experience led him to believe that suffering produces insight, and that it is only at the point when suffering becomes nearly unbearable that transformation takes place.

There are very few monks in Japan now. Nemoto's monastery, whose training is particularly harsh, has only seven. Each year, new monks present themselves for training; each year, many of them run away. This year, five came and four ran away. The focus of Nemoto's Rinzai Zen sect is individual enlightenment; when a monk leaves with the intention of doing work in the world, the *roshi* is disappointed.

Some years ago, a woman, R., contacted Nemoto through his website, and they also met in person several times.

DATE: 01/17/2008

Actually, R. was almost dead yesterday LOL. I thought of taking pills for the first time in a long while. But I can't die no matter how many times I take pills, and stomach cleansing is suuuuper painful, you know, if you're conscious. It'd work if I can take pills well until I lose consciousness, but it's so hard to swallow several hundred pills LOL. . . . If I could die easily, I would have been dead! Now, R. has a reliable friend, you know, so I cried for about 2 hours and I calmed down, but to be the one who listens is also hard, right? I feel sympathy. I thought, you're going to be tired of R. someday, and I felt even more like dying, or not, LOL. It's hard. But living is hard. This is my conclusion. O.K., I'll go take a bath!

At a certain point, R. divorced her husband and moved in with her boyfriend, who had become a *hikikomori* after his father committed suicide. She sent Nemoto an essay her boyfriend had written, arguing that *hikikomori* and training priests are essentially the same:

> Long ago, becoming a training priest was recognized as a way of living, and I think that considerable numbers of the priests were people who had troubles that prevented them from living in society—people who would be called depressed or neurotic in today's terms. . . . The basic rule was to leave the family and friends, discard all the relationships and renounce the world. . . . The old society accepted these training priests, although they were thought to be completely useless. Or rather, it treated them with respect, and supported them by giving offerings. . . . In very rare cases, some attained so-called "enlightenment," and those people could spread teachings that could possibly save people in society who had troubles. In other words, there were certain cases where training priests could be useful to society, and I think that is why society supported them. . . . I think that training priests and *hikikomori* are quite similar. First, neither of them can fit in to this society—while the training priests are secluded in mountains, *hikikomori* are secluded in their rooms. They both engage in the activity of facing the root of their problems alone. . . . However, nobody accepts this way of living anymore, and that's why *hikikomori* hide in their rooms. . . . But *hikikomori* are very important beings. *Hikikomori* cannot be cured by society; rather, it is society that has problems, and *hikikomori* may be able to solve them.

After four years in the monastery, Nemoto wanted to be out in the world again, but he wasn't sure what to do, so he moved back to Tokyo and went to work at a fast-food restaurant. After four years of rice and pickles, he found the idea of flipping burgers appealing. Sure enough, it was such easy work compared with his training that he felt happy all the time. People said hello to him, they told him he was doing a good job, they asked him if he was okay back there, was it too hot, did he want some water? It was incredible! Soon his cheerful demeanor began to attract attention. Nobody could understand why he was so happy flipping burgers; everyone else at the restaurant was miserable.

People asked him what his secret was, and he told them about the monastery. They started talking to him about their troubles—some of them about how they had considered suicide—and he found he had a knack for helping unhappy people change the way they thought. After a while, the son of one of his teachers got in touch with him and asked him what he was doing at the restaurant—their sect needed monks who could become abbots of temples. There was a temple in a small town called Seki, in Gifu Prefecture, about 160 miles west of Tokyo, that would close if it couldn't find an abbot; Nemoto agreed to move there.

Seki was a collection of low-slung concrete apartment blocks and traditional-style two-story houses with pitched roofs and fluted tiles, surrounded by hills covered with scrubby bamboo. The temple was outside the town, also in a traditional style, surrounded by rice paddies, with a graveyard on one side. Inside the temple was a meditation hall in which the memorial tablets for the parish were kept, each containing a scroll on which were written the names of that family's ancestors, some dating to the seventeenth century. The rooms opened to the outside with sliding doors latticed with wooden slats and paper screens; the floors were covered with tatami mats.

Nemoto had imagined the life of a country abbot as a peaceful one, but it turned out to be so much work that he rarely had time for himself. He conducted funerals for all the families in the parish, and then there were the two-week memorials, the three-week memorials, the four-week memorials, and all the ceremonies after that. He also planted and harvested rice in the temple fields and distributed some of it to his parishioners.

At least there were no more austerities: once monks have left the monastery and become priests, the restrictions of the monastic life fall away. Priests drink, they smoke, they marry. Buddhists from countries where customs are stricter are often shocked by the habits of Japanese priests, but Nemoto doesn't believe in putting a distance between himself and other people. (Another sect, a branch of the Pure Land Buddhists, takes this further—their priests don't even shave their heads. This is a gesture of humility: Pure Land priests consider that they are common idiots like everybody else.) When Nemoto is conducting a funeral ceremony, he wears his robes; older people feel comforted by the sight of a priest in traditional dress. But when he leaves the temple, he wears what he likes: baggy jeans, old boots, a kerchief tied over his shaved head. This is not just a matter of reducing formality: in Japan, Buddhism has become so exclusively associated with funerals that a priest in robes appears to many like a herald of death.

DATE: 04/22/2010

Dear Chief Priest of Daizenji Temple,

My recent life hasn't really changed much [since my husband committed suicide], but I still manage to continue living. I will ramble on about what I'm thinking now. Please forgive me that it's rather long. My mother was very devout. She never failed to put her palms together in prayer and chant a sutra in front of the Buddhist altar every morning and night. My father liked sake, and he acted violently ever since I could remember. I grew up, seeing my mother suffer for decades. However, my mother never complained. She worked very hard, and prayed for the happiness of our family single-mindedly and devoted herself to taking care of my father until he died. I couldn't understand my mother very much. All I thought was she was impressive. I hated my father all the time. . . .

After my father's death, my mother's health declined. She was finally released from troubles with him, but then I started giving her trouble. My marriage failed, and nothing went well in my life, and the older I got, the more I lost the meaning of life, and I just wanted to die. My heart was in a rough mood, and I started using violent words toward my mother. . . . Then she caught pneumonia and passed away. I was in despair. I felt like I was crushed by my severe regrets. I couldn't forgive myself, I felt so much pain, and I couldn't bear it anymore. I attempted suicide.

My mother suffered for decades because of my alcoholic father, and I made her suffer when she was finally released. In her entire life, she was never rewarded. Why did she, who was so devout, and sacrificed her own body and life, end up having a life so full of suffering? I know all I gave her was suffering. It was my fault. And yet I couldn't help myself. So, when I think about my mother, I feel rage, wondering if there are no gods or buddhas in this world, wondering how can such a good life be so unrewarded. I feel like I don't care anymore about anything, if you can't become happy by living virtuously. The last words my mother said after regaining consciousness were "I feel grateful." . . .

I'm alone. I know it's pathetic, since I'll be fifty in a few years. I work as a temporary employee. I can sustain my finances now, but I don't know what will happen in the future. I have absolutely no idea how to live. I feel extreme anxiety. I talk to my mother's picture every day. Every time I wake up in the morning, I feel disappointed at myself because I am still alive. I won't be able to go where my mother is when I die. That's what I think. Still, while I want to die, I also feel like finding a way to live. I have been looking for a job since the beginning of this year. Since I can't do anything but office work at this age, all I get is rejections. That's normal. So, in the end, I feel like I want to run away. I don't know what I'm doing. I don't even know if I want to live or die. I might be looking for a job to lie about the fact that I want to die. . . . At night, I think about my future and I think about my mother, and I can't help but cry.

It is hard to talk about wanting to die. Most people you talk to can't handle it; it's too disturbing. If you call a suicide hot line, the person can handle it, but he will be some stranger who knows nothing about you. There isn't much talk therapy in Japan—if you go to a psychiatrist, he will usually see you for just a few minutes and give you a prescription. Nemoto wanted to help suicidal people talk to each other without awkwardness, and so he created a suicide website. It was originally called "For Those Who Want to Die," but then it was suggested to him that it might become a place where people went to find strangers to commit suicide with—that had become quite common in Japan—so he changed its name to "For Those Who Do Not Want to Die." People communicated with one another on the site, and they also wrote to him.

He responded to everyone. He wrote back to all e-mails, and often, when he wrote, a reply would arrive within minutes, and he would reply to the reply. He answered all phone calls, day or night; many came in the night. People would call and want to talk to him, but they didn't know what to say; they didn't know how to describe what was happening to them. What would come through the phone over hours of talking was an inarticulate, urgent, and bottomless anxiety that seeped into him and didn't go away when the phone call was over. He tried to practice what he thought of as Zen listening—letting the words and emotions flow through him, taking up all the space in his mind so there was no room for any reaction of his own. He felt that in order to help people he had to feel what they felt—he had to feel that he wasn't an adviser but a fellow sufferer, trying, as they were, to make sense out of life—but this affected him more and more, as their anxiety became his. He tried to meditate in order to purge himself of these emotions, but he could never purge himself completely.

He thought about the suicidal people all the time. How could he help them? What could he do? He wasn't sleeping enough. It was grueling, but his practice in the temple had been grueling, too, and he believed that this was a continuation of his practice. After three years, he sensed that he was near a breakdown, and he started to think about ways to take care of himself. He took up karate again. He meditated more, did more chanting. But new people kept asking him for help, and the people from before kept calling back, and few cases were ever resolved; he felt responsible for more and more people who wanted more and more from him.

In the fall of 2009, he began to feel a heaviness in his chest. He felt that his neck was constricting, and he found it harder to breathe. When it got very bad, a few months later, he went to the hospital and received a diagnosis of unstable angina. Five arteries were blocked; his doctor told him he could die of a heart attack at any time. Over the next two years, he had four angioplasties. During this period, Nemoto's father became suicidal. Ten years before, the father had had a severe stroke and become partly paralyzed. By the time Nemoto was hospitalized, his father had lost the will to live. Then, a few months later, he died, of heart failure.

All this time, the e-mails and the phone calls kept coming, but for long periods Nemoto was too sick to respond. At first, he didn't say why he had gone silent. Then, as the weeks went by, he felt he had to explain. From the hospital, he wrote to his correspondents and told them he was sick. When he checked back in to see how they'd responded to his announcement, he was shocked. They didn't care that he was sick: they were sick, too, they said; they were in pain, and he had to take care of them. Lying in the hospital, he spent a week crying. He had spent seven years sacrificing himself, driving himself to the verge of a breakdown, nearly to death, trying to help these people, and they didn't care about him at all. What was the point? He knew that if you were suicidal it was difficult to understand other people's problems, but still—he had been talking to some of these people for years, and now here he was dying, and nobody cared.

For a long time, his thoughts were too dark and agitated to sort out, but slowly the darkness receded, and what remained with him was a strong sense that he wanted to do the work anyway. He realized that, even if the people he spoke to felt nothing for him, he still wanted something from them. There was the intellectual excitement he felt when he succeeded in analyzing some problem a person had been stuck on. He wanted to know truths that ordinary people did not know, and in suffering it felt as though he was finding those truths. And then there was something harder to define, a kind of spiritual thrill in what felt to him, when it worked, like a bumping of souls. If this was what he was after, he would have to stop thinking of his work as something morally obligatory and freighted with significance. Helping people should be nothing special, he thought. It should be like eating—just something that he did in the course of his life.

Having arrived at this conclusion, he went online to look at his website, and saw that there were some messages of support that he'd missed the first time, in his shock at the others. That was a relief. But he still needed to make changes in his life. Clearly, he had been doing something wrong. He thought about all the e-mails and all the phone calls and how those conversations could go on and on for years in circles with no progress at all; and he also thought about how strange and disorienting it was to take into himself terrible emotions from people he had never even seen.

He decided that, from then on, he would not communicate with people until he had met them. If they wanted his counsel, they first had to come to his temple. It would be difficult for many of them—his temple was in a remote place, far from the nearest city, Nagoya, quite far even from the local train station, and he had been talking to people all over Japan. It would cost them quite a bit of money to get to him. But that was the point. If they didn't want his help badly enough to get to the temple, it was unlikely that he could help them.

The new strategy reduced the number of people who came to him for help, and it also changed something for those who did. Was it meeting face to face, or was it the longer, more concentrated time he was able to give them? He wasn't sure. But after these meetings he often felt that he and they had achieved some kind of resolution. And this meant, too, that he didn't spend his life filled with anxiety, with the fear that any one of the many people he had spoken to or written to that week might be killing himself at any moment. As time went on, he developed other techniques. He started taking notes when he was listening to people, which helped him to maintain a certain distance from their despair. It also allowed him to remind them of things they had said before, to remind them of past happiness, and to help them to construct a story that moved from one point to the next, rather than endlessly circling, and this allowed them to view their suffering from a distance.

Once, a man walked for five hours to get to Nemoto's temple. The walk was a heroic journey for this man, because he had been living as a *hikikomori*, and now, suddenly, he was outside in the sun, sweating and feeling his body move. As he walked, he thought about what he was going to say. It had been so long since he had really spoken to anyone, and now he was going to be expected to explain his most intimate feelings to a stranger. He sweated and thought as he walked, and when, at last, after five hours, he arrived at the temple, he announced that he had achieved understanding and no longer needed Nemoto's help. He turned around and walked back home.

THE CHILDREN OF STRANGERS

"Home is the place where, when you have to go there,

They have to take you in."

"I should have called it

Something you somehow haven't to deserve."

—ROBERT FROST, *"The Death of the Hired Man"*

When Sue Hoag was twelve she read a book, *The Family Nobody Wanted*, about a couple in the 1930s who adopted a multiracial posse of twelve children, despite having very little room or money. It seemed wonderful to Sue to be part of such a family, and she begged her parents to adopt. What a thrill it would be, she thought, to take children who had been abandoned to friendless institutions and bring them home and play with them and love them and make them happy. They had only four kids in their family, she pleaded—surely there was room for more. Her parents said no. But Sue kept thinking about the book, and by the time she was fifteen she had met her future husband, Hector Badeau, and by the time she was eighteen she and Hector had planned their family: they would have two kids and adopt two. By the time they were four years out of college and four years married, they had had the two kids and adopted the two kids and thought their family was complete.

But there were more than two children in the world who needed parents. There were so many children who, because they were too old, or too violent, or too traumatized, or unable to walk, or too close to death, or the wrong color, or had too many brothers and sisters, were unlikely ever to be adopted; and when Hector and Sue thought about what those children's lives would be like without parents, lives that were already unimaginably difficult, they could not bear it. So, by the time Sue was twenty-eight and Hector was thirty, they had had two kids and adopted seven, and by the end of the following year, they had had two kids and adopted fourteen; and long before they adopted their last, twenty-second child, eleven years later, the four-child family they had imagined in high school was a distant memory, and something wilder and more explosive, more exhilarating and more crushing and unfathomably more complicated, had taken its place.

Terrible, painful things happened over the years that they were not able to prevent—three children dead, two in jail, teenage pregnancies, divorces. But there were also birthday parties and weddings and graduations; there were grandchildren and great-grandchildren, most of them still living in the same neighborhood, within a few blocks of each other and their parents, in and out of each other's homes all the time, minding each other's children. And every Easter and Fourth of July and Thanksgiving and Christmas and New Year's, the children and the grandchildren and the great-grandchildren gathered with Sue and Hector in the big house they still lived in, although they couldn't afford it, and ate a meal together. And though some were missing—three dead, two in jail—still, most were there year after year, and for everything that had happened, they were a family.

Twenty-two children didn't seem as strange to Hector as it did to most people, because he came from sixteen. His mother, Delvina, was born on a farm in Sainte-Cécile, in Quebec, and went to school through the eighth grade; his father, Philorum, left school in Montreal at nine to go to work chopping wood. Philorum married Delvina and moved to Vermont in search of work, though neither of them spoke English. He found a job in the quarries as a stone cutter. Of their sixteen children, fifteen lived—the fifth died at three, falling downstairs. Hector was the twelfth, born in 1956.

They were poor: the most Philorum ever made, toward the end of his working life, was a hundred dollars a week. The younger boys slept six to a bed.

Delvina read the Bible every day; the kids went to church every Sunday, said their rosary, went to confession. Years later, after her husband died and her children were grown, Delvina began taking homeless lodgers into her house and fed them out of her husband's Social Security money, that was the sort of person she was, but while Philorum was alive, he was in charge. He was a harsh father, strict and unloving. He had boxed for money when he was younger, and he made his boys fight each other. Hector hated that. The children weren't allowed to bring friends to the house; they weren't allowed to go on dates or to school dances.

Philorum drank a lot, and was often gone all weekend on a bender. When he came home, sometimes he was happy and played the violin; sometimes he was angry and beat the kids with a horsewhip or an electrical cord. He beat Delvina, too. By the time Hector was twelve, he had decided that he disliked his father, and that when he grew up he would be a father who spent time with his kids and told them he loved them.

The Badeau boys were known for hockey, but Hector was the best of them, the record-setting goal scorer, the star of Spaulding High School. He was always getting written up in the papers. He had curly hair, and in high school he grew it out into a giant seventies Afro with a mustache to match. The coach wanted him to try out for the pros, but by then he had meet Sue.

Hector spotted Sue in the fall of 1973, playing field hockey. She was tiny—not even five feet tall—though she was a sophomore. By the standards of their town, Sue was rich. She found out later, when she went to college, that she was not rich at all—barely middle class, in fact—but in Barre, Vermont, her family seemed well off. Her parents had both gone to college; her father was an engineer for the state highway department, her mother was a dental hygienist. Her parents taught in Sunday school and were the sort of people who were called pillars of the church, though they didn't talk much about God. They led Brownie troops and Girl Scout troops and coached Little League. They had four children, of whom Sue was the eldest, and their house was nicely decorated and exceptionally clean.

When she was in her early teens, Sue was chubby and bookish and didn't have many dates, but then she grew up and got pretty. She was crowned Junior Miss of Barre, and was first runner-up in the state beauty pageant. And then the school's star athlete and future Prom King, Hector Badeau, asked her out on a date and became her boyfriend. She wrote a poem—"Hockey Player"—about this astonishing event. Despite being a hockey star, Hector didn't have many close friends, and he'd never had a proper girlfriend before, but he found he could talk to Sue. She came from the kind of family he wanted to belong to: he saw that her father treated her mother right and showed his love for his kids. After six months, he knew that Sue was the girl for him.

Sue had always gone to church with her parents, but she started getting religious in a more serious way around the time she met Hector, when her ballet teacher started inviting her to Bible-study classes. To Hector, God had been someone you bargained with: you would obey His rules if He got you stuff; God was for Sundays and holidays, not the rest of the week. But he and Sue came to believe that the teachings of Jesus required them to support the oppressed, to care for the least, and to seek justice.

Of Hector's siblings, only his sister Irene had gone to a four-year college; she became a nurse. One of his brothers sold cars; two worked in the quarries; one did deliveries and sales for Cabot Creamery; one was a postman. A couple of them drank and went on welfare. But Sue was going to Smith College to major in child development, and she persuaded Hector to go to a four-year school, too. He went to New England College, NEC—Not Exactly College, he called it—and spent a lot of his time drinking in a toga, but when he visited Sue at Smith he was well behaved, and they got engaged that year. Hector thought Sue's parents were probably upset that she was marrying a working-class lowlife like him, rather than some guy from Amherst or Harvard, but they got used to him, and he and Sue married right after graduation, in the summer of 1979.

The first thing they did was take out a large loan to buy a Christian bookstore in Northampton, where Sue had worked while she was in college. They thought that having their own business would be a good way to have time to spend with their children. Massachusetts had recently deinstitutionalized its mental patients, and there were a lot of homeless people wandering around. Several stores put up no-loitering signs to keep them out, so Sue and Hector decided to set aside a room in the back of their store for homeless people to sit in. They put out an ashtray and had a pot of coffee going all day. Sometimes they took someone home to sleep on their sofa. They talked to the homeless people and discovered that a lot of them didn't have families, and they wondered whether they would be homeless if they did.

They had planned to wait a few years to have kids, taking time to pay off their loans for college and the bookstore, but Sue got pregnant a few months after the wedding. The child, Chelsea, was born in the summer of 1980. A few weeks later, two college students visited their church and talked about how they'd spent a summer working for Mother Teresa. This seemed to Sue and Hector like a sign from God. They had planned to adopt the child who was, as Hector put it, "most in need of a home and least likely to get one." And who could be more in need of a home than a destitute Calcutta orphan?

HECTOR: Sue and I, for better or for worse, we—
SUE: Act.
HECTOR: Just would come up with an idea and would do it. And it seemed like the thing to do, so we called the agency the next day.
SUE: We didn't even call, we walked in. Walk-ins to an adoption agency!

They told a social worker at the agency that they wanted to adopt a baby from India. The social worker looked at the tiny infant in Sue's arms and asked them why they wanted to do this, but she didn't laugh at them or tell them to go away.

The process turned out to be more complicated than they had anticipated. The social worker told them that India had placed a temporary ban on foreign adoptions, but there were two- and three-year-old children from El Salvador, where a civil war had begun the year before, in need of families. Would they adopt one of those? Sue and Hector had not imagined adopting an older child, but they talked about it and prayed on it and said yes. They adopted a boy, Jose. He arrived in bad shape: he cried out in terror if he saw a bridge or a dog; he sobbed at night and woke up screaming. He insisted on keeping either Sue or Hector in his sight at all times. Little by little, he grew calmer.

Six months after Jose arrived, Sue discovered she was pregnant again. She was horrified—she left the doctor's office and started to cry. Life with two children was good, but she couldn't cope with three, she was sure of it; she would go crazy. But now she had no choice. To make things worse, money was getting very tight: sales at the bookstore were bad. Hector got a job as a short-order cook at a diner at night, then started working the early-morning shift on the line at a factory. But after the first shock of her pregnancy receded, Sue forgot that she'd been frightened to have three children, and Hector had never worried about it. So, when the adoption agency called them, not long before the new baby was due, to ask if they still wanted to adopt a baby from India, they said yes. They also signed up to be foster parents and started taking teenagers into the house. The baby from India, Raj, arrived: he had been born prematurely and had mild cerebral palsy; when he arrived, at the age of four months, he weighed seven pounds.

In the beginning, Sue and Hector both worked at home and in the bookstore. Then, after Isaac was born, Sue decided that she wanted to try being a full-time mother, and stayed home with the four babies. She hated it. In a real crisis Sue was calm, but her self-control disintegrated rapidly when she was faced with smaller domestic challenges such as diapers or head lice.

HECTOR: I had two jobs. I had to go to work, and then I had to come home and do hers. Sue had never been really big on—

SUE: I liked baking bread or something.

HECTOR:—laundry and cleaning toilets.

SUE: We just realized that wasn't where each of our areas of strength were best used.

After a few months, it became clear that she was never going to try that again. She and Hector made a deal that, from then on, she would do all the paperwork and he would change all the diapers. And, over the years, it became clear that Sue, with her degree from Smith and her aptitude for management and public speaking, was better equipped to make money outside the house; Hector, who didn't mind diapers and disliked having a boss, was better staying home. She looked at her mother's life and he looked at his father's life, and they both did the opposite.

SUE: He wanted to be around more, I wanted to be around less.

Around this time, their money situation had grown so bad that they decided they had no choice but to move. It seemed impossible to be foster parents to teenagers while trying to work several jobs, but they realized they could combine the two by running a group home. They got a job at a home for six delinquent teenage boys in foster care, sold the bookstore, and moved back to Vermont.

SUE: There were kids in there that were sixteen, seventeen, eighteen, and we were in our early twenties.

HECTOR: It was scary at first, not knowing how this kid's gonna respond. Sue was more scared than I was.

SUE: I was not scared!

HECTOR: Whenever I went out and there were a few kids in the house, she'd say, How long are you gonna be? You better not be long.

Once they got used to it, they found that they liked being surrounded by teenagers, but the group home was depressing. In the two years they were there, twenty-three boys passed through—boys who had spent an average of eleven years in foster care. Some had been placed in more than twenty-five families by the time they were fifteen. Most of them, Sue and Hector knew, would never have a real family, and probably some would end up homeless. The more they thought about it, the more it seemed to them that foster care was a dreadful thing. Children needed permanent families. A child who was kicked out of one home after another for his whole childhood—well, there wasn't much hope for a child like that.

They thought they should be trying to get other people to adopt, so they decided to found an agency, which they would finance by fund-raising in churches. They named it Rootwings, because children needed both roots and wings. They moved to a house in Cabot, taking with them as foster kids the five boys who were at the group home when they left. The house was cheap, it was heated only by a fireplace, but it was big enough so the older kids got their own rooms, and there were five acres of land to play in. To make some money, Hector began breaking down old barns and silos and selling the wood to a salvage company; what was unsalable he kept to heat the house.

It was at this juncture that their plan to have two and adopt two began to go awry. On a trip to an adoption conference, Sue and Hector had dinner with a family that had adopted twelve children, including two sets of siblings, and they felt that the children in this house were secure and loved. And then Chelsea, in a house with three brothers and five teenage boys, began asking for a sister. Sue thought that they had enough children with four, but Hector wasn't convinced. Which was why, while Isaac was still a toddler and in the hospital recovering from a nearly fatal episode of spinal meningitis, they adopted an eight-month-old black baby girl from Florida who had fetal alcohol syndrome and had been born very prematurely, weighing two pounds. They named her Joelle. They also decided that Sue should get her tubes tied. There were moments when they were tempted to have another biological child, but it was their calling to adopt, and if they filled up their family with more biological children, their mission would be compromised.

With the four small children, the tiny baby, and the three remaining teenage foster boys, Sue and Hector decided to take a vacation. They couldn't afford to stay in hotels or eat in restaurants, so they drove across the country for five weeks in a camper. They ate peanut-butter-and-jelly sandwiches and drank Tang and camped in state and national parks for two dollars a night. They visited Yellowstone Park, Yosemite, the Grand Canyon, the Great Salt Lake Desert, and the Cherokee Trail of Tears.

Their destination was another adoption conference, in Albuquerque. There, they heard about the awful fate of sibling groups: kids who would never be adopted because there were too many of them, or who would be separated into different foster and adoptive homes and maybe never see each other again. By the end of the conference, Sue and Hector were convinced they had to do something. Soon afterward, Sue was leafing through *Los Niños*, an adoption newsletter from New Mexico, when she saw the photographs of four siblings—two boys, two girls. Something about them pulled at her. Another group caught her eye, too, a group of six teenagers, but they still had teenagers from the group home, and six more would be too many. The four younger kids seemed to fit: Abel was ten, SueAnn was nine, George was eight, and Flory was six.

HECTOR: It's hard to explain. It was like instant love.

SUE: It was as if they already were our kids, but they were somehow not with us and we had to go get them.

Every time they adopted a child, they felt new love for him. Sometimes they felt the beginnings of love even before they met the child, even before they saw his photograph. It was like the feeling you had when you learned you were pregnant, Sue said: you didn't know the child, you couldn't see or feel the child, the child barely existed; and yet you loved him.

The four children had moved around a lot. For a while they were living in a group home, but the group home separated boys and girls, so that the sisters and the brothers rarely saw each other and could not be sure that the other two were still living there. The girls were separated from each other, too, because Flory slept in the baby room. At night, SueAnn would run to the baby room and hide under Flory's crib to make sure that nobody took her away while she was asleep. She hoped that Abel was keeping an eye on George in the same way, but she didn't know. At this group home, four or five kids were assigned to a room, sleeping in bunk beds. There were shifts of workers: one person would turn the lights out and another person would wake you up; one person would tell you it was time to eat, and another that it was time to work.

Then they were taken out of the group home and placed with foster parents, one home after another, about four in five years. They didn't know why they kept moving—whether it was because they'd been bad, or because four children were too difficult, or it was just the way things were. Some of the foster parents hit them; some just didn't treat them like their own kids. Their last foster parents really loved them but couldn't afford to adopt, so they knew they couldn't stay there.

> FLORY: Family members were always trying to adopt us, but the courts wouldn't let them. I don't know why.
> SUEANN: I don't think they actually ever took any action.
> FLORY: Maybe.
> SUEANN: To be honest.

They weren't sure why they were taken from their mother, because they had heard many stories and didn't know which one was true. Abel, the eldest, remembered that for a while they and their mother were living in a car. A social worker told SueAnn that one day when the bus came to pick the children up for school George was outside playing in the mud in a diaper and the door was wide open. Inside, Abel, who was six, was trying to light the stove to cook something; Flory was in her crib with a dirty diaper, crying and hungry; and SueAnn was wandering around. They were all dirty, and there was no adult in sight, so the police came and took them.

The state told their mother that she had six months to get her children back, and then another six months, and then another six months, but she had not had much schooling and didn't know how to fill out the forms she had to fill out or how to go to her court hearings; maybe she could not even read the letters that the state sent, telling her where her children were and who was taking care of them. Or maybe she could have done those things but just didn't want her children back. A few times, the children were taken to see her on visits at a McDonald's, but then the visits stopped.

The children weren't sure if they had three or four fathers between them. Abel's father didn't speak English and was long gone. SueAnn's father did speak English, but he wasn't around. Flory's father was living with their mother when they were taken away, but he was in Mexico at the time, visiting family, so he didn't know about what happened until later, and when he got back he left their mother, and Flory never saw him again.

When the children first met Sue and Hector, they knew two facts about them: that they wanted to take all four of them, and that they wanted to adopt, which meant that they would never have to move again. Sue and Hector seemed nice, but Abel and SueAnn had their guard up: they had met a lot of people who at first seemed nice and turned out not to be. They met in a hotel in Albuquerque and went swimming in the hotel pool, and George threw up in the pool and then SueAnn threw up in the pool, but otherwise it was a fine day. It was the middle of winter when they arrived in Vermont, and freezing cold; they saw snow and mountains for the first time.

There was something about the difficulty of new children that Sue loved. Right at the beginning, everything was a challenge. How soon would the child feel that she and Hector were his parents? How could they get him to feel that this was his family, not just another foster home that he'd get kicked out of in a few months? Would he get along with the other children? These emotional questions were the most complicated part, but there were also the logistical and administrative aspects of new children: What special services should she arrange? Did the child need counseling? Physical therapy? Academic tutoring? There was always the risk that things would go badly, and this risk drove and excited her: she felt a rush of energy and purpose that she didn't feel at other times, because nothing was harder than this, and this was what she was good at.

> SUE: It was almost like a high, that new time, getting to know them and the challenge of finding the right school and the right this and the right that. It's something that, after everyone's settled, you sort of miss, and you say, Oh, it's time to do that again.

It was particularly difficult when new children came, but everything was difficult, and she and Hector liked that. They never wanted an easy life. They were always exhausted and always broke and it was rare that they had any time alone, but they knew that they were needed: they could give love and food and shelter to children who needed those things and who loved them back. They were doing God's work. Their days were crowded and unpredictable, and charged with fervor and purpose.

To manage so many children, they had to be organized. Sue

was, as Hector put it, "chart-oriented." There were chore charts and laundry charts; there were color-coded charts that listed the activities for each day. Sue planned dinner menus two weeks at a time, selecting each meal from a large computer file of options; she printed out shopping lists with the ingredients for the fourteen dinners, plus ingredients for fourteen lunches and fourteen breakfasts and fourteen after-school snacks. There was a prayer schedule posted on the bulletin board that listed who was to be prayed for each night.

Sue put together a *Badeau Family Handbook* in which she wrote down the family's values, rules, and systems, divided into several sections: "Spiritual Life," "Emotional Life & Relationships," "Education & Mental Development," "Life Management." Each year, just before school started, every child would get a copy of the updated handbook. There would be a family meeting, and Sue would go through it, page by page.

6. We will celebrate special times in each person's life like birthdays and anniversaries and try our best to make each person feel special and loved.
9. Each week, Mom will take one kid on a Friday night "date" and Dad will take one kid on a Saturday morning breakfast so we can have one-on-one time and develop our relationships with each other.

When Sue cooked, she experimented with interesting foreign recipes in order to showcase the ethnic heritage of one or another of the children; when Hector cooked, it was shepherd's pie, or spaghetti and red sauce, and sometimes, if there were leftovers of various kinds, he would tip them together into a baking tray, stick it in the oven, and call it a casserole. Hector, who had been raised in a household where the standards of domestic comfort and harmony were considerably lower than those in Sue's, was more at home with imperfection. He was also more at home with discipline. Sue

always had phrases in her head from all the social-work literature she'd read and taught classes about, phrases about how bad
anger was and how important it was to listen, and on the rare occasions when she was left alone with the children they would ride all
over her.

> HECTOR: The kids always gave her crap. I was the enforcer.
> They called me Sergeant Badeau. Sue, it just wasn't her
> thing. She did okay, she survived.

All over the house there were Bible verses on the walls, on posters
or placards, to keep the word of God in everybody's mind. The kids
had to memorize a new Bible verse each week, and there were quiz-
zes on Bible stories. But Sue and Hector wanted the children to ap-
preciate other traditions, too, so each year they celebrated Hanukkah
and Passover and Kwanzaa and Cinco de Mayo and the winter sol-
stice and Hindu and Muslim holidays. Most summers, they took a
family trip. Often Hector took the kids by himself, because Sue had
to work. In the summer of 1989, Hector drove fourteen kids in a
fifteen-passenger van (an old airport shuttle bus) to New Mexico by
way of Disney World and back again, staying at campgrounds along
the way.

Around this time, articles began to appear about their family in
newspapers and they began to win prizes; with this attention came
criticism. Some people thought they were saints, but others thought
they were publicity-seekers, or weirdoes, or had some kind of psychological disorder. People thought they were addicted to acquiring
kids to fill some need, like other people were addicted to shopping.
Some thought they were presumptuous, to imagine that they could
be good parents to so many. Even the people who thought they were
saints couldn't understand why they did it. Sue tried to explain.

> SUE: Suppose someone trains for years so they can climb
> Mount Everest. You watch a documentary about their life,

and you learn that they had to give up many things, they didn't even go to their own mother's funeral, and you think, What is wrong with that person? Why would they make those sacrifices and not live a normal life in order to pursue this goal that seems so ridiculous? I can relate to that feeling, and I don't think there's anything wrong with having that question. But then think, Why can't I just accept that person? They're driven to do that; that's their calling; that's important to them, just like what I do is important to me.

Hector's mother had at first been against the idea of his having a large family. She said to him: What are you doing? Don't do what I did! She wanted him to have a better life than she'd had. But she loved the children, and she would babysit, no matter how many kids there were. Hector's brothers and sisters were another matter. Most of them believed in blood, Hector thought; a collection of black and Hispanic and Asian children did not seem like a Badeau family to them. They couldn't understand why Hector would go out of his way to find children with mental and physical flaws. They didn't spend much time with Hector's family.

Sue felt that her mother was bewildered and intimidated by all her children; she couldn't understand why Sue had chosen a life like that. Her mother said: You cannot save the whole world. Is that what you think you're doing? Years later, after her mother died, she heard from her parents' church friends that she had been proud of her and always told people about the amazing things her daughter was doing, but until the funeral she never knew.

After Abel, SueAnn, George, and Flory arrived, there were nine children, and there were no plans for more, but a few months later, a tenth sneaked in, almost by accident. A white woman in Vermont who had had a baby with a black father wanted to give him up for adoption, but didn't want him to be in a family with only white people. She read about the Badeaus in the newspaper and decided that she wanted them to adopt her son. Hector was sick of diapers and had made a no-more-babies rule, but he figured that God had used the newspaper article to tell the mother to give them her baby. They told the children that they were going to fetch a new baby who was half black, half white. When the baby arrived, George looked at him and said, I thought you said he was half black and half white. Sue realized that he had expected the baby to be striped, like a zebra.

Some months later, they received a new copy of *Los Niños* and saw that the six teenagers they had noticed before were still there, only now there were fewer of them—the two oldest had aged out of the system. Now the six kids stood almost no chance of staying together in the same family, and the older ones might never have parents at all. Who else was going to adopt six teenagers? They decided to try for them.

The social workers said no. Hector and Sue were too young— barely ten years older than the oldest of the children—and too white. It seemed like a bad idea to bring six black kids to Vermont, and into a family that already had ten children. But Sue said to the social workers: theirs might not be the ideal family for these kids, but wasn't it better than nothing?

The teenagers were from Texas. Their mother was illiterate; she had married their father when she was sixteen and had six kids in seven years: JD, Fisher, Lilly, Renee, Trish, and David. One night when David was a baby he had such a high fever that their mother took him to the hospital, and when he came back he was deaf and couldn't talk. Their father drank a lot and was in jail a lot. He believed that his wife cheated on him while he was in jail, so when he got out he beat her. He beat the kids, too. He set the older boys against each other, competing over his love, until they became enemies. JD and Fisher thought their father was Superman.

> FISHER: When I was born my brother tried to stab me with a fork. I was my dad's favorite; he favored me over my broth-

ers and sisters. I died in the hospital when I was little and came back to life. And then a gypsy lady told me I would take on the troubles of the family.

Their father started molesting Renee when she was five. He didn't touch her sisters, only Renee. He told her he was teaching her how to be a woman. It happened in a little room at the end of the house. There was flowered wallpaper on the walls, and there was a chair in the corner. The door was white. Her mother knew what was happening—she would clean Renee up in the bathroom afterward—but she spanked her, Renee says, and told Renee it was her own fault.

Their father messed around with other women, too, and one day he messed around with another man's woman and the man shot him dead. After their father died, their mother left. JD was twelve, and all he could think about was revenge. His father had taught him that you watched out for your family no matter what, so he was going to avenge his father's death and kill the man who had killed him. He knew who the man was, and the man was going to get out of jail after a few months. He would kill him then. But the first thing was to find food. JD and Fisher left to go out and hustle. Sometimes they were gone for days, looking for food or money or work. While they were gone, Lilly stole and begged food and made sure the younger kids kept going to school. No one was paying the electricity bill, so the house was dark.

They had an idea where their mother was, because people in the neighborhood had seen her around. She was partying, and sleeping at their aunt's house, or else at a cousin's house, or at the house of someone else she knew. JD knew that his mother got a check at the end of the month, so, when that time came around, he told everyone to get in a taxi. He didn't have any money, but he told the driver he'd get money where they were going, although he didn't know if they would find their mother there or not. They did find her, but she was not happy to see them and asked them what they were doing there. JD told her they were hungry. She took them to a grocery store and bought them some food. She stayed with them for a couple of weeks and then she left again.

After a few months of this, somebody reported them to the state, and the six of them were split up. David was sent to Santa Fe, to a school for the deaf. Renee was abused in a foster home and said she wanted to kill herself, so she was put in a mental hospital in Amarillo. Trish's foster parents locked her in a closet. Sometimes when Trish was riding on the school bus she would look out the window and see her mother on the street. She would scream to her, Momma! And her mother would say, Hi, Patricia, and keep on walking.

Sue kept badgering the social workers. At first she and Hector were permitted to adopt only the youngest of the six, David, who was thirteen. When Sue and Hector went to pick him up, they persuaded the social workers to let them take the next two youngest as well—Renee, who was sixteen, and Trish, who was fifteen.

> RENEE: When I first met Hector, I'm, like, you got an Afro like a black man! Trish goes, "Renee, he black, I think he's black and white." I said, "Trish, I don't think he's black and white, I think he's all Caucasian." And she goes, "No, he had to have some mix, you see his 'fro?"
>
> TRISH: It was freezing. It was December, and they were driving us from the airport, and I remember my dad driving up to this old abandoned house, and I'm sitting there: Oh my God, these white people are going to use us for slaves! I'm so scared! I started crying in the back. And Hector was, like, Oh, stop crying back there, I'm just joking—this is where we live, over here.

At first it felt to Trish like a group home. She liked having all the little kids around—she liked doing the girls' hair and playing with Barbies, and she thought Isaac was cute, a little roly-poly blond kid—but they didn't feel like brothers and sisters yet. The thought of calling Hector and Sue her parents was strange. But they were always doing something, sledding or playing sports or running around in the grass outside the house, and getting their clothes and shoes and toys mixed up, and if you were in a fight with one person there were many others to play with, and it worked; they were happy.

RENEE: God, we used to do everything! We used to play hide 'n' go seek. We used to get in trouble with my mom and dad, and we used to hide in the big old tall grass, and they knew we was doing it. Chelsea, Flory, Renee, Trish! Where are you? I was, like, Shhh. My mom lookin' out the window. You better not be hiding in the tall grass! I'm, like, How does she know we in the grass? And Chelsea goes, 'Cause she got eyes in the back of her head. And Flory goes, Mom ain't no Slyclops! She meant to say the other word, Cyclops. Me, Chelsea, and Trish was laughing, we was rolling, we was cracking up so hard in the grass.

The following winter, Sue and Hector invited the three older kids—JD, who was nineteen, Fisher, who was eighteen, and Lilly, who was seventeen—out to visit. They arrived in a blizzard, wearing New Mexico clothes; the car wouldn't go up the hill because the snow was so deep, so Sue told the kids they had to get out and walk the last mile to the house.

JD: I was curious about what they were all about. This is my brothers and sisters these people were going to have. His name is Hector, so I'm thinking someone Hispanic, and all of a sudden I meet this light-skinned white dude, I'm thinking, What's that about? So, anyway, I watched them. I was cautious of them, let's put it that way. And also wondering, Is this really gonna stay? I was wondering if they bit off more than they could chew.

At the end of that visit, even though JD was already an adult, and Fisher and Lilly were in their senior year of high school, they decided to leave New Mexico to join them, and Sue and Hector adopted the last three.

> SUEANN: They made me give up my room. I was the oldest girl, and I had my own room, finally, once in my life—we all, me, Chelsea, and Flory, had our own rooms—and Lilly took mine, Trish took Flory's, and Renee took Chelsea's, and we three all ended up having to share a room with Joelle. My dad was, like, Don't worry, someday you'll get your own room again. And I did, eventually.
>
> FLORY: But I loved them.
>
> SUEANN: We loved them.
>
> FLORY: They used to braid our hair.
>
> SUEANN: They used to do our hair and play music and dance, they were so much fun. And Lilly liked to shop; she would always tell us about this good fashion that just came out.

> LILLY: I felt like they were my brothers and sisters. I mean, they were kids I didn't know, but they were in the same boat as me and they needed somebody to love, too. They needed a big sister. I felt I had to protect them.

All the teenagers were nervous about being black in Vermont, but Fisher and Lilly were wildly popular in high school: Lilly was a track star, and Fisher was cool and good-looking.

> FISHER: I was popular. It went to my head, I won't lie to you. All the little white girls saw I was the best dancer in the school, and I was the only black guy.

Years later, Lilly noticed that nearly every one of her brothers and sisters had married or paired off with someone of a different race.

When Lilly first joined the family, she asked Sue how she knew she could trust her. Sue said: We have made a commitment to you. That commitment is just as serious to us as our marriage vows. We are making a promise not only to you but also to God, and it doesn't matter what you do, you are our family, we are your parents, and we'll all be in this together.

To Sue, a promise made to God was unbreakable. But it was odd to think about parenthood in those terms. The reason Lilly's mother's abandoning her children was wrong was not that she had broken a promise. She was their mother; and being a mother meant, or ought to have meant, that she had no choice but to take care of them. Promising was what you did with strangers. You tried to keep promises; sometimes you failed. But to Sue and Hector there was no difference: promising meant you had no choice.

This was one of the differences between them and other people. For most people, some duties you were born with, or became part of you when your children were born, and others you undertook; and it was the family duties that were part of you that counted most. But for Sue and Hector, the duties they took upon themselves were as irrevocable as birth. For them, choice and promises were everything, and this was a source of enormous strength. They rejected the lives that their parents and everyone else they knew had led, and chose a life that they invented, because they wanted it and because they believed it would be pleasing to God. They knew that they were human and were constrained that much, but they struggled against even those limits: sleeping less, eating worse, working harder.

The people who called them saints saw this struggle and admired it; but to call them saints was also to betray an ambivalence. To many people, the love of a parent for his child should be urgent, primal, beneath thought. That love should come from longing, from a selfish clutching for happiness, not from compassion or an intention to help. Compassion, like promising, was for strangers. It was not just that altruism was not enough; altruism seemed antithetical to what a parent's love should be. A parent might sacrifice himself for a child, but because he was driven to do it, not out of duty. The love of a parent must be selfish or it was worthless, even repugnant.

To Sue and Hector, self-sacrifice came easily. To live a moral life in the usual way, resisting temptation and embracing righteous difficulty, was not hard. But what was required of them was more complicated than asceticism. To sacrifice pleasure for duty's sake was to get everything wrong. To fulfill their parental promise they must feel delight; they must take pleasure in their children or their efforts would be useless; if they felt no joy, they would have failed.

RENEE: It took me two and a half years to trust my dad. I didn't want him to touch me. I used to wake up having nightmares, and they both would come in, and he'd be standing at the door, and I'd say, What he want? I didn't mean to say it like that. And he goes, Sue, is she okay? My mom would rub my back and say: All right, you safe, you safe. Nobody can't hurt you, nobody can't touch you like this no more. And I would cry, and I would see him, I would see my father, Hector, standing at the door and tears coming out of his eyes, and he goes, What kind of man would do that to his own daughter?

I had to sit back and watch how he was with my brothers and sisters. And I wasn't warming up to him, but I would hug my mama all the time. And he goes, She not ready to hug me yet, is she? My mom goes, No. He'd be saying, When is she gonna hug me, Sue? My mom goes: Not yet. Give her time. Remember. He goes, All I want to do is hug her and let her know she's safe in my arms.

Finally, Christmas in 1990, Chelsea goes, Renee, let's go hug Mom and Dad. She goes, You been here for two years, come on. I said, Uhhh, should I hug him or should I not hug him? And Chelsea and Flory say, Come on! Hurry up! Then I hugged him. I said, Dad, thank you for my gift. After I got done hugging him, I looked at him, I said, Are you crying? He goes, Yeah. I've been waiting for this hug for two years. I said, I know. I'm sorry it took me two years to trust you.

The trouble with running an adoption agency was that it confronted Sue and Hector every day with photographs of kids who had no parents and might never get any. They kept pictures of these children stuck on the refrigerator at home, for the family to look at when they prayed for them in the evenings. One of the photographs was of a tiny doll-like black girl in Texas named Alysia, smiling and reaching out over her crib. She had severe cerebral palsy and was expected never to walk. One day, Hector told Sue that every time he prayed for Alysia the words "she's ours" came into his head. They decided to adopt her.

Their health insurance covered only eight sessions a year of physical therapy for Alysia, so they brought the whole family to the eight sessions, so everyone could learn the exercises. Night after night, the children stood Alysia on the dining table and walked her from one person to the next, using a yardstick as a railing. Within a year, she had begun not only to walk but to dance.

Rootwings received a referral for a four-year-old white boy who'd been shaken as a baby. The shaking had blinded him and left him with brain damage that would prevent him from developing past the stage of a six-month-old. He was in a foster home, but the foster mother couldn't handle him, and if he wasn't adopted soon he would be placed in an institution. The social worker who referred him told Sue that she felt in her gut that the boy was a Badeau.

Sue told the social worker that they weren't adopting any more children, but Hector saw the boy's photograph and wasn't so sure. When they went to meet him at his foster mother's house, Hector decided he wanted to do it. It would be difficult to feed the boy, to get the consistency of his food just right, and he was on a lot of medications. He bit people, so they'd have to be careful with him around the other children. But he liked being in a car, his foster mother said, so he would be fine on the summer camping trips. Hector felt that they had done so much good with Alysia, who knows what they might do with this boy? So they brought him home. They named him Dylan.

The children thought he was cute, and right away Flory, who was ten, asked to be taught how to feed him.

FLORY: Dylan was mine. I fed him, I changed him; I fed him his milk.

SUEANN: Dylan was not yours. Don't even do that.

FLORY: He was mine! I fed him.

SUEANN: All right, I'll give you, you fed him. But I prepared the food. How about that?

FLORY: I prepared the food, I fed him, I changed him, I bathed him, I washed his hair. He would only eat for me.

At first Dylan cried a lot. He had been beaten, and whenever someone approached him he looked scared. But after a while, he began to recognize voices and began to unstiffen and smile.

TRISH: My dad said I had to give Dylan his bath. I didn't want to touch him because of the way his body was, and I kind of freaked out, thinking I was going to hurt him. But they made me give him a bath, and—I knew he didn't see me, because he can't see—I can't explain it, but it looked like he looked at me in my eyes, and something just came over me, this different bond that I'd never had before, with him. It was like he was telling me, You're okay, I'm not hurt, just take care of me, don't let me drown. After that we had this little thing with each other. And that's why I wanted to be a nurse.

The year after they adopted Dylan, a social worker asked them to adopt a Chinese American boy named Wayne who had Sanfilippo syndrome, a disease that made a child hyperactive and sleepless, then gradually destroyed his physical functions until it ended in early death. Wayne was three years old and had lost his hearing, but he could still walk. At first Sue and Hector both thought that adopting Wayne was out of the question. They had too many kids already, and bringing into the family a child who was certain to die—it was a terrible thing to imagine, not only for them but for their other children. But they told the social worker they would think and pray on it.

They thought about the children they had so far, and how none of them had turned out quite as they expected, and how they had tried to adapt to that without thinking about it as disappointment. They thought about how all love meant pain and grief and loss of some kind. They thought about how they knew now, as they hadn't known when they were younger, that neither love nor faith was enough to rescue a child damaged by harrowing experience, and so, if they could love a child who was forever damaged in that way, why couldn't they love a child whom they were equally helpless to save, but who without their love would end up somewhere worse? A few weeks later, they were convinced that God meant Wayne to be their son.

Three years after that, a friend called to tell them about Adam, a six-year-old white boy from Florida who needed a family. Adam had the same terminal disease that Wayne did, but he also had fetal alcohol syndrome and took medications through a chest port. He had been in several different foster homes, and he had been abused.

Each time Sue and Hector were considering adopting another child, they held a family meeting to discuss it. At first, Jose was the only one who openly questioned the need for more kids. Jose said, There has to be another family, our family can't take every kid in the world. The others might have had the same thoughts, but they came out at other times, in other ways. When Chelsea was twelve, she was delivering newspapers, and on a steep hill the brakes of her bicycle failed and she was thrown violently over the handlebars onto the street. She yelled at her parents, If you didn't adopt so many children, I could have had a new bike, and this wouldn't have happened to me. But usually, at the family meetings, the children were in favor. A new small child was cute, a new big child was exciting, a new child of your own age was someone else to play with. This time, though, the kids weren't sure.

> TRISH: We got to a point where we were, like, All right, Dad and Mom, you've got to stop adopting. Some of us got tired of it; we felt like we were helping taking care of everybody. I would feel bad because I would think to myself, How would I feel if they didn't want to adopt me because they thought we had too many kids? But I would still feel, like, That's enough.

> ISAAC: I understand that there's people who need help, but you can only stretch yourself so thin. We'd ask them, Are you sure this is something that you want to do? And they said it was something they needed to do, that if they didn't help this boy, then nobody was going to. And that's not something they felt they could live with, I guess.

Sue and Hector told the children they would consider their opinions and pray on it. Not long afterward, Sue flew down to Florida to bring Adam home.

This was another thing that made Sue and Hector different from most people. Most people would think first about how an adoption would affect the children they had; but to Sue and Hector, the need of the child who was still a stranger weighed equally in the balance. They never told themselves that because a child was a stranger he was not their problem: if they heard about a particular child who was suffering, they felt he was as much their problem as if he were drowning at their feet, or had been left on their doorstep.

To Sue and Hector, a child in distress was not yet family, but not quite a stranger either. It was a third, intermediate category of person, morally speaking, between family and stranger: a person whom it was their *duty* to help, in the same way that it would be their duty to help a wounded person right in front of them on the street. The child was not in front of them in a physical way, but because they had decided that children without homes were their mission, that child was standing in the place where they had built their moral lives; the place where they were standing also, waiting, in case a child like that should come along. It didn't matter that they hadn't yet met the child, and didn't yet love him. Parents didn't have duties to their children because of love—even parents who did not love their children had duties towards them—but because, of all the people in the world, parents were *closest*; and there was no one else around in quite the same way.

Sue and Hector didn't tell themselves that someone else would adopt the child if they didn't. They knew that wasn't true. If they decided not to adopt a child—and there *were* many that they did not adopt—it was because they felt they could not be good parents to him for some reason, or because they worried that bringing him in would make everybody's lives worse. This was another way in which their mission was complicated: they wanted to help as many children as they could, but if they tried to help too many then they would do harm; and there was nobody to tell them where to draw that line.

Adam was different from Wayne. Wayne had been loved, and he was always laughing. Adam almost never laughed or smiled—he was angry. When someone approached him, he flinched. He was stiff and bleak.

Adam had a brother, a four-year-old named Aaron. Sue and Hector had tried to adopt Aaron, too, so the brothers could grow up together, but Aaron was small and cute as well as white, and the social worker thought she could do better for him; she said no. Besides, she told Sue, Adam was too damaged even to know he had a brother. But it turned out that Aaron was not so cute as he had appeared—he was so angry and difficult that his adoptive family sent him back after six weeks. The social worker called Sue and told her if she still wanted Aaron she could have him. A week later, Aaron arrived. He was there to greet the bus that brought Adam back from therapy; as Adam's wheelchair touched the sidewalk, Adam caught sight of his brother and smiled the biggest smile Sue had ever seen on his face.

Aaron was indeed a difficult child, and Sue and Hector were resolved that, with twenty-one children, they had reached their limit. But then, one day, when Hector was out delivering firewood, a woman he was delivering to asked him to come inside. She had seen a television program about the family and recognized him. She told him that she knew of a fourteen-year-old girl named Geeta who had been adopted as a baby from India, but her mother couldn't handle her, and she had ended up in foster care, moving from family to family. When the woman saw the Badeaus on television, she thought that they were the family that would stick by the girl no matter what. Hector told her they weren't going to adopt again. But, not long after, Sue and Hector decided that the girl was meant to be theirs after all. Sue had always believed that they would have a second child from India.

The next year, Hector received a letter from a group that was trying to resettle refugees from Kosovo. He called Sue and told her that he didn't even need to pray about it, he knew God wanted him to help. He reminded her that they had an empty room—a family could stay in that. He was taken aback when they were assigned a family of eight—a mother, a father, a grandmother, and five kids. He figured they would still fit in the one big room, however; the social worker had assured him that the family preferred to live in close quarters. It would only be for a few months. Things worked out well with the Kosovo family, so a year or so later, Hector signed up to host four boys from Sudan.

That was when they reached their peak: twenty-two children plus the refugees. They would adopt no more themselves—but there were still many children in need of a home, so, in an effort to persuade other people to adopt, they wrote a book about their family, *Are We There Yet?* And then the numbers began to go down again.

Adam was the first to die, at age eleven. Dylan died next, on his twenty-fourth birthday. Wayne died a year and a half later, at twenty-five, having outlived his life expectancy by more than ten years. Everybody grieved, but it was hardest for Hector. For twelve years he had woken up at dawn every morning to feed and change his three sick sons, and caring for them had been his most constant duty.

> SUE: It was like losing your child and your career on the same day.
> HECTOR: My whole life was changed; my whole flow was messed up. I needed to feel that I had some worth.

He and Sue needed money, as they always did, so he decided to take a job working the overnight shift at a group house for homeless men.

The other trouble with running an adoption agency—beyond the constant confrontation with needy children they either couldn't help or had to help—was that it didn't pay for itself. Sue, who was always optimistic, started paying Rootwings expenses out of their personal bank account; but their bank account was tiny, and soon it was empty, and checks started to bounce. Sue hid this from Hector for a long time, nearly two years.

When Sue finally told him about the money, she did what had to be done: shut down Rootwings. They both took a series of jobs to try to work their way out of debt.

> HECTOR: Sue worked with a—
> SUE: Facility for adults with mental illness.

HECTOR: Adult facility.

SUE: You worked for UPS.

HECTOR: I worked at UPS. And I was a job coach for a mentally retarded adult. You had that traveling-saleswoman job, selling gift cards, and you did some tutoring of Hispanic kids.

SUE: In Holyoke.

HECTOR: Holyoke.

SUE: Good lord, we did so many weird things.

They didn't have to live on their earnings alone. Some of the children came with adoption subsidies, the amount depending on the state they came from and what kind of services they needed. A healthy kid might receive anywhere from two hundred and fifty to five hundred dollars per month; a severely disabled kid might receive seven or eight hundred. The subsidies covered food and some clothing, but then there was heating and everything else.

Slowly, they began to pay off their debts, and then Sue was offered a job in Philadelphia as an adoption caseworker. It would mean more money—she would earn about sixty thousand dollars—and living in a place where their children would not be almost the only nonwhite kids in school. They decided to go. JD, Fisher, Lilly, and Trish were already living on their own by then and decided to stay behind in Vermont, but the rest packed up and went.

They found a house in Mount Airy, a vast stone edifice with a wide porch and Tudor gable roofs. It had been a bed-and-breakfast, and before that it had been a convent. Inside, the rooms were dim, paneled in dark wood, with enormous fireplaces and stained-glass windows. There were ten proper bedrooms, but Sue and Hector carved out more: some of the closets were big enough to be bedrooms, they figured. In the back was a lawn large enough so they made a bit of extra money renting it out for weddings. At first they had heat in the winters, though they couldn't really afford it because the house was so big, but then the furnace broke, and they started heating the house with the fireplace in the living room, a wood stove in the front hall, and space heaters elsewhere. This meant that most of the house was freezing; in the evenings, they huddled together in the living room, where it was warmest, around the TV.

When they bought the house, four teenage boys were squatting there. They told the boys they could stay, and they became unofficially part of the family. Over the years, the family acquired more unofficial members—foster kids who came and went, a teenage girl who was an illegal immigrant from Guatemala, friends of Badeau children who weren't getting along with their own parents and came to live in the house, sometimes for years at a time. Sue and Hector never made any distinction between these unofficial children and the official ones. Sue felt that the ones who had been around longest were part of the family: not by adoption, but by means of an unspoken commitment formed over years of being together and sharing family life, like a common-law marriage. Sometimes when Sue included these unofficial kids in intimate family occasions, the official kids would object. What did family mean if everyone was included?

This was another ambivalence that hovered when people called Sue and Hector saints. Saints were notorious for caring as much about strangers as about their families. Some claimed that this impartial, universal love for all people was a noble, if difficult, thing, something to aspire to, even if only saints could achieve it. But to most people, partiality to one's own—loving family and friends more than strangers—was at the heart of what it meant to be human.

Sue was good at her job, and after a few years she was offered a new one, doing training, advocacy, and policy work at the National Adoption Center. A couple of years after that, she applied for and was offered a fellowship at a foundation in Washington, D.C., working on foster-care and disability policy in the Senate. It meant that she would be in Washington five days a week, home only on weekends, but it would pay a lot better than the job she had, and she really wanted to do it. She persuaded Hector that it was the next stepping-stone on God's path for them—first the group home, then Root-wings, then her Philadelphia advocacy job, now this, each one allowing them to help more and more children. When the foundation job ended, after a year, Sue was offered a different job that meant staying in Washington for another year, and she took it.

> HECTOR: I had all the energy in the world, and I guess I was in the frame of mind at that time that this is what I was supposed to be doing. As time went on, to be honest with you, I got a little envious of Sue. I was on twenty-four/seven, and I was resentful some nights when I was dealing with all the crap here and she could go to bed. But the hardest part, where I developed a little anger, was, a lot of the time she came home and worked. I kinda liked her and wanted to spend time, and we both got the crappy end of each other. We were always dead tired, and even if we had a little bit of time there was always a kid interrupting.

When that job ended, Sue came back to live in Philadelphia, but she was gone often, speaking all over the country, doing trainings on the importance of adoption and giving children a permanent home. She was a prominent person in the field now; her talks and trainings were much in demand. Sometimes she would take a child on the trips with her, but mostly she went alone.

> TRISH: Sometimes I wish my mom was there more around with us. She was gone a lot. I understood she had her work, but I guess I felt I didn't have a mom then. When I had my biological mom, she was always leaving us, and I almost kind of felt that way with my mom, my adopted mother, thinking, okay, she's always gone. I felt like I needed her, it was hard to talk to my dad about girl stuff. I'm embarrassed— I want to talk to mom, when is she coming back?

Sometimes Sue would come home with all her training and her reading in the social-work literature, and tell Hector that he should be doing something differently, and he would feel that he had been in the trenches day in and day out, cleaning toilets and doing laundry while she was staying in hotels, and he would yell at her, Don't give me this textbook shit! I know what it's like. If a child was screwing up, Sue always wondered how she could support the child better; Hector thought the child ought to be punished, because if there weren't any consequences the child would never learn. The kids figured out pretty quickly that if they wanted something they should ask Sue. She would come home from a trip feeling guilty for being away and couldn't bring herself to say no, and then, the next week, she would be away again, and Hector was the cop.

> JOSE: I think my parents were way too easygoing. Account-ability was not very high on their list. It's hard for them to punish kids. I think that's one thing they really didn't get right, and that's why various scenarios happened over and over again in our family, like stealing, getting preg-nant, getting in trouble with the law. It wasn't drilled in hard enough that that's not okay, that there will be conse-quences.

Not long after they adopted the six teenagers, the troubles began. First JD got his girlfriend pregnant. Lilly went off to college, but she got pregnant and quit. Then Fisher dropped out of college and got sent to jail for drugs.

Fisher wasn't often in touch, especially once they moved to Phil-adelphia and he stayed in Vermont. He got a girlfriend pregnant—he was seductive and charming, he always had girlfriends. He asked Sue and Hector for money, and when it wasn't enough, he stole. He had another child with his girlfriend, then a child with another girl, then another child with another girl. Finally, he got arrested for beating up a girlfriend and got sent to prison for a long time. His brothers and sisters wouldn't visit, they were sick of him, his stealing and lying and beatings—only Sue and Hector did. Lilly said he had turned out just like their biological father, and she thought he would die in jail.

> FISHER: I have dreams of me being a different person. I keep having these dreams.

Trish was raped and had a baby, but Hector took care of the child and Trish graduated from high school. Renee got pregnant and moved back home. These were bad things, but Sue and Hector felt that they'd had so little time with these kids before they were grown that there'd been only so much they could do. Then SueAnn got pregnant at fifteen. Sue and Hector's fury was terrible: they raged at SueAnn, and she wept. Had she learned *nothing* from seeing her sisters blight their chances? Had she heard none of the Christian teachings they had tried for so many years to instill in her? Hector told her she had two choices: give the child up for adoption, or drop out of high school to take care of it. SueAnn allowed some family friends to adopt her baby and she went to college.

But then Flory got pregnant at nineteen. Geeta got pregnant. SueAnn got pregnant again and quit college. Geeta got pregnant again. Alysia got pregnant. Flory got pregnant again. Alysia got pregnant again. Then it started with the next generation: JD's eldest daughter got pregnant at eighteen; JD's second daughter got pregnant at seventeen; Lilly's daughter got pregnant at seventeen.

Each time, Sue felt that the failure was hers: if she'd been a better parent, it wouldn't have happened. She told herself this was a stupid way to think, she was playing God, she couldn't possibly control everything, but she felt it all the same.

FLORY: I was sleeping on the couch one night when I was pregnant because I was uncomfortable up in my room, and I woke up to my mom crying over me. She was really crying, and just sitting on the couch watching me sleep. That was the only time I seen her break down. But she did it while I was sleeping. She didn't do it to my face or tell me that she was disappointed in me.

Hector and Sue weren't naïve—they knew that kids were going to be kids, which was why they had talked to the children about sex and contraception.

JOELLE: I don't remember the sex talk. I remember a talk, maybe, but I kind of have a short attention span, and my mom can talk a lot, so if she was talking about it maybe I just was zoned out by the time she started talking about that.

Some of the girls, Hector and Sue had even got on contraceptives at fifteen because they were worried this would happen—the kind of contraceptives that you didn't have to remember to use, shots in the arm, implants—but it happened anyway. Nothing they did had made any difference at all.

Hector believed abortion was a sin, but as the pregnancies came one after another he told his daughters that it was up to them. He didn't think any of his daughters had had an abortion, but he wasn't sure that they would tell him if they did, knowing how he felt about it. He liked to think that they knew he would love them just the same, but he wasn't sure.

For a long time, Chelsea and Joelle were the holdouts. Hector was sure they would be careful. They were both in college, and they had ambitions—Chelsea wanted to make films, Joelle wanted to be an actress. But then Chelsea got pregnant, and finally Joelle did, too. When Joelle told Hector she was pregnant, first he shouted at her, then he started to cry, then he left. He went to the train station and bought a ticket, and all day he rode the train, all the way to Trenton and back, and all over Philadelphia, and for hours and hours he sat in his seat and cried. At first he raged at God. Why couldn't they get even *one* of their kids to wait until she was married before she had children? Why had every single one ignored what they had taught her about the importance of raising kids in a stable home?

Then Hector heard God reminding him of John 8:7—"Let anyone among you who is without sin be the first to throw a stone"—and he remembered his own sins and was ashamed. He thought about how Joelle had been born weighing two pounds at twenty-seven weeks and it was a miracle that she was alive at all. He thought about the funny things she'd done when she was little, and how tender she had been with Dylan and Wayne. He thought about how hard she'd worked to get into college, and how she was about to graduate, and how it was small of him to feel humiliated at the thought of her walking across the stage with a big belly. At the end of the day, he went home.

A few years later, something much worse happened. Alysia's teacher at school called Hector to tell him that Alysia said she was in love with her brother Abel. The teacher had determined that something sexual had happened between them. Abel was twenty-eight and Alysia was sixteen, though because of her cerebral palsy the teacher said she comprehended at a third-grade level.

Hector thought about what a good kid Abel had been, how he'd tried so hard in school and always followed the rules.

> ABEL: It was a really bad time in my life. I was going through divorce. What I did was illegal, mostly because of her age and because she had cerebral palsy. They said that she comprehended at a third-grade level, but if you knew her,

nobody thought that. I felt like I let the whole family down, and I was really depressed, but it wasn't like I attacked her or nothing like that.

Family loyalties were split. Even Renee, who had been sexually abused by her father, couldn't bring herself to condemn Abel completely.

RENEE: I started crying, because I think that somebody did that stuff to him. Somebody touched him like that, that he thought it was okay to do that to Alysia. But she did some stuff, too, they both was wrong. I can't put all the blame on him.

There were social workers and doctors and psychologists. There were lawyers and police. At the end of it, Abel was sentenced to eight years in prison.

HECTOR: I almost left. I almost left. I almost just walked away from everything. It was the worst thing that could have happened to us. I was so naïve, because it happens—I'd heard about it in other families and thought, That doesn't happen in my family. But it did. I was so totally unaware. I felt like such a failure. Where the hell was I? How did we not see the signs? There must have been something there, and we failed to see it. I just felt, Screw this, I'm done. I can't take this anymore; somebody else can take over. I wanted to beat somebody up. I don't think I've ever had a breakdown, but I was close to one then.

SUE: It was like falling off your boat in shark-infested water and just trying to survive until the sharks went away. I don't know. I was too depressed to even—I couldn't think about what I could do next. I couldn't think about doing anything.

Sue became more depressed than she had ever been. Sometimes she felt that her whole life had been a mistake; that she had misheard what God was saying to her, she wasn't supposed to be doing this at all, she was the wrong person. At other times she felt that she had heard just fine, and she raged at God.

SUE: You set us up for this. You told us to do this, so You should protect our kids and us from these kinds of things happening. *How dare You set us up for this?*

There was no answer. She wrote to a friend:

I try to pray but I feel like I am praying into a black hole. Reading the Bible does nothing more for me than reading the newspaper. I still "believe," but I feel nothing, no connection to God, no reality of the Holy Spirit in my life. This must be what Hell is like.

Very slowly, she returned to life. She thought about what had happened and how it was only one of the terrible things that had happened in the world, and she thought about the question of how a good and all-powerful God could allow such things. She thought that the world was an unfolding story whose ending was unknown to her, and without knowing the ending, she could never hope to understand why things happened the way they did. She knew that she was just a small part of that story, a small creature laying a few bricks of what might someday be a cathedral. She was going to die before the end of the world, so she was never going to know how things turned out. She had faith that ultimately God would make sure things turned out for the good, but how He would do that was a mystery, so she had to accept the world as it was. It was not for her to judge.

2005

Dear Abel,

These are the pictures we wanted to send you. I hope
you will be allowed to keep them. I am glad Dad and I got
to visit you although seeing you in there broke my heart. I
continue to pray for you every single day. . . . I have made
the following decision about how I am going to
demonstrate my love for you and support you in the
remaining time you are in prison—I make the following
promises to you:

- I will continue to pray for you every day, every week.
- I will write to you as often as I can. . . . My letters
  will focus on the positive, share upbeat news
  from home, information about how the family is
  doing. . . .
- From time to time, when I am able to do so, I will
  send you some money so you will have enough to buy
  the basic necessities like soap, or deodorant, or
  stamps.
- I will send you cards and gifts on your birthday and
  special holidays. . . .
- I will arrange to visit you periodically as my work and
  family schedule permit. . . .

It really is sad and a shame that you are in jail, it breaks
my heart every day. But since you are there, you have to
decide how you will use your time. Will you use it being
angry and bitter and defensive? Or will you use your time
trying to make a positive difference? You have a wonderful
opportunity to spend big amounts of time in prayer—
praying for each of us—how wonderful that would be to
know that someone is praying for me and Dad and each
of the kids every day! . . . What a gift God has given you

if you choose to use it that way. Amazing Grace! You have a great opportunity that in some ways I wish I had. The choice is yours—how WILL you spend your time?

Love Mom.

2006

Dear Abel,

I hope you're doing OK. Just a short note to wish you Happy Birthday. I'm sure you've had better but I hope it's the best it can be. Mom and I will be thinking of you.

How are things going. I'm sorry I've not written more often. I think the last time was when Mamie died. That was a hard, sad time. . . . It's been hard on Mom. She keeps everything in. A lot like you.

The last 3 months have been hard. Real problems with Aaron. He's on run-away now. He left Friday night, he stole $135 from Chelsea. In January he was on runaway and broke into a car and got arrested. I think he has a real drug problem. Things just disappear around here. A lot like when Fisher was here. I feel for Aaron. It looks like he's headed for jail because he broke his 1st time offender's agreement with the D.A. It's very hard living with him. I can never trust what he'll do next. It's very sad. . . .

I had my top teeth pulled and now have dentures. They look good but are painful till I get used to them.

I miss you and hope at some point soon to come see you.

Love
Dad.

2009

Dear Abel,

I don't know where to begin, so I will start with what is on my heart—I love you. Really, truly, sincerely with all my heart. And I miss you so very, very much it is a huge ache in my heart. So why then haven't I been faithful about writing? Why haven't I found a way to get out there to visit you? I have no answers and no excuses. I truly cannot even explain it to myself. . . . I feel as though I have failed you as a mother in the last few years but I truly hope and pray that you will give me more chances to make up for that over all the years of both of our lives that are still ahead of us. . . . Certainly I have forgiven you for any and all of the things that are in the past. I hope you will do the same for me. . . .

Now I will tell you a few updates about the family, going from kid to kid by age, I hope you will like that. . . .

Once again, I can't tell you how sorry I am for neglecting to communicate with you in the past couple of years and I ask for your forgiveness and understanding. I do love you so very, very much and I look forward to renewing our relationship.

Much love and many prayers—MOM

ABEL: When I first got back, it was really hard for me to get that bond back with my parents. It was easier for me to just bury it and let it go than to feel like it was there every time I was around them. I just let them know that certain stuff I had learned about myself—I just let them know I wouldn't do something like that again. My dad picked me up from prison and it was like a seven- or eight-hour drive, and we talked about it on the way back. They always tell me now, Good to see you're doing well, we see you've changed.

As the pregnancies came one after another, and especially after Abel went to prison, Hector began to drink. It was his escape from everything that was unbearable. No matter what he drank, he was always up at five to tend to Adam and Dylan and Wayne when they were still alive. He never let things slide, though sometimes he would go to bed hammered and realize next morning that it was a good thing nothing had happened in the night.

Sue was away so much, working, and knowing that Hector was drinking, she always worried that this trip would be the one during which something bad would happen at home. She worried that this was all her fault, because she was the mother and she wasn't at home taking care of her children, as she should have been. And every time there was a wedding or a big family event, Hector would get rowdy and Sue felt humiliated.

Sue didn't drink; instead, she got migraines, and she got depressed. Sometimes she would fall into depressions so bleak that she couldn't get out of bed; sometimes she continued to function but realized afterward that for months she had been living in a fog, barely feeling anything except anger.

Early one morning, Sue tried to wake Hector to drive her to the train, but he'd been drinking and wouldn't wake up, so she walked by herself and was mugged. That was the end. When she got home from her trip, she told him that if he didn't stop drinking she would leave him. Hector didn't really believe she would leave him, but it was enough that she had said she would. He promised her he would stop drinking completely, and he did. But that feat didn't take away the sadness that had got him drinking in the first place.

> HECTOR: I had a tremendous amount of energy when I was young, and always saw things, you know, cup half full. But I started feeling tired. Dealing with the same shit over and over and over as each generation of kids went through—

ahh, not this again. Kid got kicked out of school, or this one got arrested. Maybe ten years ago, when things were getting really hard, I started to get a little cynical and wondering: Is it worth it? Why do I keep getting up every day and doing the same thing? You get the same results. What's that thing about insanity?

It wasn't just the awful stuff that hadn't worked out the way they'd hoped. Only a few of the kids still went to church; Isaac was an agnostic, and Raj had started going to meetings for atheists. None of the kids had adopted kids of their own.

CHELSEA: I always thought in the back of my head that I would maybe adopt, but I've never wanted a huge family. I've witnessed firsthand everything that's gone into adopting, and I'm not sure I'm ready to deal with that. My parents have a calling that I don't feel like I inherited.

Sue and Hector had been so sure that they could change things for their children; but their kids' parents had had children as teenagers and gone on welfare and gone to jail, and now many of their kids had had children as teenagers and were on welfare and going to jail. When Hector felt most despairing, he told himself that at least they were better off than they would have been in foster care. It was a low bar, but they had surely done that much. And then he would think: Well, it wasn't up to us to break the cycle. It is up to God; and as long as we're doing what we believe God wants us to be doing, that's the best that we can do.

In the hard times, when they felt that they'd failed, it was difficult for Sue and Hector to remember why they'd chosen to do what they did.

JOSE: When my parents were young, they were cool: she was the beauty queen, he was the sports star. I remember how they hung out with friends, they went out for picnics, the stuff you see in a movie from the sixties—they all brought their kids, they had dinners at their friends' houses, they were very social, they had a group of friends. But with so many kids, to maintain relationships becomes harder, and not everybody wants to be associated with them, because things happen, and there are black people in their family, not everyone feels like their family is so cool anymore, and that changes your circle of friends and how you behave.

SUE: If someone came over for dinner, they would always leave saying something like, This was actually really nice. The way they would word it was, We didn't expect it to be nice.

JOSE: My parents lost their mojo. They paid that price for having such a family. I think my dad feels it the most. My mom travels for her job and has a network, but my dad is at home, and my dad went from being a really, really cool guy—even now, if you go to Barre, everyone knows who he is—and then, as life went on, they became kind of outcasts. I think my dad wishes he had more friends.

ISAAC: He had us; we were his friends, as far as going out to play pool or go bowling or ice skating. But he didn't have a group of guys, like normal people go out with their friends through life. He never had that.

In the hard times, it was difficult for Sue and Hector to remember how unlikely it was that anyone else would have adopted their children, and how much worse those children's lives would have been if they'd not had a family and a home. In the hard times it was easy for them to forget how many good things had happened in their children's lives. Misery is a stronger emotion than happiness; and catastrophes punctured their minds and reshaped their sense of their lives in a way that ordinary contentment did not. But there had been many good things.

After Lilly got pregnant, she went to work on the line at the Cabot Creamery factory, and it turned out she loved her job—twenty years later, she was still there and had been promoted to manager. She'd been with the same man for many years. Sometimes when she'd had a drink or two she would cry and tell her parents how much she loved them, and how grateful she was, and how she would never have this life without them.

Trish managed to graduate from high school, with Hector taking care of her baby, and now she had two more children, was living with a man who had also been adopted, and was a home health aide to elderly people; she loved her work, too. JD was a plumber and was engaged to his girlfriend. He knew that if Sue and Hector hadn't adopted him he would have spent his life in jail for murdering the man who killed his father.

Renee and David worked in the kitchens of local schools and were living on their own. Although David was deaf and mute, he was maybe the happiest of the family: everyone loved him, and he was always beaming; he had an otherworldly radiance that seemed to bear no trace of his difficult life. SueAnn dropped out of college to have her second baby, but she was happily married and liked her work at the Hair Cuttery; she had her cosmetology license. Flory had also been married for years. Isaac was married and had joined the military. Joelle had a steady job supervising special-needs children in schools. Jose and Chelsea were the biggest successes in worldly terms: Chelsea worked at a large media company in Philadelphia, as a director of their website, and Jose was a computer programmer at a bank in Zürich. Even Abel had found his feet after his release from jail: he was working as a chef at a Japanese restaurant.

When Sue and Hector had been married for twenty-five years, the children pooled their money and arranged for them to spend a week camping by the same lake in Vermont where they had spent their honeymoon. The place hadn't changed much. They made bonfires and swam and rowed on the lake and played backgammon. When they got back, a surprise party was waiting for them. The whole family was there—even Jose had flown in from Switzerland. There was a cake that looked just like their wedding cake. SueAnn had made centerpieces and name cards, and Renee read a poem she had written for that day. Chelsea had made a family video. Alysia danced, and people cried to see her.

And every year there were birthday parties and weddings and graduations; there were grandchildren and great-grandchildren, most of them still living in the same neighborhood, within a few blocks of each other and their parents, in and out of each other's homes all the time, minding each other's children. And every Easter and Fourth of July and Thanksgiving and Christmas and New Year's, the children and the grandchildren and the great-grandchildren gathered with Sue and Hector in the big house they still lived in, although they couldn't afford it, and ate a meal together. And though some were missing—three dead, one in jail—still, most were there year after year, and for everything that had happened, they were a family.

THE ASPIDISTRA IS THE TREE OF LIFE

THE UNDERMINING OF DO-GOODERS,
PART THREE

> Our civilization is founded on greed and fear, but in the lives of
> common men the greed and fear are mysteriously transmuted into
> something nobler. The lower-middle-class people in there, behind
> their lace curtains, with their children and their scraps of furniture
> and their aspidistras—they lived by the money-code, sure enough,
> and yet they contrived to keep their decency. The money-code as
> they interpreted it was not merely cynical and hoggish. They had
> their standards, their inviolable points of honour. They "kept
> themselves respectable"—kept the aspidistra flying. Besides, they
> were *alive*. They were bound up in the bundle of life. They begot
> children, which is what the saints and the soul-savers never by any
> chance do. The aspidistra is the tree of life, he thought suddenly.
>
> —GEORGE ORWELL, *Keep the Aspidistra Flying*

This is the core of it. There is decency, and honor, and ordinary humanness, and family, and children, and life—and then there is saintliness. There is everything you love about the world—everything that, if you found yourself shipwrecked on a distant planet, or close to death, you would most inconsolably remember of your earthly life—and then there is saintliness. If there is one place more than any other where do-gooders are set up as enemies of humanness, it is in fiction, particularly in modern novels. It's in novels that the allegiance to humility and decency and human fellowship is strongest; in novels, moral extremity and a devotion to abstract ideals are nearly always regarded with suspicion. "I hate the idea of causes," the novelist E. M. Forster wrote in 1938. "If I had to choose between betraying my country and betraying my friend I hope I should have the guts to betray my country." It is in fiction that the case against do-gooders—their spiritual hubris, their distance from ordinary life, their presuming to attempt to triumph over human failure and suffering and weakness—is made most moving and powerful.

Take Ralph Eldred, a do-gooder in Hilary Mantel's 1994 novel *A Change of Climate*. Ralph is stubbornly blind to the evil in people, and refuses to see how impossible it is to change them. He holds himself responsible for everyone, but no one responsible for themselves. He believes that human society is growing steadily more benevolent, and that humans are perfectible. His wife, Anna, doesn't worry about small injustices she inflicts by mistake; she knows that man is fallen and the world is imperfect. But Ralph finds this attitude repulsive:

> It is fatalistic, he thought, it releases us from the responsibility which we should properly take. We should do our best, he felt, always our best—consult our consciences, consult our capabilities, then, whenever we can, push out against unjust circumstance. . . . If we are not mere animals, or babies, we must always choose, and choose to do good. In choosing evil we collude with the principle of decay, we become mere vehicles of chaos, we become subject to the laws of a universe which tends back towards dissolution, the universe the Devil owns. In choosing to do good we show we have free will, that we are God-designed creatures who stand against all such laws.
>
> So I will be good, Ralph thought. That is all I have to do.

Ralph works for a home for damaged and unwanted children, and is too busy working for those children to pay much attention to his own. He will always give away household money to someone who needs it more. Every summer, he brings some of his damaged children home for a visit, and his family is forced to endure their nastiness, their thefts, and their violence. But Ralph is determined to love even the most vicious of them. He has "made a study of love, a science"; his love is stubborn, willed, combative.

Everything about his life and Anna's is shadowed by what happened to them years before. They left England together as newly marrieds in the 1950s to work as missionaries in Johannesburg. They had very little money, but Ralph was troubled that they lived better than the locals, and considered abandoning their house to live in a hut. They never sat down alone to dinner together. Whenever they came home in the evening, there were always people waiting for them on their stoep with a problem that was difficult to solve—they needed shelter or food or someone bailed out of jail. Whenever someone knocked in the night, they always opened the door. They gave out food, even knowing that some of the people who came for it didn't really need it; they just took it because it was free.

Things started to go missing. They suspected their menacing gardener, Enock. Anna gave birth to twins, a boy and a girl. Soon after that, one stormy night, Ralph heard a knock on the door and a female voice begging to come in. He realized that Enock was around and threatening, but he chose charity over safety and opened the door. Enock pushed in. Ralph was bludgeoned and stabbed and almost killed, and then he and Anna discovered that both their babies were missing. They found the girl, sometime later, nearly drowned and frozen in muddy water. They never found the boy.

There aren't many do-gooders in fiction, which is odd, because many fiction writers, like do-gooders, are driven by moral rage. But most such writers would rather show the thing that enrages them than show a character trying to fix it. You could say that do-gooders are rare in life, so their rarity in realistic fiction is not surprising—though they are rarer in novels than in life. Real people are bad, but fictional people are worse. It could be that the absence of do-gooders increases a story's moral force by directing it outward: if there is no character to help, then only the reader is left. It could be that do-gooders are considered boring. But there seems something more at work; it's as if there is something about do-gooders that is repellent to fiction.

There are exceptions, of course, such as the heroic doctor, Rieux, in Albert Camus's novel *The Plague*. But it's striking that many of these exceptional good characters go out of their way to scorn do-gooders, and to reject ethical aspiration. When they perform their good deeds, they say that they are merely doing their job, and consider their moral mandate to be quite limited. "There's no question of heroism in all this," Rieux says. "It consists in doing my job." Elsewhere, he says: "You know, I feel more fellowship with the defeated than with saints. Heroism and sanctity don't really appeal to me, I imagine. What interests me is being a man." Another such exception is the atheist, pragmatically minded Doctor Colin in Graham Greene's *A Burnt-Out Case*. Colin works in a leper colony in Congo. One day Querry, a celebrated architect, turns up, looking for somewhere remote to hide from his fame; Colin is suspicious of Querry's motives and interrogates him. "You want to be of use, don't you?" Colin asks sharply. "You don't want menial jobs just for the sake of menial jobs? You aren't either a masochist or a saint."

Many of the singularly good characters in fiction are chaste innocents rather than do-gooders—characters like Dostoyevsky's holy fool Prince Myshkin in *The Idiot*; even Alyosha, the monk of angelic disposition in *The Brothers Karmazov*, is more innocent than do-gooder. And most of the do-gooder characters that do exist have a crucial flaw that ensures that nobody can take them seriously. Either they are personally repellent, like Walter in Jonathan Franzen's *Freedom*; or ineffective, like Miss Birdseye in *The Bostonians*; or weak and die young, like Georges Bernanos's country priest, or Millie in

Wings of the Dove, or Stephen Blackpool in *Hard Times*; or else they are so completely ridiculous that they make nonsense of the whole do-gooder enterprise, like Don Quixote, or Mrs. Jellyby in *Bleak House*. George Eliot introduced Dorothea in *Middlemarch* as a "foundress of nothing" who, despite a certain spiritual grandeur and a loving heart, failed to achieve anything significant.

Preachy do-gooder characters are nearly always ridiculed for their self-righteousness, their puritanism, and their efforts to change other people. "A character who possessed all the seven great virtues would never do as the hero of a novel," the novelist Robertson Davies wrote. "He would be perfect, and in consequence unsympathetic, for we are impatient and suspicious of human perfection." The sentiment seems so obvious and banal, coming from a novelist, that it barely needs to be said. In fiction, it often seems that the imperfect and sinful are more profoundly human than the good, and so the preachy do-gooder is guilty not only of sanctimony but of a deeper failure to understand human nature.

Characters whose emotions are stirred by ideals as much as people are not to be trusted: a character who is any kind of philosopher or theorist is likely to be deplored, either for foolish unworldliness or, if his ideas are effective, for violence. Wise characters are devoted to the complex, the particular, the intimate: to the densely drawn place, the ephemeral moment, and most of all, through love, to the individual person. Here is George Eliot, criticizing, in a review, the poet Edward Young, comparing him with William Cowper:

> . . . in proportion as morality is emotional, *i.e.*, has affinity with Art, it will exhibit itself in direct sympathetic feeling and action, and not as the recognition of a rule. Love does not say, "I ought to love"—it loves. . . . In Young we have the type of that deficient human sympathy, that impiety toward the present and the visible, which flies for its motives, its sanctities,

and its religion, to the remote, the vague, and the unknown: in Cowper we have the type of that genuine love which cherishes things in proportion to their nearness, and feels its reverence grow in proportion to the intimacy of its knowledge.

When these elements are brought together—the embracing of messiness and imperfection, the dislike of preaching, the prizing of the complex and particular and distrust of the abstract, the injunction to love real people close to you rather than an ideal of people in general—what they amount to is an implicit exhortation to accept the human condition. You should love humans as they are, not as they should or could be. You should embrace human nature, with all its suffering and sin, and accept that it will always be thus. You should accept the role of fate and luck in human life, and the limits of man's ability to alter his lot. To fail to do these things is to become the sort of do-gooder who doesn't love the world as it is, or the imperfect humans in it—only ideas inside his head.

Some fiction writers, of course, reject this ethos. J. M. Coetzee's *Elizabeth Costello* is an unabashedly unclothed novel of moral ideas—so much so that it teeters at the brink of the genre. But as an exception, it is moved to acknowledge the rule. "Realism has never been comfortable with ideas," observes a character near the beginning of the book. "Realism is premised on the idea that ideas have no autonomous existence, can exist only in things." The character Elizabeth Costello is a novelist, and although she is unabashed about her preaching (about animal rights), she is aware that this preaching is considered bad form in the literary circles in which she moves. At the end of the book, Costello meets her sister, a nun, whom she has not seen for many years. "I do not need to consult novels," the sister says, "to know what pettiness, what baseness, what cruelty human beings are capable of." The sister wonders, in effect, why there are so few do-gooders in fiction—she wants more moral ambition. "If the study of mankind amounts to no more than picturing to us our darker potential, I have better things to spend my time on," she says.

"If on the other hand the study of mankind is to be a study in what reborn man can be, that is a different story."

George Bernard Shaw and Leo Tolstoy also embraced explicit and abstract moralizing—a stance that in both cases took the form of an attack on Shakespeare, for what they took to be his amoral acceptance of the human condition. Shaw railed against Shakespeare for the weakness and pessimism of his characters. He could show vanity and passivity and despair, Shaw felt, but not virtue or real heroism. "What a crew they are," Shaw wrote,

> . . . these villains, fools, clowns, drunkards, cowards, intriguers, fighters, lovers, patriots, hypochondriacs who mistake themselves (and are mistaken by the author) for philosophers, princes without any sense of public duty, futile pessimists who imagine they are confronting a barren and unmeaning world when they are only contemplating their own worthlessness . . . But search for statesmanship, or even citizenship, or any sense of the commonwealth, material or spiritual, and you will not find the making of a decent vestryman or curate in the whole horde. As to faith, hope, courage, conviction, or any of the true heroic qualities, you find nothing. . . .

Shaw, who prefaced his own plays with essays explaining the moral he intended, found Shakespeare's philosophical agnosticism frustrating and reprehensible. If he could see the world so clearly, how could he be so bizarrely incurious about ways to fix it—and, indeed, hostile to anyone who might be less so? In this, Shaw found Dickens equally astonishing: the supreme chronicler of social depravity, so awash in sentiment, Shaw felt, as to be unable to think coherently about what a slightly better world might look like. These two were "concerned with the diversities of the world instead of with its unities," he wrote. "They have no constructive ideas; they regard those who have them as dangerous fanatics; in all their fictions there is no leading thought or inspiration for which any man could conceivably risk the spoiling of his hat in a shower, much less his life."

Tolstoy in his early years was known as a naturalist, an anti-moralist, an aesthete. In 1865, just as he was beginning to publish *War and Peace*, he wrote in a letter: "The aims of art are incommensurate (as the mathematicians say) with social aims. The aim of an artist is not to solve a problem irrefutably, but to make people love life in all its countless, inexhaustible manifestations." When he first began to write *Anna Karenina*, eight years later, the book was to be about Anna and Vronsky—it was a conventional novel about romantic love. Levin, who was in large part autobiographical, first appeared about a year into the writing, and became a means for Tolstoy to fill the book with all kinds of social aims and irrefutable solutions to problems. But Tolstoy was careful to distinguish an abstract sort of social aim from the kind that springs naturally from personal feelings and the work of daily life. Although small, limited social aims were now admitted, abstraction was still bad, as was any sort of attempt to help strangers or change society.

> OBLONSKY: She has a little English girl now, and a whole family she's interested in.
> LEVIN: Why, is she some kind of a philanthropist?
> OBLONSKY: There you are—always looking for trouble! It's nothing to do with philanthropy, it's just her warm heart.

Both Levin and his wife, Kitty, at different times try to live a moral life—in Kitty's case, by ministering to repellent sick people; in Levin's, by working in various ways for "the common welfare." But both discover that no good can come of following principle: one can only live according to one's heart. Without a personal interest, either selfish or loving, philanthropy is only hypocrisy, or empty intellectualism that cannot succeed because it has no urgent drive behind it. Tolstoy writes:

Levin looked on his half-brother as a man of enormous intellect and education, who was noble in the loftiest sense of the word and had the gift of being able to work for the common welfare. But in the depths of his soul, the older he got and the better he came to know his brother, the more often the thought came into his head that this capacity of working for the common welfare, which he felt himself to be completely devoid of, might not be and was not so much a quality as the contrary, a lack of something. It was not a lack of kind, honorable, noble desires and tastes but of some vital force, of what is called heart, of that impulse that forces a man to choose, out of the countless ways of life presented to him, just one, and to desire that one alone.

Anna Karenina was a hinge work for Tolstoy, between the aestheticism of his early work and the moralizing that came after. By the time he was finishing its last installments, in 1877, Tolstoy had decided that a novel had to justify itself by serving as "a vehicle for establishing a correct point of view on all social problems." He had come to hate *Anna Karenina*, and only finished it unwillingly. He was in a terrible, anguished state of mind. He began putting away guns and ropes for fear he would kill himself. He was beginning to feel a puritanical revulsion toward art, for the very qualities—its natural, physical vigor, its amorality—that he had valued in it before.

From here it was only a few steps to his condemnation of Shakespeare. Sometime shortly after the turn of the century, when Tolstoy was in his seventies, he wrote a pamphlet in which he described his bafflement at the universal adulation conferred upon the playwright. He identified a number of aesthetic flaws in the plays that had always irritated him—the characters all talked alike, they were always giving long speeches that bore only a tenuous relationship to the action, their motivations made no sense (he considered Lear particularly inane). But the worst sin of which he held Shakespeare guilty was a moral one—the same moral agnosticism that had irritated Shaw.

The plays represented without judgment, observed without conclusion. In Shakespeare's world, Tolstoy felt, there were no moral principles that held true in all situations—human life in its infinite complexity did not admit of certitude. The only thing one could be reasonably sure of was that moderation was good, aspiration was bad or ridiculous or both, and if you behaved more or less like everyone else you wouldn't go far wrong. Shakespeare, he wrote, "did not approve of limits of duty exceeding the intentions of nature. . . . He preached a reasonable mean natural to man, between Christian and heathen precepts, of love toward one's enemies on the one hand, and hatred toward them on the other. That one may do too much good (exceed the reasonable limits of good) is convincingly proved by Shakespeare's words and examples. Thus excessive generosity ruins Timon, while Antonio's moderate generosity confers honor. . . . Shakespeare taught . . . that one *may be too good*."

Among the more startling moments in Tolstoy's railings against Shakespeare was his claim that *Uncle Tom's Cabin* was a greater work than any Shakespeare play, because it flowed from the love of God and man. This claim was particularly scandalous because *Uncle Tom's Cabin* was such a lowbrow book, a sentimental best seller whose literary merit was rarely defended. But the outrageousness of the comparison was not just due to Tolstoy's cantankerous perversity. If Tolstoy was going to make an argument against Shakespeare's amoral naturalism, the way to do it was with a lowbrow book, because in lowbrow books, the anti-moralizing literary ethos that he objected to in Shakespeare did not apply. This was, indeed, one of the qualities that defined them *as* lowbrow: in a lowbrow book, a character could be very good or very bad; unambiguous morals could be clearly drawn; and there was no sense of emotional propriety to restrict the flow of sentiment. There need be no sense, in a lowbrow book, that the complexities of the world and the human heart were such that do-gooders must be, at best, naïve, and, at worst, violent. A lowbrow character in a lowbrow book could try to change the world.

Uncle Tom's Cabin did, of course, change the world. Published in 1852, it was the best-selling book of the nineteenth century, and was enormously influential in spreading the abolitionist cause from a cadre of marginal zealots to the American public. Uncle Tom is a Christ figure—deeply pious, self-sacrificing, brave, incorruptible, loving. When his original owner sells him down the river, separating him from his family, he doesn't complain—he believes that it's better that he be sold than anyone else. He tells his wife that he loves his master because he, Tom, cared for the master when he was a baby. He tells his wife to pray for the slave dealers because their souls are imperiled, and it is a thousand times worse to be sinful than sold. He is not merely passive, however—he helps those who need help, at great risk to himself, and when he is told to whip his fellow slaves, or to stop reading the Bible, he will not. When he refuses to tell his master where some slaves have run away to, he is killed.

There were always those who hated *Uncle Tom's Cabin* for literary reasons, and others who hated it for racial-political reasons, but when James Baldwin wrote an essay in 1949 to explain why he despised the book, he argued that its racist violations and its literary failures were one and the same. Like other lowbrow novels, *Uncle Tom's Cabin* was guilty of caricature: it was populated not by complex humans but by absurd cartoons. But this was not due to Stowe's limits as a writer, or even to her placing political goals over literary ones: it was due, Baldwin felt, to something far more pernicious. "Sentimentality, the ostentatious parading of excessive and spurious emotion, is the mark of dishonesty, the inability to feel," he wrote. "The wet eyes of the sentimentalist betray his aversion to experience, his fear of life, his arid heart; and it is always, therefore, the signal of secret and violent inhumanity, the mask of cruelty."

The violence here is done most obviously to the humanity of the black man Tom, reduced to a pasteboard Jesus, but also to men as such, to the complicated truth and freedom of the human being. "In overlooking, denying, evading [a man's] complexity," Baldwin wrote, "which is nothing more than the disquieting complexity of ourselves—we are diminished and we perish; only within this web of ambiguity, paradox, this hunger, danger, darkness, can we find at once ourselves and the power that will free us from ourselves. It is this power of revelation which is the business of the novelist, this journey toward a more vast reality which must take precedence over all other claims."

This is the novel's anti-do-gooder ethos at its most passionate and Manichean: on the one side, there is complexity, life, and feeling; on the other side, sentimentality, moralizing, and violence. In this scheme, infinite complexity can seem like the only good, the only kind of truth, and Hamlet is the only hero. All action begins to look like violence, all principles like lies; all people must be novelists or murderers.

Explicit moralizing in fiction did not end with Victorian sentimentality. There are still whole worlds of lowbrow and genre fiction in which ideas dressed as characters continue to act out moral dramas. But these more recent novels tend to be self-conscious about their philosophizing and make excuses for it, as if they sense that it violates some unspoken literary rule.

Around the same time that Baldwin wrote his essay, for instance, another moralizing and world-changing novel appeared, whose message was more or less the opposite of *Uncle Tom's Cabin*'s but which, according to his idea of literature, was just as offensive: Ayn Rand's *The Fountainhead*. This book was also preoccupied with selflessness and raising up the weak, but for Rand both were anathema. Her villain was Ellsworth M. Toohey, a wily socialist architecture critic who believes that artists should subordinate their taste to that of the masses; he believes that personal love is unjust because you should love all men equally. Her hero was Howard Roark, a brilliant, eccentric architect whose principles are the opposite of altruistic—he has a horror of involving himself in another person's life, akin to the horror he would feel if anyone interfered with his. "This is the motive and purpose of my writing," Rand wrote: "*the projection of an ideal man*. The portrayal of a moral ideal, as my ultimate literary goal, as an end in itself—to which any didactic, intellectual or philosophical values contained in a novel are only the means."

Rand's argument about selflessness was taken up in 1977 by Marilyn French in *The Women's Room*, a feminist novel that sold twenty million copies. Mira, the heroine, reads *The Fountainhead* as a schoolgirl in the 1950s, and it ignites in her a desire to reclaim her self, which she feels has been smothered and forbidden by a morality that teaches women to be selfless. Mira feels guilty reading *The Fountainhead* because she is aware that it's a lowbrow book, inferior to the literature she is assigned in school. But she also begins to suspect that it is only because it is a lowbrow book that it has the power to affect her morally. "Good literature, what her teachers would call good literature, was not involved with the world," she thinks. "To be involved with the world is lower than not to be." It seems to her that the inferiority of bad novels is akin to the inferiority of bad women: to be respected, literature, like women, must remain chaste.

There was nothing chaste about James Baldwin, and he was very much involved with the world. No writer was more driven by moral rage, and in his nonfiction he describes that rage, and the institutions and wickedness that provoke it. And yet, in his novels, as in many literary novels, this rage is transfigured, as though something about the form compels a different way of expressing what is wrong and what is right and what a man should do. Moral beauty, in his fiction, becomes smaller, more concrete, more intimate—something that exists between one person and another. "Some moments in a life, and they needn't be very long or seem very important, can make up for so much in that life," he writes in *Tell Me How Long the Train's Been Gone*, "can redeem, justify, that pain, that bewilderment, with which one lives, and invest one with the courage not only to endure it, but to profit from it; some moments teach one the price of the human connection: if one can live with one's own pain, then one respects the pain of others, and so, briefly, but transcendentally, we can release each other from pain."

FROM THE POINT OF VIEW
OF THE UNIVERSE

Do not be excessively righteous and do not be overly wise. Why should you ruin yourself? Do not be excessively wicked and do not be a fool. Why should you die before your time? It is good that you grasp one thing and also not let go of the other.

—ECCLESIASTES 7:16–18

Shortly after she turned thirty, Stephanie Wykstra decided that she no longer believed in unlimited altruism. This was the third momentous transformation she had undergone in ten years, and at the end of it she was left feeling stripped and alone. She had grown up with a sense of utter moral clarity, certain that she understood what was required of her, but this had gradually withered and rotted until, at last, it fell off her like an old skin. In her twenties, she embarked on a series of quests, looking for clarity of a different sort, and twice she thought she had found it, but in both cases she was mistaken. After the last quest failed, she accepted that she might never know again the unshakable moral certainty she had known as a child.

She grew up in Holland, Michigan, a small town in the western part of the state, near Grand Rapids. It was a very Dutch place. There was a tulip festival every year, and lots of tall, blue-eyed people and Calvinist churches. Her mother taught at a Christian college; her father taught philosophy at a college where the professors were required to sign a Christian covenant of faith. Although her father was a philosopher, he and her mother presented Christianity to her not as a set of theological beliefs, or as a way to live morally, but as an emotional relationship to Jesus. Stephanie was devout and unquestioning and loved God.

When she was in eleventh grade, her parents took a sabbatical on the East Coast and sent her to a boarding school in Massachusetts. The schoolwork was more difficult than she was used to, and at first she worked so intensely that her hair began falling out. She also discovered that many of her friends at the school were not Christian, so she tried her best to bring them to God. She carried around a book of Bible verses, and would pull it out and share it with people—while hanging out with friends, at midnight in the dorm. She wasn't a say-nice-things Christian; she took her mission very seriously. She got into a terrible argument with a girl in the dining hall when she said that God would not create a type of person just to send that person to hell, so homosexuality had to be a choice.

She had a crush on an atheist boy, and he liked her back and started calling her on the phone in the evenings. One night, he asked her what she would do if she woke up one morning and knew with absolute certainty that God didn't exist. She told him that she wouldn't want to live anymore; there would be no point. The conversation ended soon after that, as did their friendship. To him, that wasn't anything they could talk about—it just sounded crazy. She had another friend who was a Jewish agnostic, and as she and he went for long walks around campus, she tried to persuade him of the existence of God. She didn't know any of the formal arguments, so she told him that when she sang Christian songs she felt the presence of the Holy Spirit. One evening, her friend said, If there is a God, why did he allow my relatives to die in the Holocaust? This hit her hard. She felt dizzy and disoriented, and couldn't think of anything to say. It wasn't the first time she had encountered the problem of evil, but it was the first time someone had confronted her with it in such a direct and personal way.

At the same time that she was trying to convert people, she herself was wavering. She had never lived before with people who weren't Christian, and she found it strange and exciting. She started swearing, and tried pot. These things didn't feel extremely sinful to her; that feeling was reserved for sex. At a Christian rock concert, she had signed a pledge not to have sex before marriage; but she stored away in the back of her mind an experience she had had when she was fourteen or fifteen. She was sitting in a coffee shop around the corner from her grandmother's apartment in New York when she saw a women's magazine lying on a table and picked it up. In it, she found an article by a woman from a Christian background. The woman addressed the reader directly and said: If you have sex before marriage you are not going to disappear in a puff of smoke. You are not going to die or cease to exist. Life will continue and you will be fine. I did it, I know. At the time, this felt to Stephanie like a revelation. Of all the sins she could commit, sex before marriage, she knew, was one of the very worst; and yet here was a Christian woman who had done it and survived. She thought about that article for years.

The summer before she went to college, she wrote the word "fuck" in an online post, under a pseudonym. Her father, searching the browsing history on their computer and guessing her pseudonym, confronted her. He told her that she needed to pray hard for strength to stop this sin. She started crying, and went outside to the backyard and lay down on the trampoline, and looked up at the night sky; just then, she saw a shooting star. She felt that God was speaking to her, asking her to come home. He had found her and embraced her and brought her back to the fold. It was a joyful feeling, a feeling of being held and being good again—even though it involved cutting off all the thrilling new parts of herself that had emerged over the past two years.

When she got to college, she immediately took steps to shore up her renewed commitment. She read the Bible every night before she went to sleep. She wrote a note to God promising never to look at pornography and carried it around in her wallet. She joined a Christian a cappella singing group that met on Saturday mornings to read the Bible and talk about theological questions. She wanted to know why God listened to prayers. Wouldn't it make more sense for Him simply to arrange things for the best, all things considered? Wasn't it a little odd for fate to depend upon whether a person happened to pray for something or not?

She went to graduate school to study philosophy, and there she met another philosophy student, named Geoff. She explained a point about Leibniz to him, and they fell in love. They talked about philosophy or religion for eight or ten hours at a stretch—they went for long walks, they stayed up all night.

Geoff was from Pennsylvania. When he was in high school, he had been an active entrepreneur—at sixteen, he raised around ninety thousand dollars to start a company—but he wasn't after money for its own sake. He wanted to have an impact on the world, and figured that, however he did this, a lot of money would be useful. He majored in business at Wharton as an undergraduate, but then decided to study philosophy instead. As he read Kant, he began to develop his own moral system. He began to develop his own theory of psychology as well. He believed that the human mind was so underutilized that, with the help of a few psychological tricks, it could do exponentially more than it was currently capable of. The example he always cited was Memory Palace, a method that enabled people to remember many more objects than they otherwise could.

When Stephanie was with Geoff, she was happy. But she was again struggling with her faith. She could not reconcile herself to a God who condemned human beings to eternal hell. She thought, I do not want to worship a God like that. She never mentioned these doubts to her father, but he sensed them. One day, he confronted her on the phone: Do you still believe that Jesus died for your sins? She ended the conversation screaming at him, and didn't talk to him for several months. It was a terrible time. She realized that if she was going to leave Christianity she had to be prepared never to be close to her parents again. But she also felt she had to protect her father, because she knew her abandonment would be devastating to him. One night she dreamed that he was wandering in the desert and she knew he was going to die and she could have saved him but she didn't.

Not long after she arrived at graduate school, she started to become disillusioned with metaphysics. Philosophers seemed to think that, by using only their intuitions about the nature of things, they could arrive at real knowledge—but why should that be so, when studies had shown that people in different cultures had completely different intuitions about the same questions? And when philosophers in the same culture, even in the same *department*, had conflicting intuitions, how were you supposed to adjudicate between them? She switched to epistemology—studying how we justify our beliefs—but soon she began to suspect that a lot of those discussions were pointless.

Around this time, on a family trip to Italy in which Geoff was included, her mother discovered that Stephanie had started taking birth-control pills. Her mother was horrified, and tried everything she could think of to prevent this terrible sin. She prayed over Geoff and laid hands on him and tried to bring him to God. She made them promise not to have sex in Italy. At last, she and Stephanie had a terrible fight, which ended with her mother running after her and Geoff, not letting them out of her sight—as though, Stephanie thought with rage and bewilderment, she expected them to have sex in the street. Later, when she found out that Stephanie had slept with Geoff, her mother told her that she had turned her back on God and He would not forgive her.

For months afterward, she and her parents argued over the phone about Stephanie's relationship to God. Her parents felt her faith was dying, and they fought for her soul, but they lost. She no longer believed, and she told them so. The following summer, she and Geoff went to Michigan for a wedding and stayed at her parents' house while they were away. She arrived to discover that all the photographs of her, which had been everywhere in the house, were gone. Every trace of her had been removed. Her mother had left a note explaining how to find the grocery store, as though she were a stranger, as though she had not grown up in that house, going to that grocery store every week. The note also informed her that her belongings had been packed in boxes in the basement and she should take them with her when she left.

Stephanie and Geoff got married. Her parents attended the wedding but she knew they were unhappy about it, and she didn't ask her father to walk her down the aisle. At the reception, she saw that a cousin had put out some photographs of her as a child, including one in which Stephanie, aged about twelve, was trying on her mother's wedding dress. The photos seemed to show a happy continuity between that child and her now, and she recoiled. There was no continuity, she thought. She had made a choice to break away from that childhood, and the choice had been hard and painful. She gathered up the photographs and hid them.

For a while after the wedding, it seemed as though her life was finally settling down. She and Geoff got jobs teaching at a small college in suburban Massachusetts, and moved together into a house nearby. But she wasn't satisfied—she felt she should do something better with her life.

While she was still a graduate student, she had signed up to be a big sister to a thirteen-year-old girl living in foster care in Perth Amboy. They went to museums and movies and cooked together, and she became attached to the girl. She started researching foster care and discovered that an enormous percentage of foster children became homeless after aging out of the system. One summer, she interned with a couple of organizations that worked with foster kids and tried to help them make their way as adults, but although these organizations were well intentioned, she noticed that they rarely looked into how well their programs were working. There was no real research, no data, no evidence. She realized that this was something she would love to do—conduct research on the effectiveness of good intentions.

Searching around in this field, she discovered GiveWell, an organization entirely devoted to such research, and to finding organizations that improved the most lives for the least money. It had been started up a few years before by a couple of young men who had been working at a hedge fund and were frustrated by the near absence, in the nonprofit world, of the sort of data that they used to evaluate investments. Many charities talked about lives saved for some tiny amount of money, because it was good for fund-raising, but in fact the notion of a saved life didn't make much sense. To count a life as "saved," how much longer would the person have to live? It wouldn't be much use curing a person of malaria if he died of polio the following week. And if you prevented him from dying of malaria one week and of polio the next, did that count as two lives saved or one? The unit of measurement that GiveWell liked to use was the DALY, which stood for Disability-Adjusted Life-Year. This took into account not only *that* a person survived but how long he survived, and in what condition. A year of perfect health counted for more than a year spent blind, say, or with an amputated leg. This was helpful in choosing which diseases and problems to focus on. Stephanie started by volunteering for GiveWell, and then, forcing aside her fear that her parents would never respect such work, as they did philosophy, she quit her academic job to work there full time.

Meanwhile, Geoff was changing, too. He had also quit teaching, to found an organization called Leverage Research, with which he intended to change the world. He allied it with the effective-altruism movement that Toby Ord had started at Oxford, and which had been establishing outposts in America, at colleges and through people like Julia Wise and Jeff Kaufman. Geoff and Stephanie moved to New York and rented a group house with a few other people who had also signed on with Leverage, so the organization, and Geoff's ambitions for it, were with them all the time.

In order to change the world, Geoff believed, he had to change himself. He became more and more concerned with productivity. He began to sleep only three hours a night, with three twenty-minute naps spaced evenly through the day. Stephanie watched him nodding off at his computer and worried that he would make himself seriously ill. His ambition was boundless. He wrote in his Leverage bio: "Geoff thinks and acts from first principles. He has derived, and is enacting, a course of action to create a flourishing world for all." What this meant was that he didn't believe in building on any work that anyone else had done in a subject. He was going to come up with an original moral theory and an original theory of the human mind, and he was going to start from scratch.

His ultimate plan was to create an ideal world. Stephanie argued with him about this. She would say, You could achieve one part of your plan—you could work on disease, or war, or famine, or problems between people—but you can't do all of those things, even though you're very smart, because the world is complicated. But Geoff was good at arguing, and he would defeat her points one after another; even though he never convinced her that he was right, she couldn't persuade him, either. She would write up long series of numbered arguments, and he would send back replies such as: "I disagree with premise 4 of your argument, please clarify how you are using the word 'difficult,' here are five possible definitions of the word, which one do you mean?" She felt helpless and frustrated and, over time, she began to avoid these arguments. He sensed her disengagement and felt betrayed: surely, if you loved someone, either you supported his goals or you worked hard to dissuade him—you didn't just look away. She agreed with this, and felt guilty. Part of her wished that the critical part of her mind that made her skeptical of his ambitions would just shut down—then they would be happy together again, and she could stop struggling—but it wouldn't.

Stephanie loved her work at GiveWell, but always nagging at the back of her mind was the Geoff-inspired thought that it wasn't enough. She ought to be doing something bigger. She didn't know what the something bigger was: Working to defeat death, like Aubrey de Grey? Preventing malevolent computers from attacking mankind, like the people at the Machine Intelligence Research Institute? But it was certainly something more than she was doing. Geoff felt that GiveWell's work was too short-term, too limited. It was performing a useful function, he conceded, but it was only suggesting little fixes to the world as it was—not really changing things. If only she worked harder and stopped worrying about adopting unconventional views, he told her, she would be able to live up to her potential.

But this thought made her sad. If she truly committed herself to saving the world as she ought to, she thought, she would never have fun anymore—she wouldn't be able to travel, she would never go to beautiful places. She would have to be as single-mindedly devoted as Geoff was. She would have to work all the time. She would have to cut out of her life the things she loved, one by one, until there were none left. If she were truly going to commit herself, it had to be all or nothing—but a commitment of that magnitude horrified her, and she dreaded the day when she would have to make it. She always felt guilty; yet, at the same time, some things about effective altruism had begun to bug her. She disliked feeling that she was obliged to focus only on the most effective possible ways to do good—that more personal but less efficient ways, such as being a big sister to a girl in foster care, were not a good use of time.

Stephanie and Geoff started couples therapy, and after some months they separated. She dreaded telling her parents, but to her amazement they were not angry. She began to talk more often with them on the phone. Those were not easy conversations—she still felt distant—but she felt that she and they were moving slowly closer again, groping uncertainly about, trying to reach each other. Her mother said, We think about you every day. Stephanie thought that what she meant, though she was careful not to say it, was, We pray every day that you find your way back to God.

Although Stephanie was sure that separating was the right thing to do, she was miserable, and felt herself begin to fall apart. One evening, she was supposed to meet her mother for dinner at her grandmother's apartment, but she was so disoriented that she took the wrong subway and ended up in the wrong part of town. She called her mother, crying, and said that she could not come to dinner, she could not face her judgment. Her mother said, Come. And Stephanie did, and all that evening she lay and cried and her mother sat next to her and stroked her hair, and Stephanie felt that she was no longer hiding any part of herself but still her mother loved her exactly as she was.

Around this time, the couples therapist recommended a book to Stephanie called *Radical Acceptance*, and it changed her life. It was a Buddhist book, and she wasn't particularly interested in Buddhism, but its basic message was: You are an okay person just as you are right now. You can change, but you don't have to. When she first read it, this idea struck her as insane. But then she thought: If you saw a tree, you wouldn't think, That tree isn't as flowery as another sort of tree, it's not good enough. You wouldn't think, if you saw a small dog, You ought to be bigger, what's wrong with you? Maybe people were the same—they were a certain way, and that was fine.

All her life, she had believed that there was something fundamentally bad about her; but now she thought that maybe she had simply been wrong about this. The book described the way many people went through life in a "trance of unworthiness." This reminded her of a line she had read long ago about how God covered you with His cloak to hide your sin. This had startled and horrified her, the thought that man was so repellent to God that He would cover him rather than look at him directly. That was one of the moments when she had felt herself starting to leave the church.

As she began to accept herself, she began to reject what had been the foundation of her moral life since she rejected Christianity: utilitarianism. She rejected Peter Singer's shallow-pond argument about how much we are obliged to give, because accepting it, she had come to realize, meant rejecting herself. She didn't have a philosophical refutation of the argument, but she no longer believed that she had to have one. It took her a long time to get to this point—several years of guilt and self-laceration—but at the end of it, she no longer believed that she was obliged to dedicate every waking moment to saving the world, or to pry ever more waking moments from her hours of sleep.

She still longed to be part of a community of people who shared her values, but was she ever going to be able to find one that she didn't disagree with? She read a sociology book about how all human groups have semi-arbitrary rituals and beliefs that held them together. Maybe, in trying to justify her beliefs, she was misunderstanding their purpose, and how human society worked. Maybe you were just supposed to accept this stuff, or at least not to question it too much. She wanted to belong somewhere and believe something. She didn't want her whole life to consist of joining followed by rejection, an unending series of departures.

She had rejected Christianity, she had rejected philosophy, she had rejected unlimited altruism. Now she had nothing left—only herself. It made her happy to think about doing things she wanted to do, but it was also frightening. She felt less guilty than before, but more anxious. She had spent her whole life castigating herself for failing to live up to one set of established principles or another; now she was going to have to figure things out on her own. This way of thinking did not come easily to her, but she accepted that its vertiginous uncertainty was the price of her freedom.

"Is it somehow legitimate to say what is valuable is what I consider to be valuable?" she wondered. "Is that okay?" It sounded so subjective to her—so flimsy, so groundless. It was disturbing to think about. She had spent her life looking for a foundation. When she no longer believed in a divine plan, she had looked for objective moral truth, but she hadn't found it, and now she doubted that there was such a thing. But what was left? Could you base a life on ideals that you invented? Nothing larger—nothing more than that? She had rejected moral systems built on centuries of the thought and faith and obedience of millions of people, and now her foundation was going to be *herself*? It sounded ridiculous. But it was all she had. Is it okay to say, These are the things that I value, this is what I'm going to pursue in life? she wondered. Or, was it possible to live without a foundation at all, knowing that she no longer knew what was right, and maybe never would? She didn't know.

SOMETHING QUITE DIFFERENT FROM LIFE

When an upright man is in the greatest distress, which he might have avoided if he could only have disregarded duty, is he not sustained by the consciousness that . . . he has no reason to be ashamed of himself in his own sight, or to dread the inward glance of self-examination? This consolation is not happiness, it is not even the smallest part of it, for no one would wish to have occasion for it, or would, perhaps, even desire a life in such circumstances. But he lives, and he cannot endure that he should be in his own eyes unworthy of life. This . . . is the effect of a respect for something quite different from life, something in comparison and contrast with which life with all its enjoyment has no value.

—IMMANUEL KANT, *The Critique of Practical Reason*

I f there is a struggle between morality and life, life will win. Life itself will win, and so will the things that make life worth living. Not always, not in every case, but life will win in the end. Sometimes a person will die for a cause; sometimes a person will give up for duty's sake the things that are to him most precious. But most of the time, the urge to live, to give to your family, to seek beauty, to work for your own purposes, to act spontaneously, to act without any purpose at all, or to do any number of things other than helping people, is too strong to be overridden.

How much life is threatened by morality depends on what you think life is. In most ancient traditions, a good life *is* a moral life (though most traditions also distinguish between an ordinary moral life and that of a saint). The idea of life most threatened by too much morality is a newer, romantic one—one that values emotion more than reason, spontaneity more than willed intent, and the search for an original, authentic self more than careful molding of a moral one. To a romantic, desire is less something to be restrained, as a do-gooder would restrain it, than the very stuff of life. "Those who restrain desire, do so because theirs is weak enough to be restrained," wrote William Blake, one of the first Romantic poets, with contempt. "And being restrain'd it by degrees becomes passive till it is only the shadow of desire." To a certain kind of Romantic, the struggles of a do-gooder with himself can look misguided to the point of suicide.

Blake was reacting here to the piety of *Paradise Lost*, in which Milton described the revolt of Satan against the authority of God. Satan wanted power and freedom; but the angel Abdiel told him that, even now that he had fled from heaven, he was still not free: he was enslaved to a new master—himself. That was the old view of desire, the inward slave driver; but Blake and Romantics who followed him rejected it.

The goodness that Satan revolted against was an angel's goodness, consisting of obedience to God. But the do-gooder's goodness is not usually obedience—it is often, on the contrary, a revolt against the rules and customs he grew up with. Part of the reason do-gooders seem so strange is that they're acting on their own. They are following rules that they laid down for themselves, driven by a sense of duty they have felt since they were too small to know what duty was, much less how anybody else thought about it. The people they came from thought they were as weird and extreme as anyone else did. They didn't come from a community in which their sacrifice was normal, part of the order of things.

In some circumstances, do-gooders do not look so odd. For do-gooders, it is always wartime; and in wartime, do-gooders look less zealous, their commitments less severe. But war itself has changed, which may be one reason do-gooders look even odder now than they used to. War no longer demands sacrifice from everyone. War for some rich countries is now, as often as not, something that happens to other people, somewhere far away. For most of human history, the sacrificing of self or child or work for something larger was ordinary, because conscription was ordinary. But many countries got rid of the draft decades ago. Not for a long time has it been a common experience in those countries to be expected, as a matter of course, to risk your life, or those of your family members, for the sake of your country. It may be that, in the absence of this older form of duty, the sense of duty to family has expanded to take its place, so that sacrificing family for a cause now seems unnatural and extreme.

In 1906, the philosopher William James gave a speech titled "The Moral Equivalent of War." James had come to realize, he said, that pacifists like himself had been so caught up in deploring the gore and violence and waste of war that they failed to see that these arguments never even touched their opponents. "The military party denies neither the bestiality nor the horror, nor the expense," he said. "It only says that war is *worth* them; that, taking human nature as a whole, its wars are its best protection against its weaker and more cowardly self." What pacifists didn't understand was that it was not just the base desires for mastery and plunder that drove nations to battle. The soldier lived *in extremis*, a hard, strenuous, courageous life, and was prepared to sacrifice everything. To such a person, peacetime could seem like a lazy, soft, degenerate existence, with no purpose higher than the pursuit of pleasure, and in which nothing more was required of a man than to leave his neighbor alone. "Where is the sharpness and precipitousness, the contempt for life, whether one's own or another's?" James imagined this soldier asking. "Where is the savage 'yes' and 'no,' the unconditional duty?"

There was, James felt, something deeply right about this military contempt. If war was ever to end, there must be something as honorable, and as difficult, to take its place. Such a thing was not unthinkable: why should it be only in wartime that people felt bound to risk their lives for something larger than themselves? James proposed a peacetime conscription to hard labor—"to coal and iron mines, to freight trains, to fishing fleets in December, to dishwashing, clotheswashing, and windowwashing, to road-building and tunnel-making, to foundries and stoke-holes"—that would both toughen up a country's youth and go some way toward righting the unfairness by which some people lived a life of ease while others were humiliated by poverty. Why shouldn't people be spurred to action as much by the existing shame of their country's injustices as they are by the threatened shame of conquest? he wondered. Why shouldn't the commitment and fellowship and urgency of war be grafted onto the morality of ordinary times?

When people heard that I was writing about do-gooders, many of them said, But aren't they mentally ill? An extreme sense of duty seems to many people to be a kind of disease—a masochistic need for self-punishment, perhaps, or a kind of depression that makes its sufferer feel unworthy of pleasure. Surely those who suffer from a disease like that must live dark, narrow lives, overcast by responsibility, forcing themselves always to think about the misery of others and to endure misery themselves. Surely they must be perpetually crouched in some dank office, bolting a bowl of reheated noodles before racing off to the next emergency.

In fact, some do-gooders are happy, some are not. The happy ones are happy for the same reasons anyone is happy—love, work, purpose. It's do-gooders' unhappiness that is different—a reaction not only to humiliation and lack of love and the other usual stuff, but also to knowing that the world is filled with misery, and that most people don't really notice or care, and that, try as they might, they cannot do much about either of those things. What do-gooders lack is not happiness but innocence. They lack that happy blindness that allows most people, most of the time, to shut their minds to what is unbearable. Do-gooders have forced themselves to know, and keep on knowing, that everything they do affects other people, and that sometimes (though not always) their joy is purchased with other people's joy. And, remembering that, they open themselves to a sense of unlimited, crushing responsibility.

Of course, any do-gooder who is not dead or irredeemably jaundiced by the age of thirty has learned to acquire a degree of blindness in order to get by. Aaron Pitkin no longer sees a starving child next to every vending machine. Sue and Hector Badeau decided not to adopt a twenty-third child, no matter how desperate. Do-gooders learn to codify their horror into a routine and a set of habits they can live with. They know they must do this in order to stay sane. But this partial blindness is chosen and forced and never quite convincing. It takes a strong stomach to see the world's misery, feel a sense of duty to do something about it, and then say to yourself, I have done enough, now I'm going to shut my eyes and close my ears and turn my back. Do-gooders who last have strong stomachs.

The do-gooders in this book have lasted. Many things are better for many people (and chickens) because of that. All these do-gooders ventured close to the brink of what for them would be self-destruction, but they stepped back again before they reached it. Either they found their limit and accepted it, or they were lucky. Dorothy Granada did not fast to the death and was not shot by Contra soldiers. Aaron Pitkin did not remain homeless or alone. Julia Wise did not stay childless. Baba Amte did not contract leprosy, and his children were not eaten by panthers. Prakash Amte was not forced to cut his baby to pieces to save his wife, and was not killed by one of his animals. Kimberly Brown-Whale's son did not die in Mozambique of his heart condition, and her daughter was not kidnapped. Ittetsu Nemoto did not die from overwork. Sue and Hector Badeau held their family together. But any of these stories might have turned out differently. One step over the brink and their commitment might have looked like craziness, or cruelty.

Do-gooders are different from ordinary people because they are willing to weigh their lives and their families in a balance with the needs of strangers. They are willing to risk the one for the sake of the other. They, like anyone else, believe that they have duties to their families, but they draw the line between family and strangers in a different place. It's not that they value strangers more: it's that they remember that strangers have lives and families, too. When this willingness results only in calculated sacrifice, that's one thing; when it results in destruction, it's another. How things turn out depends partly on the choices of the do-gooder, but partly on luck. It might seem that moral judgment shouldn't depend on luck—surely you can't be blamed for something you have no control over. But, in fact, luck affects moral judgments all the time. Someone who attempts murder but fails is judged differently from someone who succeeds. And someone who lives the life of a do-gooder, attempting to relieve the pain of strangers without ruining the lives of those he is close to, is judged, too, on his success.

What would the world be like if everyone thought like a do-gooder? What would it be like if that happy, useful blindness fell away and suddenly everyone became aware, not just intellectually but vividly, of all the world's affliction? What if everyone felt obliged to put aside the work he had chosen and do something about that affliction instead? What if everyone decided that spontaneity or self-expression or certain kinds of beauty or certain kinds of freedom were less vital, or less urgent, than relieving other people's pain? What if everyone stopped believing it was his duty to protect and comfort and give to his family as much as he could, no matter what, and started thinking that his family was no more important or valuable than anyone else's?

If everyone thought like a do-gooder, the world would not be our world any longer, and the new world that would take its place would be so utterly different as to be nearly unimaginable. People talk about changing the world, but that's not usually what they mean. They mean securing enough help so there is less avoidable suffering and people can get on with living decent lives; they don't mean a world in which helping is the only life there is.

If there were no do-gooders, on the other hand, the world would be similar to ours, but worse. Without their showing what a person can do for strangers if he sets himself to do it, fewer would try. It may be true that not everyone should be a do-gooder. But it is also true that these strange, hopeful, tough, idealistic, demanding, life-threatening, and relentless people, by their extravagant example, help keep those life-sustaining qualities alive.

ACKNOWLEDGMENTS

The people most essential to this book are, of course, its subjects. I am extremely grateful to them for talking with me at such length, in most cases over the course of several years. I want to thank them all for trusting me with their stories, and I hope they feel that their trust was justified.

In the course of researching this book I interviewed many extraordinary people who helped me to understand the joy and difficulty of living with a strong sense of moral duty. I am grateful to all of them for talking with me, particularly Frida Berrigan, Jerry and Molly Mechtenberg-Berrigan, Elizabeth McAlister, Daniel Berrigan, Joe and Leah Pullaro, Rabbi Ephraim Simon, Richard Semmler, Judi Buchman and Richa, Brenda and Paul Muessig, Mark Lee, Jill Warren, Pilar Gonzales, Ben Lawent, and especially Ela Bhatt.

I am indebted to several people who helped me to find my subjects: Anne and Christopher Ellinger, Sylvia Hart Wright, and Jonathan Watts (who also acted as my interpreter in Japan). Chanda Athale, a nurse who travels to Anandwan and Hemalkasa each year to work in the clinics and visit the Amtes, was a boon companion during my time in those places. Many other people helped me in the course of writing. Anna Hartford, Heather Rogers, and Julia Longoria assisted me with research. Mallory Falk, Merrell Hambleton, Veronica Simmonds, and Sam Nichols transcribed interviews. Jennifer Stahl and Celia Barbour each fact checked parts of the book with care and skill. Andrea Munoz translated articles about Dorothy Granada.

Two people with interests uncannily similar to mine—Benoît Monin, a psychologist at Stanford, and Kelly Sorensen, a philosopher at Ursinus College—heard about my book as I was writing it and got in touch; discovering their work was a delightful surprise. Several generous and wise friends read and commented on chapters: David Bezmozgis, Harriet Clark, David Grann, Chris Jennings, and Judith Shulevitz. I particularly want to thank Mary Karr, who in an act of truly supererogatory friendship read the whole manuscript not once but twice.

The Dorothy and Lewis B. Cullman Center at the New York Public Library supported the writing of this book for nine months. I am very grateful to Lewis Cullman for his gift, and I have Jean Strouse, Marie d'Origny, Sam Swope, and Paul Höldengraber to thank for making that year fun as well as useful. I want to express my gratitude to Susan Neiman, Eric Beerbohm, Larry Lessig, Arthur Applebaum, Charles R. Beitz, Andreas Morgensen, Eric Banks, and Stephanie Steiker for inviting me to give talks on my book while it was in progress; it was a great honor to speak to those audiences. I want also to thank Susan Neiman for her enlightening comments on a chapter. I am particularly grateful to Rob Reich for his unflagging interest in this book; for reading and commenting on the manuscript; and for inviting me several times to Stanford's Center for Ethics in Society. Joan Berry always made me feel at home on those visits.

Some of the material in this book was first published in somewhat different forms in *The New Yorker*. I'm extremely lucky to have had as my editor there for eighteen years the omniscient Henry Finder, who has read everything I've written with perceptive care and astonishing speed, including most recently this book, which was beyond the call of duty. I want to thank Ann Goldstein for reading everything I've written with astonishing slowness, and with her acute understanding of language. Rhonda Sherman generously invited me to talk about my book at the New Yorker Festival. And I'm hugely grateful to David Remnick, the editor of *The New Yorker*, for his encouragement; for giving the go-ahead to unlikely ideas with no more than a raised eyebrow; and for granting me a leave to write this book, which he would have finished in a quarter of the time.

Sarah Chalfant at the Wylie Agency has been an indomitable support. I have much appreciated the assistance of Karen Mayer at Penguin, and the patience and counsel of Benjamin Platt. I want to thank my editor at Penguin UK, Alexis Kirschbaum, for her spirited backing. And I am endlessly grateful to my editor at Penguin, Ann Godoff, for her discerning and sensitive editing, and for her unswerving, inspiring, and emboldening enthusiasm.

My husband, Philip Gourevitch, is always my keenest reader in both senses of the word, and this book would have been much worse without his comments. I could not have written it at all without his constant support.

I dedicate this book to my wonderful parents, Roderick and Emily MacFarquhar. That my mother is not here to read it is the saddest part about bringing this project to a close.

BIBLIOGRAPHY

I did not use all of these sources directly in this book, but I found all of them useful, and I hope this list will lead other people to some of the marvelous work I've enjoyed discovering in the course of this project.

The student and philosophy professor (young man and older man) whom I quote in the first pages of the book are Mark Lee, the leader of THINK—The High Impact Network, an organization that promotes effective altruism, and Jeff McMahan, White's Professor of Moral Philosophy at the University of Oxford.

FOR DO-GOODERS, IT IS ALWAYS WARTIME

The works listed below I found illuminating on the do-gooder or saintly personality and attitudes toward it.

Day, Dorothy. *The Long Loneliness: The Autobiography of the Legendary Catholic Social Activist*. New York: HarperOne, 2009.

DeNicola, Daniel R. "Supererogation: Artistry in Conduct." In *Foundations of Ethics*, edited by Leroy S. Rouner. Notre Dame, IN: University of Notre Dame Press, 1983.

Flanagan, Owen. *Varieties of Moral Personality: Ethics and Psychological Realism*. Cambridge, MA: Harvard University Press, 1991.

Franklin, Benjamin. *The Autobiography of Benjamin Franklin*. Mineola, NY: Dover Publications, 1996.

Haidt, Jonathan, and Selin Kesebir. "Morality." In *Handbook of Social Psychology*, edited by Susan T. Fiske, Daniel T. Gilbert, and Gardner Lindzey. Hoboken, NJ: Wiley, 2010.

Hawley, John Stratton, ed. *Saints and Virtues*. Berkeley: University of California Press, 1987.

James, William. *The Varieties of Religious Experience*. New York: Penguin Classics, 1982.

Keltner, Dacher, and Jonathan Haidt. "Approaching Awe, a Moral, Spiritual, and Aesthetic Emotion." *Cognition and Emotion* 17, no. 2 (2003): 297–314.

Mecklin, John M. *The Passing of the Saint: A Study of a Cultural Type*. Chicago: The University of Chicago Press, 1941.

Minson, Julia A., and Benoît Monin. "Do-Gooder Derogation: Disparaging Morally Motivated Minorities to Defuse Anticipated Reproach." *Social Psychological and Personality Science* 3, no. 2 (2012): 200–207.

Monin, Benoît, Pamela J. Sawyer, and Matthew J. Marquez. "The Rejection of Moral Rebels: Resenting Those Who Do the Right Thing." *Journal of Personality and Social Psychology* 95, no. 1 (July 2008): 76–93.

Murdoch, Iris. "The Sublime and the Good." *Chicago Review* 13, no. 3 (Autumn 1959): 42–55.

Nelson, Juanita. *A Matter of Freedom and Other Writings.* San Francisco: Peace & Gladness Press, 1988.

Orwell, George. "Reflections on Gandhi." In *A Collection of Essays.* San Diego: Harcourt Brace Jovanovich, 1946.

Paul, Ellen Frankel, Fred D. Miller, Jr., and Jeffrey Paul, eds. *Altruism.* Cambridge, UK: Cambridge University Press, 1993.

Payton, Robert L., and Michael P. Moody. *Understanding Philanthropy: Its Meaning and Mission.* Bloomington: Indiana University Press, 2008.

Sorensen, Kelly. "The Paradox of Moral Worth." *The Journal of Philosophy* 101, no. 9 (September 2004): 465–83.

———. "Effort and Moral Worth." *Ethical Theory and Moral Practice* 13 (2010): 89–109.

Strachey, Lytton. "Florence Nightingale." In *Eminent Victorians.* London: Penguin Books, 1948.

Wolf, Susan. "Moral Saints." *The Journal of Philosophy* 79, no. 8 (August 1982): 419–39.

THE BODIES OF STRANGERS

Andersen, Dorothy N., ed. *Downwardly Mobile for Conscience Sake. Ten Autobiographical Sketches: Each a Personal Search for Justice, Peace, and Eco-Sanity.* Eugene, OR: Tom Paine Institute, 1995.

Brooks, Svevo, John Burkhart, Dorothy Granada, and Charles Gray. *A Guide to Political Fasting.* Eugene, OR: Nonviolent Tactics Development Project, 1981.

Gray, Charles. *Toward a Nonviolent Economics,* 2nd ed. Eugene, OR: The Author, 1994.

Hart, Sylvia. *An Oral History of Charles Gray.* Eugene, OR: University of Oregon Special Collections and University Archives, 2009.

Mahony, Liam, and Luis Enrique Eguren. *Unarmed Bodyguards: International Accompaniment for the Protection of Human Rights.* West Hartford, CT: Kumarian Press, 1997.

Mogil, Christopher, Peter Woodrow, and Anne Slepian. *We Gave Away a Fortune: Stories of People Who Have Devoted Themselves and Their Wealth to Peace, Justice and a Healthy Environment.* Philadelphia: New Society Publishers, 1992.

THE MOST OPPRESSED OF ALL

Singer, Peter. *Ethics into Action: Henry Spira and the Animal Rights Movement.* Lanham, MD: Rowman & Littlefield Publishers, Inc., 1998.

DUTY! THOU SUBLIME AND MIGHTY NAME THAT DOST EMBRACE NOTHING CHARMING OR INSINUATING, BUT REQUIREST SUBMISSION

There is a substantial literature in Anglo-American moral philosophy on "demandingness"—how much morality can demand from a person. There is a smaller, related literature on "supererogation" and the question of whether some acts are beyond the call of duty—i.e., morally praiseworthy but not required. The list below is by no means comprehensive, but it includes the articles and books I found most helpful in those two areas. The chapter title is taken from Kant's *Critique of Practical Reason* (trans. T. K. Abbot, Amherst, NY: Prometheus Books, 1996, p. 108).

Adams, Don. "Love and Impartiality." *American Philosophical Quarterly* 30, no. 3 (July 1993): 223–34.

Adams, Robert Merrihew. "Saints." *The Journal of Philosophy* 81, no. 7 (July 1984): 392–401.

Anscombe, G. E. M. "Modern Moral Philosophy." *Philosophy* 33, no. 124 (January 1958).

Appiah, Kwame Anthony. *Cosmopolitanism: Ethics in a World of Strangers*. New York: W. W. Norton, 2006.

Baier, Kurt. *The Moral Point of View: A Rational Basis of Ethics*. New York: Random House, 1965.

Blum, Lawrence A. *Friendship, Altruism and Morality*. London: Routledge & Kegan Paul, 1980.

Chappell, Timothy, ed. *The Problem of Moral Demandingness: New Philosophical Essays*. Basingstoke, Hampshire, UK: Palgrave Macmillan, 2009.

Chopra, Yogendra. "Professor Urmson on 'Saints and Heroes.'" *Philosophy* 38, no. 144 (April 1963): 160–66.

Crisp, Roger, and Michael Slote, eds. *Virtue Ethics*. Oxford, UK: Oxford University Press, 1997.

Flanagan, Owen. "Admirable Immorality and Admirable Imperfection." *The Journal of Philosophy* 83, no. 1 (1986): 41–60.

Flescher, Andrew Michael. *Heroes, Saints & Ordinary Morality*. Washington, D.C.: Georgetown University Press, 2003.

Foot, Philippa. *Virtues and Vices and Other Essays in Moral Philosophy*. Berkeley: University of California Press, 1978.

———. *Natural Goodness*. Oxford, UK: Oxford University Press, 2001.

Godwin, William. "Thoughts Occasioned by the Perusal of Dr. Parr's Spital Sermon, Preached at Christ Church, April 15, 1800: Being a Reply to the Attacks of Dr. Parr, Mr. Mackintosh, the Author of an Essay On Population, and Others." London: Taylor & Wilks, 1801.

———. *Enquiry Concerning Political Justice and Its Influence on Modern Morals and Happiness*. Gloucester, UK: Dodo Press, 2009.

Heyd, David. *Supererogation: Its Status in Ethical Theory*. Cambridge, UK: Cambridge University Press, 1982.

Jackson, Frank. "Decision-Theoretic Consequentialism and the Nearest and Dearest Objection." *Ethics* 101, no. 3 (April 1991): 461–82.

Jamieson, Dale, ed. *Singer and His Critics*. Oxford, UK: Blackwell Publishers, 1999.

Kagan, Shelly. *The Limits of Morality*. Oxford, UK: Oxford University Press, 1989.

Kamm, F. M. "Does Distance Matter to the Duty to Rescue?" *Law and Philosophy* 19, no. 6 (November 2000): 655–81.

Kant, Immanuel. *The Critique of Judgment*. Translated by James Creed Meredith. Oxford, UK: Oxford University Press, 1952.

Kymlicka, Will. "Altruism in Philosophical and Ethical Traditions: Two Views." In *Between State and Market: Essays on Charities Law and Policy in Canada*, edited by Jim Phillips, Bruce Chapman, and David Stevens. Montreal: McGill-Queen's University Press, 2001.

Louden, Robert B. "Can We Be Too Moral?" *Ethics* 98, no. 2 (January 1988): 361–78.

Mayerfield, Jamie. *Suffering and Moral Responsibility*. New York: Oxford University Press, 1999.

McGoldrick, Patricia M. "Saints and Heroes: A Plea for the Supererogatory." *Philosophy* 59, no. 230 (1984): 523–28.

Melden, A. I. "Saints and Supererogation." In *Philosophy and Life: Essays on John Wisdom*, edited by Ilham Dilman. The Hague: Martinus Nijhoff Publishers, 1984.

Mellema, Gregory. *Beyond the Call of Duty: Supererogation, Obligation, and Offence*. Albany: State University of New York Press, 1991.

Murdoch, Iris. *The Sovereignty of Good*. London: Ark Paperbacks, 1985.

Murphy, Liam B. *Moral Demands in Nonideal Theory*. Oxford, UK: Oxford University Press, 2000.

Nagel, Thomas. *The Possibility of Altruism*. Princeton, NJ: Princeton University Press, 1970.

———. *The View from Nowhere*. Oxford, UK: Oxford University Press, 1986.

———. *The Last Word*. Oxford, UK: Oxford University Press, 1997.

Neusner, Jacob, and Bruce Chilton, eds. *Altruism in World Religions*. Washington, D.C.: Georgetown University Press, 2005.

New, Christopher. "Saints, Heroes and Utilitarians." *Philosophy* 49, no. 188 (April 1974): 179–89.

Parr, Samuel, L.L.D. "A Spital Sermon, Preached at Christ Church, Upon East Tuesday, April 15, 1800." London: J. Mawman, 1801.

Pybus, Elizabeth M. "Saints and Heroes." *Philosophy* 57, no. 220 (April 1982): 193–99.

Raz, Joseph. "A Morality Fit for Humans." *Michigan Law Review* 91, no. 6 (May 1993): 1297–1314.

Schaler, Jeffrey A., ed. *Peter Singer Under Fire: The Moral Iconoclast Faces His Critics*. Chicago: Open Court, 2009.

Scheffler, Samuel. *Human Morality*. Oxford, UK: Oxford University Press, 1992.

Silver, Arthur M. "May One Disinherit Family in Favor of Charity?" *Tradition* 28, no. 3, 1994.

Singer, Peter. "Famine, Affluence, and Morality." *Philosophy and Public Affairs* 1, no. 1 (Fall 1971): 229–43.

———. *Practical Ethics.* Cambridge, UK: Cambridge University Press, 1993.

———. *How Are We to Live?: Ethics in an Age of Self-Interest.* Amherst, NY: Prometheus Books, 1995.

Slote, Michael. *Goods and Virtues.* Oxford, UK: Oxford University Press, 1983.

Smart, J. J. C., and Bernard Williams. *Utilitarianism: For and Against.* Cambridge, UK: Cambridge University Press, 1973.

Stocker, Michael. "Desiring the Bad: An Essay in Moral Psychology." *The Journal of Philosophy* 76, no. 12 (December 1979): 738–53.

———. *Plural and Conflicting Values.* Oxford, UK: Clarendon Press, 1990.

Thomson, Judith Jarvis. "A Defense of Abortion." *Philosophy and Public Affairs* 1, no. 1 (Fall 1971): 47–66.

Unger, Peter. *Living High & Letting Die: Our Illusion of Innocence.* Oxford, UK: Oxford University Press, 1996.

Urmson, J. O. "Saints and Heroes." In *Essays in Moral Philosophy,* edited by A. I. Melden. Seattle: University of Washington Press, 1958.

Williams, Bernard. *Moral Luck: Philosophical Papers 1973–1980.* Cambridge, UK: Cambridge University Press, 1981.

———. *Ethics and the Limits of Philosophy.* Cambridge, MA: Harvard University Press, 1985.

———. *The Sense of the Past: Essays in the History of Philosophy.* Princeton, NJ: Princeton University Press, 2006.

Wolf, Susan. "Self-Interest and Interest in Selves." *Ethics* 96, no. 4 (July 1986): 704–20.

———. "Above and Below the Line of Duty." *Philosophical Topics* 14, no. 2 (Fall 1986): 131–48.

———. "Morality and Partiality." *Philosophical Perspectives* 6, Ethics (1992): 243–59.

AT ONCE RATIONAL AND ARDENT

MacAskill, William. "Replaceability, Career Choice and Making a Difference." *Ethical Theory and Moral Practice* 17, no. 2 (April 2014): 269–83.

Singer, Peter. *The Life You Can Save: Acting Now to End World Poverty.* New York: Random House, 2009.

AN ACCIDENTAL CAPABILITY PRODUCED, IN ITS BOUNDLESS STUPIDITY, BY A BIOLOGICAL PROCESS THAT IS NORMALLY OPPOSED TO THE EXPRESSION OF SUCH A CAPABILITY

THE UNDERMINING OF DO-GOODERS, PART ONE

There is an enormous quantity of academic work on altruism, across many disciplines—biology, evolutionary psychology, sociology, psychology, and anthropology, to name just a few. To do justice to this literature would require many books; I have only noted some of the major landmarks in this area.

Andreoni, James. "Impure Altruism and Donations to Public Goods: A Theory of Warm-Glow Giving." *The Economic Journal* 100, no. 401 (June 1990): 464–77.

Anonymous. "The Failure of Altruism." *Fraser's Magazine* XX (July–December 1879): 494–503.

Atwood, George. "The Loss of a Loved Parent and the Origin of Salvation Fantasies." *Psychotherapy: Theory, Research and Practice* 11, no. 3 (Fall 1974): 256–58.

———. "On the Origins and Dynamics of Messianic Salvation Fantasies." *International Review of Psychoanalysis* 5 (1978): 85–96.

Batson, C. Daniel. *The Altruism Question: Toward a Social-Psychological Answer.* Hillsdale, NJ: Lawrence Erlbaum Associates, 1991.

———, Michelle H. Bolen, Julie A. Cross, and Helen E. Neuringer-Benefiel. "Where Is the Altruism in the Altruistic Personality?" *Journal of Personality and Social Psychology* 50, no. 1 (1986): 212–20.

Baumann, Donald J., Robert B. Cialdini, and Douglas T. Kenrick. "Altruism as Hedonism: Helping and Self-Gratification as Equivalent Responses." *Journal of Personality and Social Psychology* 40, no. 6 (1981): 1039–46.

Budd, Louis J. "Altruism Arrives in America." *American Quarterly* 8, no. 1 (Spring 1956): 40–52.

Cialdini, Robert B., Mark Schaller, Donald Houlihan, Kevin Arps, Jim Fultz, and Arthur L. Beaman. "Empathy-Based Helping: Is It Selflessly or Selfishly Motivated?" *Journal of Personality and Social Psychology* 52, no. 4 (1987): 749–58.

Freud, Sigmund. "The Economic Problem of Masochism." Trans. James Strachey. In *The Standard Edition of the Complete Psychological Works of Sigmund Freud XIX (1923–1925): The Ego and the Id and Other Works.* London: Vintage, 2001.

Green, André. "Moral Narcissism." In *On Private Madness.* London: The Hogarth Press, 1986.

Kant, Immanuel. *Observations on the Feeling of the Beautiful and Sublime.* Translated by John T. Goldthwait. Berkeley: University of California Press, 1960.

Kitayama, O. "The Wounded Caretaker and Guilt." *The International Review of Psycho-Analysis* 18 (1991): 229–40.

Krebs, Dennis L. "Altruism—An Examination of the Concept and a Review of the Literature." *Psychological Bulletin* 73, no. 4 (1970): 258–302.

Mandeville, Bernard. *The Fable of the Bees and Other Writings.* Indianapolis: Hacket Publishing Company, Inc., 1997.

Mauss, Marcel. *The Gift: The Form and Reason for Exchange in Archaic Societies.* Translated by W. D. Halls. New York: W. W. Norton, 1990.

McWilliams, Nancy. "The Psychology of the Altruist." *Psychoanalytic Psychology* 1, no. 3 (1984): 193–213.

Monroe, Kristen Renwick. *The Heart of Altruism: Perceptions of a Common Humanity.* Princeton, NJ: Princeton University Press, 1996.

Nietzsche, Friedrich. *On the Genealogy of Morals.* Translated by Walter Kaufman and R. J. Hollingdale. New York: Vintage Books, 1969.

Oakley, Barbara, Ariel Knafo, Guruprasad Madhavan, and David Sloan Wilson. *Pathological Altruism.* Oxford, UK: Oxford University Press, 2012.

Oliner, Pearl M., Samuel P. Oliner, Lawrence Baron, Lawrence A. Blum, Dennis L. Krebs, and M. Zuzanna Smolenska, eds. *Embracing the Other: Philosophical,*

Psychological, and Historical Perspectives on Altruism. New York: New York University Press, 1992.

Oliner, Samuel P., and Pearl M. Oliner. *The Altruistic Personality: Rescuers of Jews in Nazi Europe.* New York: The Free Press, 1988.

Piliavin, Jane Allyn, and Hong-Wen Charng. "Altruism: A Review of Recent Theory and Research." *Annual Review of Sociology* 16 (1990): 27–65.

Post, Stephen G., Lynn G. Underwood, Jeffrey P. Schloss, and William B. Hurlbut, eds. *Altruism & Altruistic Love: Science, Philosophy, & Religion in Dialogue.* Oxford, UK: Oxford University Press, 2001.

Rushton, J. Philippe, and Richard M. Sorrentino. *Altruism and Helping Behavior: Social, Personality, and Developmental Perspectives.* Hillsdale, NJ: Lawrence Erlbaum Associates, 1981.

Sandler, Joseph, and Anna Freud. *The Analysis of Defense: The Ego and the Mechanisms of Defense Revisited.* New York: International Universities Press, 1985.

Schweitzer, Albert. *The Psychiatric Study of Jesus: Exposition and Criticism.* Translated by Charles R. Joy. Boston: The Beacon Press, 1948.

———. *Explorations in Altruistic Love and Behavior.* Boston: The Beacon Press, 1950.

Seelig, Beth J., and Lisa S. Rosof. "Normal and Pathological Altruism." *Journal of the American Psychoanalytic Association* 49, no. 3 (2001): 933–59.

Shapiro, Yakov, and Glen O. Gabbard. "A Reconsideration of Altruism from an Evolutionary and Psychodynamic Perspective." *Ethics & Behavior* 4, no. 1 (1994): 23–42.

Simmons, Roberta G. "Presidential Address on Altruism and Sociology." *The Sociological Quarterly* 32, no. 1 (1991): 1–22.

Sorokin, Pitrim A. *Altruistic Love: A Study of American Good Neighbors and Christian Saints.* Boston: The Beacon Press, 1950.

Trivers, Robert L. "The Evolution of Reciprocal Altruism." *The Quarterly Review of Biology* 46, no. 1 (March 1971): 35–57.

Weiss, Robert Frank, Jenny L. Boyer, John P. Lombardo, and Mark H. Stich. "Altruistic Drive and Altruistic Reinforcement." *Journal of Personality and Social Psychology* 25, no. 3 (1973): 390–400.

Wilson, David Sloan. *Does Altruism Exist?: Culture, Genes, and the Welfare of Others.* New Haven, CT, and London: Yale University Press, 2015.

Wuthnow, Robert. *Acts of Compassion: Caring for Others and Helping Ourselves.* Princeton, NJ: Princeton University Press, 1991.

THE HUMILIATION OF STRANGERS

I traveled to Anandwan to interview Vikas, Bharati, Kaustubh, Pallavi, and Sheetal Amte, and to Hemalkasa to speak with Prakash, Manda, Digant, Anagha, Aniket, and Samiksha Amte. But Baba and Tai Amte both died a few years before I began working on this book, so I am indebted to others' accounts of their lives, especially to Neesha Mirchandani's *Wisdom Song.*

Amte, Prakash. *Pathways to Light.* Translated by Chandrashekhar Marathe. Mumbai: Samakaleen Prakashan, 2012.

Amte, Sadhana. *Samidha*. Translated by Shobha Pawar. Hyderabad, India: Orient Longman Private Limited, 2008.

Bhave, Vinoba. *Moved by Love: The Memoirs of Vinoba Bhave*. Translated by Marjorie Sykes. Dartington Totnes, Devon, UK: Green Books Ltd., 1994.

Farrow, John. *Damien the Leper: A Life of Magnificent Courage, Devotion & Spirit*. New York: Image Books, 1954.

Gandhi, Mohandas Karamchand. *Autobiography: The Story of My Experiments with Truth*. BN Publishing, 2008.

Kainthla, Anita. *Baba Amte: A Biography*. New Delhi: Viva Books, 2005.

Manohar, Vilas. *Negal: Unusual and Interesting True Stories of Wild Species Raised in Human Surroundings*. Translated by S. A. Virkar. Mumbai: Granthali, 1991.

Marshall, George, and David Poling. *Schweitzer: A Biography*. Baltimore: The Johns Hopkins University Press, 1971.

Matthew, Grace, Purnima N. Mane, Y. D. Phadke, S. H. Deshpande, R. Ganapati, Asha A. Bhende, Roopashree Sinha, and Babu Santosh Kumar. *A Journey from Sympathy to Empathy: Baba Amte and His Work*. Bombay: Tata Institute of Social Sciences, 1990.

Mirchandani, Neesha. *Wisdom Song: The Life of Baba Amte*. New Delhi: The Lotus Collection, 2006.

Narayan, R. K. *The Ramayana: A Shortened Modern Prose Version of the Indian Epic*. London: Penguin Books, 1977.

Schweitzer, Albert. *Out of My Life and Thought: An Autobiography*. Translated by A. B. Lemke. New York: Henry Holt, 1990.

Shepard, Mark. *Gandhi Today: A Report on Mahatma Gandhi's Successors*. Arcata, CA: Simple Productions, 1987.

Staffner, Hans, S.J. *Baba Amte: A Vision of New India*. Mumbai: Popular Prakashan, 2000.

Talmon, Yonina. *Family and Community in the Kibbutz*. Cambridge, MA: Harvard University Press, 1972.

Tarnowski, Arthur. *The Unbeaten Track*. London: Harvill Press, 1971.

Tennyson, Hallam. *India's Walking Saint: The Story of Vinoba Bhave*. New York: Doubleday, 1955.

Turner, Graham. *More Than Conquerors: A Distinguished Economic Commentator Tells of 20th Century Men Made New*. London: Hodder and Stoughton, 1976.

THE LEGACY OF DRUNKS

THE UNDERMINING OF DO-GOODERS, PART TWO

Al-Anon. *Twelve Steps & Twelve Traditions*. Virginia Beach, VA: Al-Anon Family Group Headquarters, Inc., 1981.

Al-Anon Family Groups. *How Al-Anon Works: For Families & Friends of Alcoholics*. Virginia Beach, VA: Al-Anon Family Group Headquarters, Inc., 1995.

Beattie, Melody. *Codependent No More: How to Stop Controlling Others and Start Caring for Yourself*. San Francisco: Harper San Francisco, 1987.

Cheever, Susan. *My Name Is Bill: Bill Wilson—His Life and the Creation of Alcoholics Anonymous*. New York: Washington Square Press, 2004.

Cole, Teju. "The White Savior Industrial Complex." *Atlantic*, March 21, 2012.

De Vries, Manfred Kets. "Leadership Coaching and the Rescuer Syndrome: How to Manage Both Sides of the Couch." INSEAD Working Paper Collection, 2010.

De Waal, Alex. *Famine Crimes: Politics & the Disaster Relief Industry in Africa*. Bloomington: Indiana University Press, 1997.

Durham, Mary Sherrill. "The Therapist and the Concept of Revenge: The Law of Talion." *The Journal of Pastoral Care* 44, no. 2 (Summer 1990): 131–37.

Edelwich, Jerry, and Archie Brodsky. *Burn-Out: Stages of Disillusionment in the Helping Professions*. New York: Human Sciences Press, 1980.

Erikson, Erik H. *Gandhi's Truth: On the Origins of Militant Nonviolence*. New York: W. W. Norton & Company, 1969.

Furedi, Frank. "Help-Seeking: The Principal Therapeutic Virtue."

Guggenbühl-Craig, Adolf. *Power in the Helping Professions*. Dallas: Spring Publications, Inc., 1971.

Haaken, Janice. "From Al-Anon to ACOA: Codependence and the Reconstruction of Caregiving." *Signs* 18, no. 2 (Winter 1993): 321–45.

Illich, Ivan. "To Hell with Good Intentions." Address to Conference on Inter-American Student Projects, Cuernavaca, Mexico, April 20, 1968.

Irvine, Leslie. *Codependent Forevermore: The Invention of Self in a Twelve Step Group*. Chicago: The University of Chicago Press, 1999.

Jacobs, Michael. "The Therapist's Revenge: The Law of Talion as a Motive for Caring." *The Interdisciplinary Journal of Pastoral Studies* 105 (1991): 2–11.

Lipsky, Laura van Dernoot, with Connie Burk. *Trauma Stewardship: An Everyday Guide to Caring for Self While Caring for Others*. San Francisco: Berrett-Koehler Publishers, Inc., 2009.

Maren, Michael. *The Road to Hell: The Ravaging Effects of Foreign Aid and International Charity*. New York: The Free Press, 1997.

Miller, Angelyn. *The Enabler: When Helping Harms the Ones You Love*. Claremont, CA: Hunter House, 1988.

Norwood, Robin. *Women Who Love Too Much: When You Keep Wishing and Hoping He'll Change*. Los Angeles: Jeremy P. Tarcher, Inc., 1985.

Rieff, David. *A Bed for the Night: Humanitarianism in Crisis*. New York: Simon & Schuster, 2002.

Rieff, Philip. *Freud: The Mind of the Moralist*. New York: The Viking Press, 1959.

———. *The Triumph of the Therapeutic: Uses of Faith After Freud*. Chicago: The University of Chicago Press, 1966.

Springle, Pat. *Rapha's 12-Step Program for Overcoming Codependency*. Houston: Rapha Publishing, 1990.

———. *A Christian Perspective: Codependency: Breaking Free from the Hurt and Manipulation of Dysfunctional Relationships*. Houston: Rapha Publishing, 1994.

Steinbeck, John. *The Grapes of Wrath*. New York: Penguin Books, 1976.

Tillett, Richard. "The Patient Within: Psychopathology in the Helping Professions." *Advances in Psychiatric Treatment* 9 (2003): 272–79.

Tracy, Sarah W., and Caroline Jean Acker, eds. *Altering American Consciousness: The History of Alcohol and Drug Use in the United States, 1800–2000.* Amherst: University of Massachusetts Press, 2004.

Travis, Trysh. *The Language of the Heart: A Cultural History of the Recovery Movement from Alcoholics Anonymous to Oprah Winfrey.* Chapel Hill: The University of North Carolina Press, 2009.

Vaux, Tony. *The Selfish Altruist: Relief Work in Famine and War.* London: Earthscan Publications, 2001.

Wilson, Lois. *Lois Remembers: Memoirs of the Co-Founder of Al-Anon and Wife of the Co-Founder of Alcoholics Anonymous.* Virginia Beach, VA: Al-Anon Family Group Headquarters, Inc., 1979.

Woititz, Janet Geringer. *Adult Children of Alcoholics.* Pompano Beach, FL: Health Communications, Inc., 1983.

ONE OF THOSE GOD THINGS

This book is one that Kimberly Brown-Whale has used many times in attempting to explain to others her sense of God.

Yancy, Philip. *What's So Amazing About Grace?* Grand Rapids, MI: Zondervan, 1997.

KIDNEYS

Danovitch, Gabriel M. "Who Cares?: Impact of Commercialized Kidney Transplantation on the Doctor/Patient Relationship." Manuscript.

Dew, M. A., C. L. Jacobs, S. G. Jowsey, R. Hanto, C. Miller, and F. L. Delmonico. "Guidelines for the Psychosocial Evaluation of Living Unrelated Kidney Donors in the United States." *American Journal of Transplantation* 7 (2007): 1047–54.

Epstein, Miran, and Gabriel Danovitch. "Is Altruistic-Directed Living Unrelated Organ Donation a Legal Fiction?" *Nephrology Dialysis Transplantation* 24, no. 2 (2009): 357–60.

Fellner, Carl H., and Shalom H. Schwartz. "Altruism in Disrepute: Medical Versus Public Attitudes Toward the Living Organ Donor." *The New England Journal of Medicine* 284 (March 1971): 582–85.

Fox, Renée C. *Experiment Perilous: Physicians and Patients Facing the Unknown.* Philadelphia: University of Pennsylvania Press, 1959.

———, and Judith P. Swazey. *The Courage to Fail: A Social View of Organ Transplants and Dialysis.* Chicago: The University of Chicago Press, 1974.

———, and Judith P. Swazey. *Spare Parts: Organ Replacement in American Society.* New York and Oxford, UK: Oxford University Press, 1992.

Henderson, Antonia J. Z., Monica A. Landolt, Michael F. McDonald, William M. Barrable, John G. Soos, William Gourlay, Colleen J. Allison, and David N. Landsberg. "The Living Anonymous Kidney Donor: Lunatic or Saint?" *American Journal of Transplantation* 3 (2003): 203–13.

Jacobs, Cheryl L., Deborah Roman, Catherine Garvey, Jeffrey Kahn, and Arthur J. Matas. "Twenty-two Nondirected Kidney Donors: An Update on a Single Center's Experience." *American Journal of Transplantation* 4 (2014): 1110–16.

Kissling, Frances. "Whaddaya Have to Do to Get a Kidney Around Here?" *Salon.com,* March 27, 2009.

Lawler, Peter Augustine. "Is the Body Property?" *The New Atlantis,* Fall 2006.

Meilander, Gilbert. "Organ Procurement: What Are the Questions?" Paper presented to the President's Council on Bioethics, June 2006.

President's Council on Bioethics (discussion transcript). "Procuring Organs for Transplantation: Ethical Considerations." January 16, 2003, Session 2.

———. "Organ Transplantation and Procurement—Literary and Philosophical-Anthropological Perspectives." June 22, 2006, Session 2.

———. "Organ Transplantation and Procurement—The Ethical Challenges." June 22, 2006, Session 3.

———. "Living Organ Donation: Outcomes and Ethics." September 7, 2006, Session 2.

———. "On the Body and Transplantation: Philosophical and Legal Context." February 15, 2007, Session 1.

Richards, Janet Radcliffe. *Careless Thought Costs Lives: The Ethics of Transplants.* Oxford, UK: Oxford University Press, 2012.

Sadler, H. Harrison, Leslie Davison, Charles Carroll, and Samuel L. Kountz. "The Living, Unrelated, Kidney Donor. *Seminars in Psychiatry* 3, no. 1 (February 1971): 86–101.

Satel, Sally. "Desperately Seeking a Kidney." *The New York Times,* December 17, 2007.

———, ed. *When Altruism Isn't Enough: The Case for Compensating Kidney Donors.* Washington, D.C.: The A.E.I. Press, 2008.

Spital, Aaron. "Evolution of Attitudes at U.S. Transplant Centers Toward Kidney Donation by Friends and Altruistic Strangers." *Transplantation* 69, no. 8 (27 April 2000): 1728–31.

Titmuss, Richard M. *The Gift Relationship: From Human Blood to Social Policy.* New York: Random House, 1971.

PLEASE REPLY TO ME AS SOON AS POSSIBLE

Benedict, Ruth. *The Chrysanthemum and the Sword: Patterns of Japanese Culture.* New York: Mariner Books, 2005.

Camus, Albert. *The Myth of Sisyphus and Other Essays.* New York: Vintage International, 1991.

Estrin, James. "Wandering in Japan's 'Suicide Forest.'" *The New York Times,* October 25, 2012.

Iga, Mamoru. *The Thorn in the Chrysanthemum: Suicide and Economic Success in Modern Japan.* Berkeley: University of California Press, 1986.

Kitanaka, Junko. *Depression in Japan: Psychiatric Cures for a Society in Distress.* Princeton, NJ: Princeton University Press, 2012.

Leenaars, Antoon A., ed. *Suicidology: Essays in Honor of Edwin Shneidman.* Northvale, NJ: Jason Aronson Inc., 1993.

Minois, Georges. *History of Suicide: Voluntary Death in Western Culture.* Translated by Lydia G. Cochrane. Baltimore and London: The Johns Hopkins University Press, 1999.

Ozawa-de Silva, Chikako. "Too Lonely to Die: Internet Suicide Pacts and Existential Suffering in Japan." *Culture, Medicine, and Psychiatry* 32 (2008): 516–51.

Pinguet, Maurice. *Voluntary Death in Japan.* Translated by Rosemary Morris. Cambridge, UK: Polity Press, 1993.

Watts, Jonathan, and Yoshiharu Tomatsu, eds. *Buddhist Care for the Dying and Bereaved.* Somerville, MA: Wisdom Publications, 2012.

Zielenziger, Michael. *Shutting Out the Sun: How Japan Created Its Own Lost Generation.* New York: Vintage, 2007.

THE CHILDREN OF STRANGERS

Badeau, Hector, and Sue Badeau. *Are We There Yet? The Ultimate Road Trip: Adopting & Raising 22 Kids!* Franklin, TN: Carpenter's Son Publishing, 2013.

Blank, Joseph P. *19 Steps Up the Mountain: The Story of the DeBolt Family.* Philadelphia: J. B. Lippincott Company, 1976.

Doss, Helen. *The Family Nobody Wanted.* New York: Scholastic Book Services, 1954.

THE ASPIDISTRA IS THE TREE OF LIFE

THE UNDERMINING OF DO-GOODERS, PART THREE

Austen, Jane. *Mansfield Park.* London: Penguin Classics, 1996.

Baldwin, James. *Notes of a Native Son.* Boston: Beacon Press, 1955.

———. *The Fire Next Time.* New York: Dial Press, 1963.

Bayley, John. *Tolstoy and the Novel.* New York: Viking Press, 1966.

Bernanos, Georges. *The Diary of a Country Priest.* Translated by Pamela Morris. New York: Doubleday, 1954.

Camus, Albert. *The Plague.* Translated by Stuart Gilbert. New York: Vintage International, 1991.

Coetzee, J. M. *Elizabeth Costello.* London: Penguin Books, 2003.

Davies, Robertson. "Literature and Moral Purpose." In *The Merry Heart: Reflections on Reading, Writing and the World of Books.* New York: Viking, 1997.

Dostoevsky, Fyodor. *The Idiot.* Translated by David Magarshack. London: Penguin Books, 1955.

———. *The Brothers Karamazov.* Translated by David Magarshack. Harmondsworth, UK: Penguin Books, 1958.

Eliot, George. "Worldliness and Other-Worldliness: The Poet Young." In *The Complete Works of George Eliot: Scenes of Clerical Life, Essays.* London: Postlethwaite, Taylor & Knowles, Ltd., 1908.

————. *Middlemarch.* London: Penguin Books, 1965.

Forster, E. M. "What I Believe." In *Two Cheers for Democracy.* New York: Mariner Books, 1962.

French, Marilyn. *The Women's Room.* London: Sphere Books Limited, 1977.

Greene, Graham. *The Heart of the Matter.* London: Penguin Books, 1962.

————. *A Burnt-Out Case.* London: Penguin Books, 1963.

Hastings, Elizabeth. *An Experiment in Altruism.* London: Macmillan and Co., 1895.

Howells, William Dean. *A Traveler from Altruria: Romance.* New York: Harper and Brothers Publishers, 1908.

Kass, Amy A., ed. *The Perfect Gift: The Philanthropic Imagination in Poetry and Prose.* Bloomington: Indiana University Press, 2002.

Koestler, Arthur. *Darkness at Noon.* Translated by Daphne Hardy. New York: Scribner, 1941.

Mann, Thomas. "Anna Karenina." *Essays of Three Decades.* Translated by H. T. Lowe-Porter. New York: Alfred A. Knopf, 1947.

Maugham, W. Somerset. *The Razor's Edge.* New York: Vintage International, 2003.

Murdoch, Iris. *The Bell.* London: Penguin Books, 1987.

Nussbaum, Martha C. "Transcending Humanity." *Love's Knowledge: Essays on Philosophy and Literature.* New York: Oxford University Press, 1990.

Pullen, Henry William. *The Ground Ash: A Public School Story.* London: Simpkin, Marshall & Co., 1874.

Rand, Ayn. *The Fountainhead.* New York: Signet, 1952.

————. *The Virtue of Selfishness.* New York: Signet, 1964.

Sand, George. "Review of *Uncle Tom's Cabin.*" *La Presse* (December 17, 1852).

Shaw, Bernard. "Why for Puritans?" *Three Plays for Puritans.* London: Penguin Books, 1946.

Stewart, Carol. *The Eighteenth-Century Novel and the Secularization of Ethics.* Farnham, Surrey, UK: Ashgate, 2010.

Stowe, Harriet Beecher. *Uncle Tom's Cabin.* Mineola, NY: Dover, 2005.

————. *Uncle Tom's Cabin.* Edited by Elizabeth Ammons. New York: W. W. Norton & Company, 2010.

Sullivan, Erin. "Anti-Bardolatry Through the Ages—Or, Why Voltaire, Tolstoy, Shaw and Wittgenstein Didn't Like Shakespeare." *Opticon 1826* 2 (2007).

Tolstoy, Leo. *Anna Karenina.* Translated by Joel Carmichael. New York: Bantam, 1960.

————. *Tolstoy on Shakespeare.* New York: Funk and Wagnalls Co., 1906.

————. *What to Do?* Translated by Isabel F. Hapgood. Gloucester, UK: Dodo Press, 2007.

————. *The Kingdom of God Is Within You.* Translated by Constance Garnett.

Tompkins, Jane P. "Sentimental Power: *Uncle Tom's Cabin* and the Politics of Literary History." *Glyph* 2 (1978).

Twain, Mark. "The Story of the Good Little Boy Who Did Not Prosper." *The Best Short Stories of Mark Twain.* New York: Modern Library, 2004.

Ward, Mrs. Humphry. *Robert Elsmere.* Oxford, UK: Oxford University Press, 1987.

Wilson, A. N. *Tolstoy: A Biography.* New York: W. W. Norton & Company, 1988.

Wilson, Edwin, ed. *Shaw on Shakespeare*. New York: E. P. Dutton & Co., Inc., 1961.

FROM THE POINT OF VIEW OF THE UNIVERSE

Brach, Tara. *Radical Acceptance: Embracing Your Life with the Heart of a Buddha*. New York: Bantam, 2003.

SOMETHING QUITE DIFFERENT FROM LIFE

As I was finishing this chapter I was thinking of a passage from Susan Sontag, which I echo in the last line. I didn't want to quote from this passage in the book because I didn't want to imply, even for a moment, that the people I write about are fanatical, irrational, and masochistic in the way that Simone Weil was. But I found Sontag's thoughts on Weil moving and significant. Here is the passage, which appears in a review of Weil's *Selected Essays* (*The New York Review of Books*, February 1, 1963):

> Some lives are exemplary, others not; and of exemplary lives, there are those which invite us to imitate them, and those which we regard from a distance with a mixture of revulsion, pity, and reverence. It is, roughly, the difference between the hero and the saint (if one may use the latter term in an aesthetic, rather than a religious sense). Such a life, absurd in its exaggerations and degree of self-mutilation—like Kleist's, like Kierkegaard's—was Simone Weil's. I am thinking of the fanatical asceticism of Simone Weil's life, her contempt for pleasure and for happiness, her noble and ridiculous political gestures, her elaborate self-denials, her tireless courting of affliction; and I do not exclude her homeliness, her physical clumsiness, her migraines, her tuberculosis. No one who loves life would wish to imitate her dedication to martyrdom nor would wish it for his children nor for anyone else whom he loves. Yet so far as we love seriousness, as well as life, we are moved by it, nourished by it. In the respect we pay to such lives, we acknowledge the presence of mystery in the world—and this mystery is just what the secure possession of the truth, an objective truth, denies. In this sense, all truth is superficial; and some (but not all) distortions of the truth, some (but not all) insanity, some (but not all) unhealthiness, some (but not all) denials of life are truth-giving, sanity-producing, health-creating, and life-enhancing.

Blake, William. *The Marriage of Heaven and Hell*. New York: Dover Publications, Inc., 1994.

James, William. "The Moral Equivalent of War." *McClure's Magazine,* August 1910: 463–68.

Milton, John. *Paradise Lost*. New York: The Modern Library, 2008.